Between War and Peace

Woodrow Wilson and the
American Expeditionary Force
in Siberia, 1918–1921

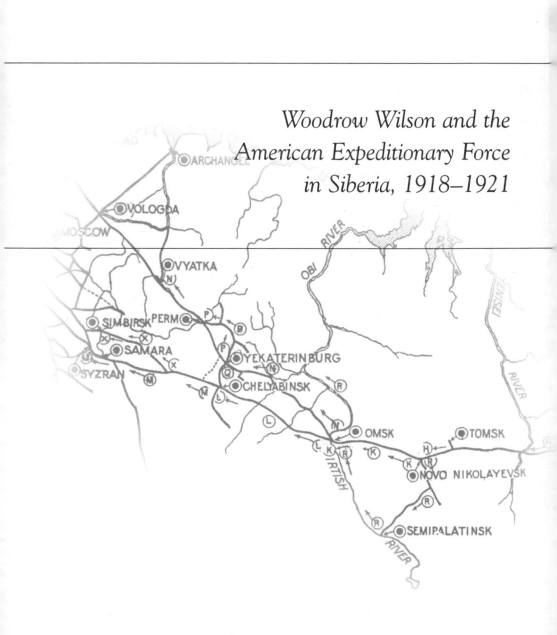

Between War and Peace

By Carol Willcox Melton

MERCER UNIVERSITY PRESS | 2001

ISBN 0-86554-692-4
MUP/H512

Published by Mercer University Press
6316 Peake Road
Macon, Georgia 31210-3960

First Edition.

∞ The paper used in this publication meets the minimum requirements
of American National Standard for Information Sciences—Permanence of Paper
for Printed Library Materials, ANSI Z39.48-1992.

Library of Congress Cataloging-in-Publication Data

CIP data is on file with the Library of Congress

ACKNOWLEDGMENTS

IF THIS PROJECT WERE A CHILD, IT WOULD NOT ONLY BE OLD ENOUGH TO drive a car, but almost eligible to vote. In the eighteen years since I began working on the AEF Siberia, I have been fortunate to have the help and support of a number people. First, I'd like to thank my husband, Buckner F. Melton, Jr., for years of proofreading, editing, and typing the various incarnations of the manuscript, and my mother, Lorraine G. Thompson, for her unflagging financial and moral support through far too many years of higher education.

I am also grateful to the members of my dissertation committee at Duke University for their comments and assistance: I. B. Holley, Jr., Joel Colton, Harold Parker, Martin Miller, and Alex Roland.

I am much indebted to Joseph Longuevan, the former head of the AEF Siberia Veterans Organization, who in the early 1980s helped me to locate the few veterans then living, and to Joseph Demastrie and Alan Ferguson for their recollections of their service in Siberia. I also want to express my appreciation to Betsy Pratt Lowe for giving me access to the papers and photographs of her of her uncle, Captain John Wilmer Blue of the US 31st Infantry Regiment.

I especially wish to acknowledge the assistance of the following individuals and institutions: Dr. Dane Hartgrove for his help in obtaining the Historical Files of the American Expeditionary Force in Siberia from the National Archives; Dr. Richard J. Sommers, Archivist Historian and the staff of the United States Army Military History Institute at Carlisle Barracks, Pennsylvania; the staff of the Manuscript Collection of the Perkins Library at Duke University; the archival staff of the Imperial War Museum in London; Dr. Marie-Jeanne Rossingnol for help with the *Service Historique Armée de terre Chateau de Vincennes les Archives de la Mission Militaire Francaise en Sibérie 1918–1920*. I am also grateful to Julia

Brooks Poblete for her help with research in the Library of Congress and to Katie Swett for her work in the William S. Graves Papers at the Hoover Institution.

For their hospitality in my travels I am indebted to the late Dr. Lyman Cotten and Patsy White Cotten, as well as Mr. and Mrs. John Fitzpatrick and Dr. Winston Fitzpatick. My thanks also to Joseph W. Wescott, II for his constant urging to have my dissertation published, and to Marjorie Temple Benbow Henry for her reading of the manuscript. My thanks also to Bill Wilkerson for his fine work restoring and enlarging the photographs, and most particularly to Dr. Anne Cipriano Venzon for her insightful comments on the manuscript, which resulted in a far better book than might otherwise have been.

For Lorraine G. Thompson and Buckner F. Melton, Jr.
And in memory of Lena Blue McFadyen Woodard

And we are here as on a darkling plain
Swept with confused alarms of struggle and flight,
Where ignorant armies clash by night.

—Matthew Arnold, "Dover Beach"

Woodrow Wilson

Four American soldiers standing on what remains of a bridge on the Suchan Branch Railroad that was burned by the Bolsheviki in June of 1919. This area of the railroad along with the coal mines was under American supervision. (Robert Eichelberger Papers, Special Collections, Duke University.)

Lt. Stewart of the Russian Railway Service Corps at Hailer, Manchuria. In the foreground is, as Robert Eichelberger described in the original caption, 'What is left of nine so-called Bolsheviks after Semenov and the souvenir hunters got through with them.' (Robert Eichelberger Papers, Special Collections, Duke University)

Major General Williams S. Graves in his Siberian winter gear. The photograph is inscribed to Mrs. Robert Eichelberger. (Robert Eichelberger Papers, Special Collections. Duke University)

The center figure is Ataman Ivan Kalmikov with his staff and colleagues. (Robert Eichelberger Papers, Special Collections, Duke University)

From left to right: General William S. Graves; General Alfred Knox, head of the British Mission in Siberia; Commodore Lin, commander of the Chinese forces; Colonel Vuchterle, Czech town mayor; and Major Broz, Czech military diplomat. Reading is the Japanese Chief of Staff, General Inagaki. (Robert Eichelberger Papers, Special Collections, Duke University)

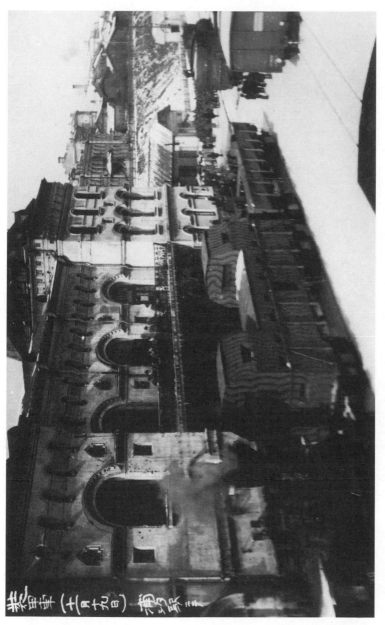

Ataman Kalmikov's armored train, standing in front of the Vladivostok railway station on November 18, 1919, shortly after a democratic revolt in the city had been suppressed with great bloodshed. Robert Eichelberger wrote on the back of this photograph that "this train is one of several that badly needs blowing up." (Robert Eichelberger Papers, Special Collections. Duke University)

The Inter-Allied parade in Vladivostok held November 15, 1918, celebrating the conclusin of the First World War. The building in the background is A.E.F. Headquarters. (Robert Eichelberger Papers, Special Collections. Duke University)

The three central figures are: General Graves, General Inagaki and Ambassador Roland Morris just before Graves and Morris left to investigate conditions at Omsk. (Robert Eichelberger Papers, Special Collections. Duke University)

White forces in Western Siberia (Collection of the author)

Czech legionnaires posing with a Bactrian camel train (Collection of the author)

A detachment of Cossack Cavalry (Collection of the author)

A Czech orchestra entertains troops in the field (Collection of the author)

An American soldier and nurse, probably in Vladivostok, taken at Christmas 1919 (Collection of the author)

A French officer examining one of the ubiquitous piles of frozen dead littering Siberia (Collection of the author)

A typical street demonstration (Collection of the author)

Ataman Gregorii Mikhailovich Semenov, a Japanese protégé and notorious murderer (Collection of the author)

Two unhappy generals: Rudolf Gajda and William S. Graves on the balcony of A.E.F. Headquarters in Vladivostok (Collection of the author)

A derailed locomotive on the Trans-Siberian Railroad (Collection of the author)

Czech legionnaires with their rifles stacked (Collection of the author)

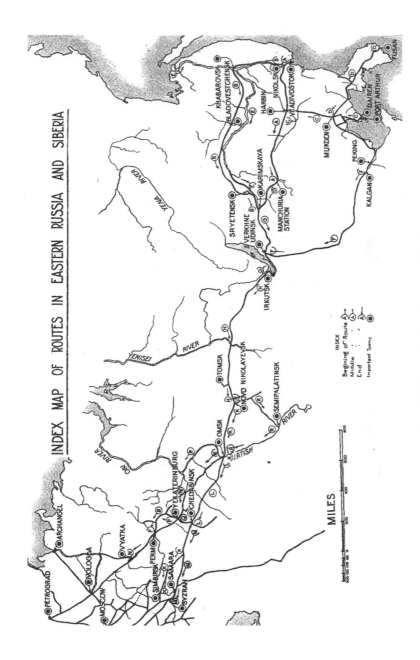

Map of Routes in Eastern Russia and Siberia

1

Wilson, War, and Revolution in Russia

IN APRIL 1917, WOODROW WILSON ENDED HIS LONG STRUGGLE TO KEEP the United States neutral in the Great War. All the major powers of the world, along with their colonies and dominions, had spent the previous thirty-four months engaged in an unequalled outpouring of blood and treasure. The intricate web of the European alliance system, which had preserved the peace on the continent since 1871 had, in 1914, ensnared the Allies and the Central Powers in the most destructive and dehumanizing war the world had yet seen. In the United States Woodrow Wilson continued his program of Progressive reform. Like so many Progressives of his generation he believed, if not in the perfectibility of mankind (a theological impossibility for a Presbyterian), at least in its steady improvement and enlightenment through education, science, and technology. Technology in the age of the machine gun and poison gas would betray the trust of millions.

Wilson both intellectually and intuitively had an advantage that few of his contemporary statesmen did in 1914: he feared war. While his European counterparts were reared on tales of honor and glory achieved on distant colonial battlefields, and reenacted on nursery floors with lead soldiers, Wilson had spent his childhood amid the grim realities of the Civil War in Georgia, and the persistent poverty of the Reconstruction South. Because he had seen war he feared it, because he feared it he was determined to avoid it, and he urged the United States to maintain an attitude of impartial neutrality.

Wilson's position was frequently challenged by German naval and foreign policy. The former was dictated by the technological demands of submarine warfare and America's own role as purveyor of war materiel to the Allies. The latter was fueled by stupidity and overconfidence. If German naval policy led to the sinking of the *Lusitania*, the *Sussex*, and several US merchant vessels, incompetence led to the sending and publication of the Zimmermann telegram, which offered American territory to Mexico in exchange for attacking the United States.

Through these crises Wilson maintained US neutrality, often in the face of heated and vigorous opposition. He convinced Germany to abandon unrestricted submarine warfare and to respect America's freedom of the seas. He calmed the public outcry over the Zimmermann affair. If the destruction of neutral Belgium by the "beastly Hun" tugged at America's heart and purse strings, it was difficult to identify the Allies as the defenders of light and liberty against German tyranny, when they included amongst their number the world's largest and most repressive autocracy–Russia.

In the spring of 1917 two events altered the political landscape. First, in February, the German government resumed unrestricted submarine warfare, gambling on the hope that it could force Great Britain to surrender before the United States, virtually certain to be provoked into declaring war against Germany, could build and transport an army to the Western Front. Attacks by German U-Boats on American vessels caused Wilson to sever diplomatic relations with the German government, by April similar attacks would cause him to request and receive a declaration of war against Germany. Secondly, in March an enormous and largely impromptu democratic revolution swept away the Romanov dynasty, which had ruled Russia for 304 years. Tsar Nicholas II abdicated for himself and his ailing son Alexei. After a period of rioting and political maneuvering among a myriad of amateur Russian revolutionaries, a provisional government was established. Prince Lvov, a committed democrat despite his title, became its prime minister, and so it appeared that the one great blessing of the war thus far had been to bring Russia into the liberal democratic fold.

Consequently, when the United States entered the World War in April 1917, the possibility of military action within the borders of Russia was something no one foresaw. Woodrow Wilson was an enthusiastic supporter of the February Revolution and the Provisional Government. This new government promised to keep Russia in the war against Germany, and it continued, with difficulty, to keep its army in the field, if not on the offensive. But this increasingly unpopular commitment to the Allied cause proved its undoing in November 1917, when the Bolsheviks overthrew the Provisional Government, signed an armistice with Germany, and began negotiating a separate peace.

These developments caused general consternation, if not panic, among the Allies. Britain and France had been prepared to accept a reduced Russian war effort, but not wholesale defection. The London Agreement, signed by the tsarist government and honored by the Provisional Government, prohibited any member of the Entente from making a separate peace. On the Western Front in 1917 the Allies faced the grave possibility of defeat. The Allied offensive in the spring brought record casualties, widespread mutinies, and mass courts-martial. The impending transfer of two-thirds of the German Army to the Western Front following the Russian armistice greatly compounded the Allies' peril.

Almost immediately after the November Revolution, various Allied officials began devising plans to avert this possibility. Marshal Ferdinand Foch, Generalissimo of the Allied armies, suggested that the Allies undertake armed intervention in Russia by seizing the Trans-Siberian Railway and using it as a means to restore the Eastern Front. The other Allies rejected his idea, but the proposal continued to dominate inter-Allied discussions throughout the following year.[1] In this way the issue of military intervention in Siberia first came before the Wilson administration.

In the first six months of 1918, the Allies besieged Wilson with requests to consent to intervention in Siberia. In January the British Embassy in Washington forwarded a memorandum from the Foreign Office urgently requesting the United States to consent to a change of Allied policy in Russia. The British government sent similar cables to Paris and Rome.

The Foreign Office said that until a few weeks before Russia had "presented a spectacle of unredeemed chaos," but that groups in South Russia, particularly the Cossacks, were now organizing and might prove useful to the Allied cause by preventing "Russia from falling immediately and completely under the control of Germany." The British argued that it was not possible to supply pro-Allied forces via the Baltic or the Black Sea. As they saw it, the only possible artery of communication left was the Trans-Siberian Railroad, but it could only be used if the Japanese, acting at the behest of the Allies, would take control of thousands of miles of track to prevent its falling under German control and neutralizing the effects of the Allied blockade.[2] This cable was followed by a message from Colonel Edward M. House, the president's close friend and advisor, who was then in London, urging Wilson to consent to the suggestion.[3]

Other appeals came from the Supreme War Council in Paris,[4] from many of Wilson's own diplomats, and from the Japanese government. The Japanese, motivated by expansionist visions, wished to be appointed Allied mandatory in Siberia. The British and French supported Japan's desire, since it was ideally situated geographically and militarily to sponsor a force in Siberia. But in February 1918 the United States vetoed the proposal.

The French and Japanese governments continued to support the British request.[5] On 13 February, Secretary of State Lansing cabled the US ambassador in London, Walter Hines Page. Lansing told him to explain to the British government that the United States felt that Japanese intervention might prove "embarrassing to the cause of the powers at war with Germany" on several grounds. First, it would antagonize the Bolsheviks, who were in control of the Russian government. Second, the US government did not believe that there was a clear necessity to intervene. Third, if intervention did become necessary, it should be Allied in composition not just Japanese. Finally any action taken, should be approved by the Chinese government which would probably wish to guard the portion of the Trans-Siberian Railroad that ran through its own country, rather than having the Japanese do it for them.[6]

The Allies, however, refused to accept Wilson's objections. On 26 February, the French ambassador urged Wilson to reconsider, claiming that reports from Irkutsk, Harbin, and Vladivostok showed conditions there were extremely serious. The French feared that the railroad would be interrupted. In their view keeping the railroad open was essential to counteracting German political and military efforts in Russia.[7]

There was growing concern in the War Department over the requests for intervention and the potential role of Japan in Siberia. General Tasker Bliss, the American military representative to the Supreme War Council and former US Army chief of staff, saw the whole question of intervention as fraught with potential hazards. On 20 February, he wrote to Chief of Staff General Peyton March that "the intervention, over a large part of Siberia, of a large Japanese Army, raises the question of when and how they can be made to get out. I have often thought that this war, instead of being the last one, may only be the breeder of still more. This Japanese intervention suggests a possible way in which another war may be brought about."[8]

Despite these warnings, Wilson considered approving Japanese intervention, if only because he felt he had already opposed too many Allied suggestions in the past. He did not wish to continue to obstruct plans that had the support of all the Allies. Disregarding the advice of his military advisors, Wilson succumbed to the pressure of Britain and France and drew up a memorandum consenting to Japanese intervention. This capitulation was only temporary; he ultimately decided not to send the memorandum, whose contents were already an open secret in Washington diplomatic circles.[9]

Wilson's momentary weakening encouraged the Allies. On 27 February, Arthur Balfour, the British Foreign Minister, asked Wilson to join the British, French, and Italians in asking Japan to occupy the Trans-Siberian Railway to protect the Allied supplies at Vladivostok and to deny the Germans access to the agricultural resources west of Lake Baikal. Balfour admitted, however, that while the Japanese wanted the status of Allied mandatory they would not tolerate Allied cooperation. Nevertheless the

British government believed intervention was an urgent necessity. The Italians had consented, and the French wanted it approved quickly. The final decision lay with the United States. If Wilson refused, common action would be impossible; on one hand the Japanese desired American support, and on the other hand the Entente governments feared that without their support the Japanese would intervene unilaterally and leave the Allies without any control over them.[10] The Japanese desired the legitimacy that their status as an Allied mandatory would give them without the restrictions of Allied supervision, or the possibility of the Allies revoking their control of Siberian or Chinese territories.

In the face of Allied pressure, Secretary of State Robert Lansing urged Wilson to agree to intervention. But Wilson resisted, afraid that it might force the Bolsheviks, who were negotiating a peace treaty at Brest-Litovsk, into an agreement with the Germans. So far no treaty had resulted, and the Allies continued to hope that the two parties might find it impossible to agree at all. Negotiations had already broken down once, and the Germans had resumed their offensive on the Eastern Front. But then, on 3 March, the Bolshevik representative, Leon Trotsky signed the Treaty of Brest-Litovsk in spite of the harsh terms the Germans imposed.

Despite Russia's formal withdrawal from the war, Wilson continued to oppose Allied intervention in Russia. Wilson's case against intervention hinged on three points. First, he feared that it would strengthen the position of the extreme revolutionary groups in Russia and further widen the breach between Russia and the Allies. Second, he believed that such action was contrary to American democratic war aims; therefore, he opposed intervention even if the Japanese promised to respect Russian territorial integrity. Third, he feared it might cause resentment in the United States by creating the impression that the Allies were using a "yellow race to destroy a white one."[11]

On 5 March, Frank L. Polk of the State Department directed Roland Morris, the American ambassador in Tokyo, a former student of Wilson's, to read Wilson's message to the Japanese government at the earliest opportunity. In this note, Wilson stressed "that the wisdom of interven-

tion seems to it [the United States Government] most questionable."
Japan would have to give "the most explicit assurances" that it was intervening as Russia's ally, for Russia's good, and with the exclusive purpose of
holding Russia against Germany and "at the absolute disposal of the final
peace conference." Otherwise, Wilson feared the situation might "play
into the hands of the enemies of Russia, and particularly of the enemies of
the Russian Revolution, for which the Government of the United States
entertains the greatest sympathy, in spite of all the unhappiness and misfortune which has for the time being sprung out of it."[12]

On 18 March, Lord Reading, the British ambassador to Washington,
asked Wilson to reconsider his stand on intervention.[13] Wilson replied
that he was "very conscious of the perplexities of the situation." Reading
reported that the Supreme War Council's most recent request urging him
to cooperate had not changed Wilson's mind.[14]

That same day Secretary of the Navy Josephus Daniels received a report
from Admiral Austin M. Knight, commander of the United States Asiatic
Fleet at Vladivostok, indicating that reports of the German menace in
Siberia were probably exaggerated. Knight reported that "no real *necessity*
exists for armed intervention in Siberia unless such intervention is desir-
able for the establishment of law and order. If for any reason, armed
intervention in Siberia should be decided upon," he added, " it is of the
first importance that Japan should not be permitted to act alone. This is
the one point upon which everybody who knows conditions and sentiment in Russia is absolutely agreed. It is universally believed by Russians
that Japan desires to take over a large part of Siberia and no arguments
can shake this belief."[15]

On 21 March the Germans began a startlingly successful spring offensive on the Western Front. The Allies felt an urgent need both to prevent
Germany from shifting reinforcements from the Russian Front and to stop
the armies of the Central Powers from obtaining supplies via Siberia, and
thereby circumventing the successful British blockade. Consequently they
increased their pressure on Wilson to consent to military intervention. By
the end of March the British Foreign Office had decided that it could

overcome American objections by proposing the use of an inter-Allied force rather than one exclusively run by the Japanese.[16]

Yet by the first of April, it seemed that American opposition to intervention had been successful. Wilson had vetoed all Allied proposals, and the Japanese were reluctant to act without American authorization.[17] The Allies, although unhappy, had to concede that Japanese intervention without American approval would lose its moral authority. Rebuffed by Wilson, the British turned their efforts, unsuccessfully, to winning an invitation to intervene from the Bolsheviks. The situation remained stymied until an incident involving the Czecho-Slovaks in Russia.

From 1914 to 1917 large numbers of Czech and Slovakian soldiers fighting in the Austro-Hungarian Army either had been captured by, or defected to, the Russian Army. Under the Provisional Government these troops were organized into the Druzina, or Czech Legion to fight the Germans on the Eastern Front. After the Bolsheviks seized power, they made arrangements to transport the legion, under the nominal command of the French Army, to Vladivostok. Once there they were to be shipped across the Pacific, the United States and the Atlantic to the Western Front to fight the Germans.

On 14 May 1918, while en route to Vladivostok, a train loaded with Czecho-Slovak soldiers stopped at Cheliabinsk, just east of the Urals in western Siberia. On the next track was a train loaded with Hungarian prisoners of war being repatriated under the terms of the Brest-Litovsk treaty. In a few minutes the traditional enmity between the two groups erupted into violence. As his train pulled out of the station, a Hungarian soldier threw a lump of iron at a group of Czechs, killing one of them. An irate party of Czechs boarded and stopped the Hungarian train, located the culprit, and lynched him. The local soviet, in turn, arrested the Czech hangmen.[18] In response to the arrests the Czecho-Slovak troops seized the town of Cheliabinsk. By 25 May, fighting had broken out all along the railroad between the Czechs and a variety of local soviets. Leon Trotsky, the commissar of foreign affairs, ordered the soviets to disarm the Czechs between Penza and Cheliabinsk; declaring that any Czech with a weapon was to be shot on sight.[19] When the Czechs learned of Trotsky's declaration, they voted to fight their way to Vladivostok—a seemingly impossible distance of about 4,000 miles.

The Czech uprising caused the Allies to reevaluate the possibility of intervention. They saw the legion's seizure of strategic points along the Trans-Siberian Railway, and the presence of 5,000 Czechs in the Volga area, as a heaven-sent opportunity to re-open the Eastern Front. Their only potential obstacle was Woodrow Wilson.

The first crack in Wilson's resolve appeared on 3 June. On that date he authorized the diversion of American troops from the Western Front to the north Russian port of Murmansk. Marshal Foch had assured him such a move was vital to the war effort.[20] The decision to send Allied troops to northern Russia was another offshoot of the presence of the Czech Legion in Russia and the desperate state of Allied affairs on the Western Front.

In the spring of 1918 a portion of the Czech Legion had begun its journey across Siberia to Vladivostok, but the rest remained in European Russia and western Siberia awaiting transportation. Sir Henry Wilson, the British permanent military representative to the Supreme War Council, recommended that the Czechs still in the Omsk area be sent to North Russia to the ports of Archangel and Murmansk to await transport to the Western Front. This route, he pointed out, was not only much shorter, but the Czechs could be used to protect the ports if the Germans in Finland attacked. In April, Lieutenant General Tasker Bliss, the American representative to the Supreme War Council, agreed to the proposal. Immediately the British Imperial General Staff sent a military mission to North Russia, supposedly to train and resupply the Czechs upon their arrival. Bliss agreed to send one battalion of US troops to serve with an inter-Allied force under British command. General John J. Pershing, the head of the American Expeditionary Force in Europe reluctantly agreed.[21] At first Wilson had opposed the move, but he too finally agreed, mainly because the British had received a request for help from the local soviet. But while Wilson agreed to send troops to Archangel, he continued to hesitate to involve the United States in Siberia.[22]

Wilson instructed General Bliss to inform the Supreme War Council that "Russia's misfortune imposes upon us at this time the obligation of unswerving fidelity to the principle of Russian territorial integrity and political independence." Wilson added that he still believed intervention via Vladivostok "impracticable" and that the idea of compensating Japan by giving up any part of Siberia was "inadmissible." Efforts in North Russia, he proclaimed, "should proceed, if at all, upon the sure sympathy of the Russian people and should not have as their ultimate object any restoration of the ancient regime or any other interference with the political liberty of the Russian people."[23]

Not everyone believed Wilson's decision to send troops to North Russia was a wise one. But when Secretary of War Newton Baker objected, Wilson told him he had "felt obliged to do it anyhow because the British and the French were pressing it on his attention so hard and he had refused so many of their requests that they were beginning to feel that he was not a good associate much less a good ally...."[24]

By 13 June, Allied diplomats and a few prominent American political figures, among them former presidents Taft and Roosevelt, were urging Wilson, in light of the Czech troops' uprising, to reconsider Siberian intervention. Meanwhile the American minister to China, Paul Reinsch, cabled Lansing that there might be an advantage in leaving the Czechs in Russia rather than transporting them to France. He and the Allied representatives in China believed that it would be a mistake to remove the Czecho-Slovaks. In his view, with very limited support they could gain control of all of Siberia and deny it to the Germans. The Czechs, he wrote "are sympathetic to the Russian population, eager to be accessories to the Allied cause, and their removal would greatly benefit Germany and further discourage Russia." He added, "if they were not in Siberia it would be worthwhile to bring them from a distance."[25]

Despite continuing pressure for intervention in Siberia from Allied diplomats, and increasing numbers of American State Department officials abroad, American military advisors continued to oppose it unanimously, believing the Western Front needed every available man.

On 19 June 1918, Wilson asked Army Chief of Staff Peyton C. March, to make a study of the feasibility of Siberian intervention by an inter-Allied force of 10,000 to 15,000 men. March, a man renowned for his austerity, efficiency, and lack of tact, offered serious objections to the proposal. In a letter to Wilson dated 24 June 1918, he declared that "as a military proposition [intervention in Siberia] is neither practical nor practicable."[26] He argued that intervention would mean giving Japan a portion of Siberian territory. Worst of all was that it would achieve nothing. March believed there was no possible way to re-invigorate the Russian army or force it back into the war. More than any other American advisor, he was qualified to make this judgment. March was familiar with the area, having been an observer in Siberia during the Russo-Japanese War of 1905. He concluded that the United States must concentrate its efforts exclusively on the Western Front and stay out of Russian affairs.[27]

The secretary of war agreed with his chief of staff. Baker told Wilson that if he had his way he would like to "take everybody out of Russia except the Russians, including diplomatic representatives, military representatives, political agents, propagandists, and casual visitors, and let the Russians settle their own affairs."[28]

Wilson's military advisors were not the only ones warning him against becoming enmeshed in Russia. Thomas Masaryk, president of the Czechoslovak National Council, was also skeptical. In a meeting on 19 June, Masaryk advised Wilson against involvement in Russia. Masaryk believed that the many proposals for intervention were not clear in their strategy or their goals. Japanese intervention in Siberia was unsound because it would aggravate and alienate the Russian people. He insisted that ultimately it would be extremely difficult to pay off the Japanese for their cooperation. Wilson pointed out that the United States would finance the Japanese expedition. Masaryk warned him that that would not satisfy them; they would demand Russian territory as well. He also told Wilson that in his opinion at least a million men would be required to intervene successfully in Siberia, and that the Japanese simply would not undertake a commitment of that size. As far as the Czech Legion was

concerned, Masaryk's position was clear. The Czech people wanted independence from Austria and they wanted the Czech Legion out of Russia
as soon as possible.[29]

By mid-June, the Japanese firmly declared what they would and would
not do in Siberia. They informed the Allied foreign ministers that no
Japanese forces sent to Siberia would go farther west than Irkutsk—slightly less than a third of the way across Siberia. They would intervene only
to prevent the spread of anarchy and German intrigue. But they would
not act unless America committed to the plan. They feared becoming
involved in a long struggle in Siberia only to be prevented by the Allies
from establishing trade there. Balfour tried to convince Wilson that the
Japanese demands were reasonable. "Since Russia cannot help herself, she
must be helped by her friends."[30] Therefore, it was logical the war council
should ask Japan, the nearest ally, to deliver that help.

On 27 June, Wilson received yet another appeal for intervention.
Marshal Foch warned him that "more than ever, in the interest of military
success in Europe, I consider the expedition to Siberia as a very important
factor for victory, provided the action be immediate, on account of the
season being already advanced, I take the liberty of insisting on this last
point."[31] Foch enclosed a proposed plan of action by the permanent military representatives of the Supreme War Council.

As June ended, events were forcing Wilson to make a decision. Thus far
he had tried to assure the Bolsheviks of his benevolent intentions, hoping
that if intervention were necessary he might receive an invitation from
the Soviets, but this policy had failed. German-Soviet relations, while far
from cordial, had failed to result in armed conflict as the Allies had hoped.
Allied ambassadors and several influential American politicians, as well as
Wilson's own diplomatic advisors in the United States and abroad, were
all pressing him to act. Wilson, moreover, could not discount the possibility that the Japanese would act independently. If they intervened on their
own, the American ability to influence them would be slight. While
Wilson continued to receive conflicting reports about a potential German

menace in Siberia, reports on the war in France were uniformly pessimistic, varying only in their increasing estimates of the length of the war.

Another consideration was the effect of Wilson's persistent rejection of the Allied schemes. The United States had been an active belligerent for only fourteen months, and Wilson had already had several major disagreements with the Allies. He had taken an independent position on war aims; he had insisted on an independent American command in France. Wilson's consent to intervention would be tangible proof of his good faith, and it would allow him to influence Allied policy in Russia.

As June ended, Wilson was still undecided. He spent the first weeks of a muggy Washington July consulting his advisors, and trying to find a satisfactory solution to what he termed "the Russian problem." The War Department still claimed that intervention was impractical and unnecessary, and that it could not reestablish the Eastern Front. Lansing was ambivalent, but an increasing number of State Department specialists, particularly the J. K. Caldwell, the American consul at Vladivostok, strongly favored intervention. Edward House, the president's closest friend and most influential advisor, was an eloquent opponent of intervention. House was spending the summer at his home in Massachusetts, where he was flooded with requests and reports aimed at persuading him (and consequently Wilson) to agree to intervention. By the end of June the alarming nature of these reports convinced House that some sort of action in Siberia was necessary, but Wilson could not just ignore the consistent opposition of the War Department, which considered the whole project futile at best, if not potentially disastrous.

As Wilson considered intervention he faced another unusual situation. The State Department, with the possible exception of Lansing, now supported intervention. If Wilson took its advice he would have to disregard the recommendations of the Army, which would then have the duty of carrying out a policy that it strongly opposed.

In an attempt to find a middle ground between Wilson and the Allies, House suggested that Wilson create a "Russian Relief Commission" under the leadership of Herbert Hoover. In 1914 Hoover had developed the successful Commission for the Relief of Belgium to feed millions of civilians in Belgium and other German occupied territory. In 1917 he had become head of the US Food Administration, whose task it was to create a surplus of food and fuel for the war effort. This new commission's objective would be to help Russia improve her food production. It would also coordinate its efforts with the Red Cross, the YMCA, and other relief organizations. To secure this objective, House argued, the relief commission would require a safe area in which to work. Wilson could thus ask the Allies to cooperate in maintaining order for the commission. The Allies, however, must promise in turn "that they will not either now or in the future, interfere with Russia's political affairs, or encroach in any way upon her territorial integrity." House argued that such a program would give Wilson control of the Russian situation, while satisfying the Allies and perhaps reconcile the greater part of Russia towards this kind of intervention.[32]

Wilson had already contemplated a Russian relief scheme, and he found House's suggestion appealing. The Allies, meanwhile, continued to press for full-scale military intervention. But Wilson was developing his own ideas for American military involvement in Russia—ideas that would bear little similarity to anything that the Allies had in mind—or to any previous incident in American military history.

While Wilson is probably best remembered for his attempts to establish world peace through the League of Nations, he was no pacifist. Nor was he squeamish about using military force if he felt American interests required it. Wilson sent American troops abroad seven different times during his eight years as president.[33] For Wilson, resorting to military force was, as Clausewitz said, "not merely an act of policy, but a true political instrument, a continuation of political intercourse, carried on with other means."[34] As president he often employed tightly controlled military force as an instrument of foreign policy. To understand the importance of this point one must review some of Wilson's views on the power of the president to conduct foreign affairs.

As a constitutional scholar, and the former McCormick Professor of Jurisprudence at Princeton University, Wilson had highly developed views on the powers of the president before he ever decided to run for that office. In his 1908 book *Constitutional Government in the United States*, he remarked "One of the greatest of the President's powers" is "his control…of the foreign relations of the nation. The initiative in foreign affairs which the President possesses without any restriction whatever, is virtually the power to control them absolutely."[35]

Not until the end of the nineteenth century and the beginning of the twentieth, however, did presidents have to concern themselves very much with the use of the military in international relations. Until the turn of the century there were only two basic uses for the American military. The first of these was that of suppressing domestic insurrection against the United States government. The Civil War is by far the best example, but the Whiskey Rebellion, the suppression of white terrorism in the South during Reconstruction, the Pullman strike of 1894, and innumerable Indian wars also illustrate the principle. The second sort of use was in a declared or de facto war against a foreign belligerent to protect immediate American interests, whether real or perceived. The Declaration of Independence served to convert the American Revolution into just such a war between sovereign belligerents (the newly sovereign United States and the now-foreign England). The undeclared naval war with France from 1798 to 1801, the clash with the Barbary States, the War of 1812, the Mexican War, and the Spanish-American War all exemplify this sort of conflict.

Since the United States continued to expand its borders throughout the nineteenth century, conflicts with American Indian tribes grew more frequent, and the legal status of the tribes tended occasionally to blur the distinction between foreign and domestic policy (and consequently the two categories of military operations). Campaigns in the Philippines also shared this ambiguity.

Military actions and occupations in Latin America before 1917, although actions of the second type, deserve special attention. William Howard Taft began this trend by dispatching troops to Nicaragua in 1910. Wilson likewise used the military once in Haiti, once in the Dominican

Republic, and once, if not twice, in Mexico, although the Punitive Expedition to Mexico has many anomalous features of its own. Wilson's policy towards Mexico to some extent foreshadowed his policy in Russia. The Taft and Wilson administrations justified these actions by arguing that these areas were vital to American interests, or that the United States would accrue some benefit by military actions there. This policy of using American troops in foreign countries in which the US had an important interest came to be known as "intervention."

Frederick Calhoun has argued that World War I and the actions in North Russia and Siberia were also interventions.[36] This seems to be so broad a use of the term, however, as to make it virtually meaningless. World War I was clearly just what the name implies—a foreign war, in the full and traditional sense of the word, against sovereign belligerents. Congress, in exercising its power to declare war (at Wilson's request), destroyed any fiction that American actions abroad were domestic in nature. Wilson agreed to the North Russian Expedition only after the Supreme War Council convinced him that it had a legitimate connection with the war with Germany.[37] Regarding this diversion, Wilson explained at the time that the United States "yields...to the judgment of the Supreme Command in the matter of establishing a small force at Murmansk, to guard the military stores at Kola and to make it safe for Russian forces to come together in organized bodies in the north. But it owes it to frank counsel to say that it can go no further than these modest and experimental plans."[38]

Actual American operations in Northern Russia, moreover, do not reflect American policy. Wilson authorized the diversion of the 339th Infantry and supporting units from the Western Front to Russia to help train and equip members of the Czech Legion who were being brought there to help defend the ports from the advancing German-supported Finns, however, the Czechs never reached North Russia, and the American troops came under the command of a British officer, Major General Frederick C. Poole. The troops actually fought Bolsheviks, not representatives of the Central Powers, until they were withdrawn in the summer of 1919. This episode, however, did not represent the true policy of the United States. It was the result of rapidly changing circumstances in northern Russia, and the fact that the American commander, Colonel George Stewart (whom the British commander outranked), found his orders unclear.

It was in Siberia alone, then, that Wilson's policies fell within neither the scope of a traditional war with a foreign belligerent nor the criteria of an intervention. Wilson seems to have been determined from the first that whatever action the United States took in Russia, it should remain neutral in Russian internal affairs. He was also determined that the expedition that he sent to Siberia, if any, should be wholly benevolent and self-abnegating. In this regard Wilson's Siberian policy differed not only from interventions, but also from all other instances in which the country had deployed troops to a foreign country.

His motives in Siberia were disinterested ones. In his "Fourteen Points" Address of 8 January 1918, Wilson said that whether "present Russian leaders believe it or not, it is our heartfelt desire and hope that some way may be opened whereby we may be privileged to assist the people of Russia to attain their utmost hope of liberty and ordered peace."[39] To that end his sixth point called for the evacuation of all Russian territory, and "self-determination of her own political development and national policy and assure her of a sincere welcome into the society of free nations under institutions of her own choosing; and, more than a welcome assistance also of every kind that she may need and may herself desire. The treatment accorded Russia by her sister nations in the months to come will be the acid test of their good will, of their comprehension of her needs as distinguished from their own interests, and of their intelligent and unselfish sympathy."[40]

Wilson wished to aid Russia. The problem was how to go about it. Throughout the first half of 1918, he watched and waited. He wrote to Charles William Eliot that "I wish most earnestly that it were possible to find some way to help, but as soon as we have thought out a working plan there is a new dissolution of the few crystals that had formed there."[41] The overthrow of the Provisional Government followed by the Treaty of Brest-Litovsk and the outbreak of civil war in Russia, each in turn destroyed his tentative plans to give aid.

Despite his concern over the Bolshevik's dissolution of the Constituent Assembly, Wilson repeatedly entertained the idea of at least de facto recognition of the Bolsheviks.[42] Meanwhile he attempted to impress upon the Allies the necessity of maintaining neutrality in Russian internal affairs. Wilson told his secretary, Joseph P. Tumulty, in effect that he did not "propose to interfere with the form of government in any other government. That would be in violent contradiction of the principles we have always held, earnestly as we should wish to lend every moral influence to the support of democratic institutions in Russia and earnestly as we pray that they may survive there and become permanent."[43]

On 8 April 1918, in his Proclamation on the National War Labor Board, Wilson commented on the necessity for respecting the self-determination of all countries, and his own policy towards revolutionary Mexico:

> Now, there isn't any one kind of government under which all nations ought to live. There isn't any one kind of government which we have the right to impose upon any nation. So that I am not fighting for democracy except for the peoples that want democracy. If they want it, then I am ready to fight until they get it. If they don't want it, that is none of my business....
>
> That was the principle I acted on in dealing with Mexico, I said that Mexico was entitled, so far as we were concerned, if she did not interfere with us, to have any kind of order or any kind of disorder that she pleased—that it was none of our business.

He concluded by saying, "A peace is not going to be permanent until this principle is accepted by everybody, that, given a political unit, it has the right to determine its own life."[44] As far as Wilson was concerned, this policy extended to Russia.

Nevertheless, Wilson believed that conditions in Russia required that the United States send some sort of civil relief commission. He still refused to consider military intervention to restore order without the invitation of the Bolshevik authorities. The American Expeditionary Force (AEF) in Siberia, to his mind, had a carefully defined mission, but that mission did not qualify as "intervention" and he expressed skepticism about such an undertaking even if the Allies were invited.[45]

By June the president and the State Department were involved in creating a commission for the relief of Russia. Lansing seconded House's suggestion that Wilson name Herbert Hoover as chairman and that the commission be organized along the lines of the Commission for Relief in Belgium.[46] Sir William Wiseman, head of British counterintelligence in the United States, in his report to Sir Eric Drummond, Balfour's private secretary, found some hope for the interventionist cause in this news. Sir William said that Hoover would take a large staff with him, and that a military force of sufficient size to protect his mission would accompany them. Hoover could then request more troops if he needed them. The British took the position that the commission might be used as an intermediate step in persuading Wilson to participate in full-scale military operations in Siberia.[47]

In early July 1918 the Supreme War Council in Paris decided to make a stronger, unified appeal for military intervention to Wilson. On the 2 July, the British prime minister, David Lloyd George, presented a final draft of the appeal to the Supreme War Council, maintaining that Allied intervention was "an urgent and imperative necessity."[48]

Lloyd George stressed that the actions of the Czecho-Slovak troops in seizing strategic points along the Trans-Siberian Railroad had transformed the situation. Fate had introduced a well-trained and highly motivated Allied force into Russia, which ought to be put to good use as the nucleus for reviving the Eastern Front. He also argued that intervention was necessary if the Allies were to win the war. "The Germans know as well as we know that there is but the smallest chance of an Allied victory on the Western Front in 1919 unless Germany is compelled to transfer a consid-

erable amount of her strength back again from West to East. It will therefore be," he said, "a primary object of her policy to prevent the re-creation
of an Eastern Allied front...." He then added, "If the Allies are to win the
war in 1919 it should be a primary object of their policy to foster and assist
the national movement in Russia in order to reform an Eastern Front."[49]

Lloyd George asserted that apart from forcing the Germans to withdraw
troops from the Western Front, and thereby shortening the war, interven-
tion would prevent Germany from benefiting from her victory over Russia.
It would "deny to Germany the supplies of Western Siberia and the important military stores at Vladivostock and render them available for the
Russian population."[50] He added that it was "the unanimous opinion of
General Foch and the Allied military advisers of the Supreme War
Council that the immediate dispatch of an adequate Allied force to
Siberia is essential for victory of the Allied armies."[51] He assured Wilson,
furthermore, that Japanese cooperation was essential, but that Japan
would not undertake effective action without encouragement and support
of the United States government. Finally, bearing in mind "the short time
available before the winter for initiating active operations in Siberia and
the rapid German penetration into Russia," Lloyd George and the
Supreme War Council appealed to Wilson to approve their recommended policy "and thus enable it to be carried into effect before it is too late."
An important additional consideration, and one the Allies believed would
appeal to Wilson, was the safety of the Czech troops in Russia. Military
intervention, they added, would also "bring assistance to the Czecho-
Slovak forces which have made great sacrifices to the cause for which we
are fighting."[52]

Apart from enumerating the reasons for intervention, the council outlined the manner in which they wanted it to be carried out. Pledges to
respect Russian territorial integrity should accompany intervention. The
council also stated that circumstances required the intervening forces to
be "adequate in number, ...and Allied in composition."[53] It recommended sending 100,000 men. Speed was the vital factor, and due to
geographical and shipping conditions Japanese troops would comprise the

largest portion of the force, "but its Allied character must be maintained and it must include American and Allied units." To prevent giving the impression of a Japanese invasion, the force was to be under a single command appointed by the power that provided the largest number of troops.[54] In a further attempt to win Wilson's favor, the Supreme War Council also suggested that the United States might administer relief programs. These programs would "supply the wants and alleviate suffering of Russian people."[55]

Wilson had resisted most of these arguments before, but the council's appeal contained a new element—the Czech Legion. It is doubtful, given Wilson's previous intransigence, that this appeal, desperate though it was, could have persuaded him to ignore the advice of the War Department. But the reportedly perilous position of the Czechs did represent a substantial change that required a review of policy. The State Department lost no time in bringing this change to Wilson's attention.

Following the Cheliabinsk uprising, the weak forces of the Maryanoka Soviet at Novo Nikolaevsk tried to carry out Trotsky's orders to halt the legion. They attempted to disarm the 7th Regiment of Captain Rudolf Gajda, one of the few Czech officers who had seriously planned for the possibility of shooting his way out of Siberia. Gajda, an able, albeit high-strung, soldier, originally served in the Austrian Army as a hospital orderly; later, in the more fluid structure of the Czech Legion, he advanced in rank. He had a decided taste for the melodramatic, and a tendency to dabble in political intrigue, neither of which was uncommon in revolutionary Russia. Gajda resisted the Maryanoka Soviet, and his troops seized Novo Nikolaevsk. He then ordered all Czech units between Omsk and Irkutsk to act likewise to secure the escape of the Czechs.[56] Thus had begun the revolt of the entire Legion.

In Washington, even by the beginning of July, Wilson was not aware of the actual position of the Czechs in Russia. He, like everyone else, believed that German and Austro-Hungarian prisoners of war released from confinement by the Bolsheviks had the Czechs trapped in Siberia. As defectors from the Austrian Army, the Czechs could expect no mercy from their former comrades.

The Supreme War Council had been correct in its assumption that a plan to rescue the Czechs would appeal to Americans. The secretary of state believed it was a significant change in circumstances. On 4 July, Lansing sent Wilson a memorandum stating that the United States's responsibility to the Czechs was particularly great as "they were being attacked by released Germans and Austrians." He advised that the United States should aid the Czechs who had reached Vladivostok by sending ammunition, arms, artillery, and supplies. He also suggested that additional troops be sent to assist the Czechs in policing the Trans-Siberian Railway, and disarming and dispersing the Austrian and German prisoners of war. These additional troops would be supplied by the United States and the Allies, but the bulk of them would come from Japan.

Lansing stipulated that the Allies should precede any action in Russia by a declaration of non-interference in Russian internal matters, and a promise of the complete withdrawal of all forces as soon as the threat from the Central Powers ended. His final suggestion was the creation of a commission to assist in the restoration of trade and industry, and to dispense aid to the Russian people. Arguing forcibly that steps must be taken to help the Czech Legion, Lansing distinguished the kind of intervention he proposed from that which the Supreme War Council recommended. He was convinced that "furnishing protection and assistance to the Czecho-Slovaks who are so loyal to our cause, is a very different thing from sending an army into Siberia to restore order or to save the Russians from themselves. There is a moral obligation to save these men from our common enemies, if we are able to do so."[57]

Wilson agreed with Lansing's assessment; on the evening of 6 July, he summoned the secretaries of state and war, along with Secretary of the Navy Josephus Daniels, Chief of Staff Peyton March, and Chief of Naval Operations Admiral William S. Benson, to a meeting to discuss a proposed solution for the Czech problem. General March recalled that the "President entered the room with a pad in his hand, and taking a position standing and facing us, somewhat in the manner of a school teacher addressing a class of pupils, read from his pad his views on the matter at issue...." This was an outline of the aide memoire he later sent to General Graves.[58] Wilson proposed that the United States share with Japan the cost of supplying the Czechs. The Japanese and Americans would land a military force in Vladivostok to guard the Czech line of communication as far west as Irkutsk. The American and Japanese detachments would each be limited to 7000 troops.[59]

The two US regiments, the 27th and 31st Infantry Regiments, stationed in the Philippines and totaling 7000 men, were the only troops the General Staff was willing to spare from duty in France. As the Office of the Chief of Staff saw it, a large number of troops would not be necessary as "the value of our troops in Siberia" was to be "*largely moral.*" The troops would serve two purposes. The first was to provide a "rallying point — which would serve as a center of development and expansion for the anti-German Russian and Czecho-Slav elements in Siberia." The second purpose of the American troops was to take part in an operation to rescue the Czecho-Slovaks. In discussing the strength of the force required, the War Department believed that "the moral effect of the two Regular United States Regiments is practically as important, when the regiments are small, as if they were at war strength. It was not expected that they will be needed for combat purposes any time in the near future...." This was the understanding of the General Staff of the situation when it completed its preliminary report on 6 July.[60]

Having presented his proposal, Wilson called for a vote. According to General March, he shook his head disapprovingly. "Why are you shaking your head, General?" Wilson asked in irritation. He then answered his own question. "You are opposed to this because you do not think Japan will limit herself to 7000 men and that decision will further her schemes for territorial aggrandizement.?" General March replied, "Just that, and for other military reasons," which he had already made plain in his earlier report. To which Wilson responded "Well, we will have to take that chance...."[61]

Baker's position was well-known to Wilson. He said little during the meeting, but his opposition to the expedition was unwavering. He believed that the Russians had to sort out their own future, and that the United States should confine its efforts to France. Years later he was still unresigned to the expedition, remarking in 1929 that "the expedition was nonsense from the beginning and always seemed to me one of those sideshows born of desperation for the purpose of keeping up morale rather than because of any clear view of the military situation."[62]

Despite General March's opposition, and Secretary Baker's disapproval, the majority of the conference members ultimately agreed on several points. First, they believed that reestablishment of the Eastern Front was impossible, even if a large Japanese force were available. Second, they thought that any advance west of Irkutsk was equally impossible. Third, they held that the Czech situation warranted action by the US government and the Allies "to make an effort to aid the Czechs in Vladivostok in reuniting with their compatriots in Western Siberia; and that the United States would be open to widespread criticism if she failed to help them."[63] The conference further decided that the United States could not furnish any considerable force in the short time required; therefore it would ask the Japanese to supply the Czecho-Slovaks with small arms and ammunition at Vladivostok, and to send 7000 troops immediately to help guard Czecho-Slovak lines of communication. The United States would dispatch a similar force as soon as possible; naval forces in Vladivostok should take the city and cooperate with the Czechs. Finally, the members stipulated that the Americans and the Japanese should jointly announce that their purpose in "landing troops is to aid the Czecho-Slovaks against German and Austrian prisoners, that there is no purpose to interfere with the internal affairs of Russia and they guarantee not to impair the political or territorial sovereignty of Russia."[64]

When the meeting adjourned, wheels immediately began to turn. Daniels cabled Admiral Austin M. Knight aboard the *USS Brooklyn*, anchored off Vladivostok in Gold Horn Bay, and ordered him to keep the city open as a route of escape for the Czechs.[65] Meanwhile, in the White

House, Wilson closeted himself with his typewriter for the next several days to compose an aide memoire, defining the role of the United States in Russia and explaining his reasons for dispatching troops to Siberia. It was the only statement Wilson ever made on his decision to intervene. Its articulation proved painfully slow.

On 8 July Wilson confided to House, "I have been sweating blood over the question—what is right and feasible (*possible*) to do in Russia. It goes to pieces like quicksilver under my touch, but I hope; See [sic] and can report some progress presently, along the double line of economic assistance and aid to the Czechoslovaks."[66]

While Wilson struggled to define American policy, Secretary of the Navy Daniels sent him a report from Admiral Knight on the Czech situation. Knight reported that in capturing the town of Nikolsk the Czechs suffered 43 killed and 233 wounded. The admiral estimated their enemies' losses at 250 killed, many wounded, and 1,000 taken prisoner. Four Czech soldiers were taken prisoner and "killed with great brutality" after being "shockingly mutilated." The Czechs' supply of ammunition was exhausted, although Japan promised to provide new supplies. In Knight's opinion, the situation was "extremely dangerous." The Czechs had to garrison the towns in their rear as they advanced; therefore, they were constantly loosing strength. He added, "the present condition cannot long continue." He urged the Allies to take prompt and decisive action. Knight believed a small force sent immediately would stay the present emergency, but accomplish nothing permanent unless it was followed by a much larger force "whose coming" he said "should be announced soon even if actual arrival is delayed." The Philippine regiments, he continued, "could be thrown in promptly with an equal force of Japanese," but they ought to be followed by a larger army with the ultimate purpose of establishing a new front. Knight pointed out that the Czechs considered the situation of their comrades west of Irkutsk so dangerous that they intended to advance regardless of all obstacles, and would fight to the last man. It was now a question, he concluded, not just of helping the Russians but of combating German aggression in Siberia. "Germany," he warned had "found the means to create a new Eastern front from war prisoners and Bolsheviki all of whom are with her. The other parties are inactive through fear of [the] results if Germany crushes the CZECHS," he concluded "We shall save Siberia in saving the CZECHS."[67]

This alarming cable did not persuade Wilson to expand the expedition beyond the limits already set. It was typical, however, of reports from Americans in Siberia about the position of the Czechs. It did, however, prompt Wilson to complete his statement. While he was contemplating American policy, Lansing contacted the Japanese government about its proposed role in Siberia.[68] Shortly after this communication, rumors that the United States was going to intervene began to circulate. In response to this embarrassing development, Wilson dispatched confidential copies of his aide memoire on the Siberian situation to the Allied governments on 17 July.[69]

Wilson's aide memoire was the most important document concerning American policy in Siberia. It served as the instructions for both the diplomatic corps and the army. Wilson never countermanded or amended the aide memoire during the two years that American troops were in Siberia. Its scope ranged far beyond a typical set of military orders; rather, it embodied Wilson's policy in Siberia. It encapsulated his views on the duty of one nation to another, and outlined his attempt to create a benevolent role for the American troops. If seen as concrete instructions for the practical application of these principles, however, it was often unclear, occasionally contradictory, and left a great deal to the discretion of the commanding general.

In this document Wilson stressed the United States's commitment to the war and her desire to cooperate with the Allies. But he pointed out that the focus of the American effort was on winning the war on the Western Front. The United States, through tremendous effort, was able to bridge the Atlantic. She could not, he emphasized, undertake a military action in the Far East at an even greater distance without undermining her efforts in Europe at a time when the situation there was already desperate.

Wilson insisted that the United States could not countenance or participate in military intervention in Russia, and he dismissed the possibility of reconstructing an Eastern Front. He stated emphatically that military intervention in Russia "would only add to the present sad confusion in Russia rather than cure it, injure her rather than help her, and that it would be of no advantage in the prosecution of our main design, to win the war against Germany." The United States could not, therefore, "take part in such intervention or sanction it in principle." In such a case "[m]ilitary intervention would...be merely a method of making use of Russia, not a method of serving her." Wilson echoed the sentiments of the War Department in this matter. Then, having apparently prepared to refuse to cooperate once again, he suddenly granted permission for the dispatch of American troops to Siberia. Their duties, however, he strictly circumscribed. Wilson defined military action as "admissible in Russia,...only to help the Czecho-Slovaks consolidate their forces and get into successful cooperation with their Slavic kinsmen and to steady any efforts at self-government or self-defence in which the Russians themselves may be willing to accept assistance."[70]

He added that the only "legitimate object for which American or Allied troops can be employed...is to guard military stores which may be subsequently needed by Russian forces and to render such aid as may be acceptable to the Russians in the organization of their own self-defense." Therefore, American soldiers were to have two specific tasks. Their primary object was the rescue of the Czech Legion, "for which there was immediate necessity and sufficient justification."[71] Wilson did not, however, specify how this was to be done; neither did he say what the American forces were to do after effecting the rescue. Their secondary task was to protect Allied supplies at Vladivostok and to assist the Russians in self defense against the Germans.[72]

There were potential problems with the duties of the American troops described in the aide memoire. They were to guard the military stores stock-piled at Vladivostok which the Russians might need in the future. But Wilson did not say which Russians were to have use of them. At that time there were more than twenty self-proclaimed governments in Russia. He did not say, moreover, for what purpose they were to be used. The aide memoire made no mention at all of the Bolsheviks, or any other Russian political faction. Wilson did make repeated references to the "Russian people," indicating that he believed there existed some basic unity of opinion within Russia to which he could appeal. Consequently, Wilson deliberately left the United States in the position of neither supporting nor opposing any Russian political party. The United States would maintain neutrality as far as Russian domestic politics were concerned.[73]

The situation was further complicated by Wilson's secondary task for the Army, which was to "steady any efforts of self-government or self-defense in which the Russians themselves may be willing to accept assistance." Wilson made no attempt to clarify this statement. He did not say what sort of self-government he had in mind, nor who was to establish it, neither did he define what he meant by "efforts at self-defense," although presumably they were to be directed against the Germans. Although Wilson's instructions were far from explicit, and left much to the expedition's commander, he did make it abundantly clear that he was not willing to permit American participation to exceed the limits he set for it. The aide memoire, as Wilson described it, was intended to be a "perfectly frank and definite statement of the policy which the United States feels obliged to adopt for herself and in the use of her military forces." He stated that the United States would "feel at liberty to use the few troops it could spare only for the purpose stated and shall feel obliged to withdraw these forces...if the plans in whose execution it is now intended that they should cooperate should develop into others inconsistent with the policy to which the Government of the United States feels constrained to restrict itself."[74]

After stating firmly that the United States would withdraw if the Allies attempted to push her into action inconsistent with the his views, Wilson forfeited any leverage the ultimatum might have given him over the Allies by amending his warning and adding that "the Government of the United States does not wish it to be understood that in so restricting its own activities it is seeking, even by implication, to set limits to the action, or define the policy of its Associates."[75] Wilson, therefore, had tied his own hands diplomatically before the expedition had even been organized, by in effect giving carte blanche to the Allies.

The president then asked the Allies for the usual assurances guaranteeing Russian political sovereignty and non-interference in Russian internal affairs. He cautioned that the Associated Powers had "the single object of affording such aid as be acceptable, [sic] and only such aid as shall be acceptable, to the Russian people in their endeavor to regain control of their own affairs, and their own destiny."[76]

In his final paragraph Wilson announced his intention to dispatch a commission of merchants, agricultural experts, laborers, advisors, and Red Cross representatives, as well as agents of the YMCA to Russia to organize "educational help of a modest sort in order in some systematic manner to relieve the immediate economic necessities of the people there in every way for which opportunity may be open."[77] Wilson rejected the idea of American "military intervention" in Russia, saying that the United States could not "take part in such intervention or sanction it in principle."[78] Yet he was sending American troops to Siberia. Clearly he distinguished the mission of the troops that he planned to dispatch to Siberia from the idea of "military intervention."

While Wilson contemplated economic and police action in Russia, the news of the Czech uprising caused him to expand his plans for the latter.[79] These were the underlying elements that influenced Wilson's policy as outlined in his aide memoire. This document delineated the extent to which Wilson was willing to compromise.

The Allies, however, were not completely satisfied with the aide memoire. Wilson had consented to send troops to Russia, something the Allies had requested for months, but the final result was not what they had anticipated. The British government in particular took exception to the aide memoire on three points. First, Wilson had ruled out the reestablishment of the Eastern Front as a legitimate object. The British government had taken the position that this was prerequisite to defeating Germany.

Second, the British objected to the implication that the Allies were thinking only of their own interests, and not Russia's. They believed that
freeing Russia from potential German domination constituted a signal service. Finally they emphatically denied that intervention in Russia had any
ulterior political purpose.[80]

A few days after Wilson dispatched copies of the document to the
Allied governments, the Japanese government released its own plan for
Siberian intervention—a plan which did not coincide with Wilson's.
Amid avowals of disinterested friendship for Russia and respect for her
territorial integrity, the Japanese government announced the dispatch of
troops to Vladivostok. However, in a conversation with Frank Polk the
Japanese ambassador told him that his country could not be bound by the
limit of 7000 men Wilson had placed upon them. Such a number would
be "too small adequately to protect the rear of the Czecho-Slovacs." He
anticipated that his government would send one division, about 12,000
men, "with the understanding that the number of troops that they would
send would depend upon the amount of resistance that they met from the
Bolsheviks, Austrian and German prisoners."[81]

On 26 July, Wilson discovered that the Japanese were proposing to send
another division to Manchuria in addition to the one they were sending
to Vladivostok.[82] As a result of the Japanese action, Wilson was compelled
to make large portions of the aide memoire public.[83] In response to the
president's complaints that Japan had acted without consulting him,
Colonel House wrote on 25 July to Wilson that in his opinion the "difficulty...is that there are two parties in Japan. The Civil Government
wishes to cooperate with us and sees the necessity for it. The military
clique sees nothing in such intervention [under Wilson's terms] for Japan.
They have not the vision to know that in the end it would be better for
the Japanese to do the altruistic thing." House added, "I hope before the
war is over we can drive it into the consciousness of individuals as well as
nations that from a purely selfish viewpoint it is better to take the big
broad outlook that what is best for all is best for one."[84]

While House and Wilson both distrusted the Japanese military and perceived its cynical attitude, they did not specifically question the wisdom of assigning it to carry out a policy to which it was hostile. It was imperative that the United States and Japan agree on the purpose of the expedition if Wilson's hopes were to have the remotest chance of being realized. By the end of July this difficulty seemed to have been overcome, when the State Department carefully defined the goals of the expedition in a declaration to which the Japanese gave full adherence.

In a statement on 2 August 1918, the Japanese government proclaimed its anxiety to fall in with the desires of the US government, and in consequence it had decided to proceed immediately to make available a suitable force for the mission. It emphasized its willingness to reaffirm its respect for the territorial integrity of Russia and to abstain from all interference in her internal affairs. The statement concluded with the pledge that "upon the realization of the objects...indicated," it would immediately withdraw all Japanese troops from Russian territory.[85] At the beginning of August the conflict between American and Japanese policies seemed to have been satisfactorily resolved. Matters seemed to be progressing smoothly when Wilson received criticism of his policy from an unexpected quarter. When reporters asked Thomas Masaryk about the proposed expedition, he responded that he had no specific knowledge of Allied plans but

> [j]udging from the reports I receive, and the news I read in the papers, I am obliged to say that it seems to me that the Allies must send a considerably greater force and that their policy towards the various Russian parties and governments (a rather dreary symptom of the Russian disorganization and lack of political maturity) should be clearer and more energetic. A precise political (and administrative) plan is also necessary for the success of military operations.[86]

Masaryk's criticism was based on his estimate of the minimum steps necessary to revitalize the Eastern Front, something which Wilson had no intention of doing. Wilson was determined to help the Czechs get out of

Siberia, but beyond their rescue he had no wish to become ensnared in any military action. He wanted to dispatch a humanitarian mission to Russia, and to use American forces to protect that mission. He had no wish to go beyond this. Wilson made his intentions plain in several interviews with Allied diplomatic representatives, including Sir William Wiseman. The British, nevertheless remained convinced, that once the US was involved in Russia they could persuade Wilson to expand his commitment and cooperate militarily with the Allies.[87] Sir William was one of the only Allied representatives besieging Wilson during the first half of 1918 who detected anything other than coyness in Wilson's attitude. He cautioned Arthur Cecil Murray at the Foreign Office Department of Political Intelligence that Wilson's policy was not whimsical.

> The President remains quite unconvinced by all political arguments in favor of Allied intervention, nor was he more impressed by the military arguments in favor of re-creating an Eastern Front. From the political point of view, he has always thought—and still thinks—it would be a great blunder for the Allies to intervene without an unmistakable invitation from the Soviet Government. Anyone who has studied his Mexican policy will understand the remarkable parallel which the Russian situation presents, and realise that this is to him more than a passing political question, but a matter of principle. I am not saying that he is right, but I think we should realise that we are up against *a new conception of foreign policy* which no amount of argument will reconcile with, for instance, traditional British policy.[88]

As Sir William saw it, at some point either Wilson would change his policy or the Allies would be bitterly disappointed. To him the latter seemed more likely. But for the present, Wilson had decided to implement his own version of a Siberian policy—a policy that broke sharply with traditional ventures of this sort.

Now he had to find someone to carry it out.

2

The Czecho-Slovak Legion and American Policy

DURING THE WINTER AND SPRING OF 1918, AS THE ALLIED AND Associated Powers debated the possibility of intervention in Siberia, and Wilson formulated the policies that he eventually set forth in the aide memoire, events in Russia were in flux. By the time American forces arrived in August 1918, the circumstances that caused Wilson to send them had changed radically. The main reasons for this change were the actions of the Czechs and of the Bolsheviks, and the arrival of Allied forces—particularly Japanese troops—in Siberia.

In March 1918 the only interest the Czech Legion had was in getting out of Siberia alive; involvement in Russian revolutionary politics was far from the Czech leaders' minds. After the Treaty of Brest-Litovsk, Masaryk outlined the Czechs' official policy in Russia. "As long as you are in Russia," he proclaimed, "maintain, as hitherto, strict neutrality in regard to Russian party dissensions. Only those Slavs and those parties who openly side with the enemy [Austria and Germany] are our enemies."[89] But a few months later, while Masaryk was in America, the young Czech military leaders in Siberia showed little regard for either the political or military implications of their actions and the ensuing complications. For the most part they remained unaware of the repercussions of the Czech revolt on Allied and American policy and strategy, and indifferent to the effect on Russian politics.[90]

In late May and early June 1918 the Czechs enjoyed spectacular success following the revolt of the legion at Cheliabinsk. Three hundred miles south of Moscow they seized Penza and within a month had control of the railroad spanning the Urals between that city and Omsk. In the towns along the railroad the Czechs found large quantities of arms and ammunition.[91] They enjoyed one quick victory after another until June, when they fought a successful twelve-day battle to recapture Irkutsk. Once it fell, the only remaining obstacle between the legion and Vladivostok was the imposing Lake Baikal. The largest fresh water lake in the world, Baikal had been a major engineering problem in the construction of the Trans-Siberian Railway. Its maximum depth is more than 5,700 feet. To complicate matters further, it is flanked on the west by the Baikal Mountains, and is fed by over 300 rivers. The lake was impossible to bridge, so the tsar's engineers had blasted their way through the rock spurs on its south shore. The track connecting Baikal and Kultuk thus passed through no fewer than thirty-nine tunnels.

The Bolsheviks were comparatively strong in the Baikal sector. They used this highly defensible area to offer stiffer resistance than the Czechs had yet encountered. Gajda's troops ultimately forced them to retreat, but the Bolshevik forces managed to blow up one of the tunnels. Gajda, by now a general, took personal command of the Lake Baikal sector. He took a month to clear the tunnel; the track was reopened by the end of July, but Bolsheviks, who had retained control of the lake continued to hinder Czech efforts using ships to bombard them on shore.

While the Czechs were engaged in clearing the railroad, the Red Forces had time to recover, and now they were considerably stronger. Gajda decided his only chance of breaking through the mountains was to prepare an ambush at a point behind the Czech lines where the tracks passed through a long, deep valley. Gajda's remaining units attacked the Red forces and then retreated, luring the Bolsheviks behind their lines. The Bolsheviks followed with three armored trains and several echelons of troop-carriers accompanied by substantial infantry, cavalry, and artillery support. Suspicious, they entered the valley cautiously, and then only after darkness fell on 4 August. The Czechs tore up the tracks behind the Bolshevik trains, while their waiting regiments attacked from both sides. Then Gajda's main force took the offensive. The Red forces fought tenaciously throughout the night and the next day. But by 6 August the

Bolsheviks, cut off, were weakening, and by the next day, they had clearly lost. To the Czechs went the spoils: sixteen engines, a large quantity of rolling stock, and most importantly, a clear line to Vladivostok and a secure line of communications.[92]

About the same time the Czechs enjoyed another stroke of good fortune in the west. On 6 August, after nearly a month-long siege, members of the Czech Corps captured the Volga city of Kazan. When the Czechs seized the rail yard, they discovered they had also captured the Imperial Russian gold reserves, which the Provisional Government had sent there a year before when it feared that Petrograd would fall to the Germans.[93] Twenty freight cars contained vast riches: 650,000,000 rubles in gold; 100,000,000 paper "Romanovs," which still held their face value; Tsar Nicholas's and the Empress Alexandra's personal gold, silver, and platinum stocks; several imperial crowns; an assortment of jewels; a priceless porcelain collection; and two old assayers, who kept the registers and lived in the boxcars with their families. The treasure had an estimated value of half a billion dollars.[94] The windfall gave the Czechs additional leverage in their negotiations with the Allies, the Bolsheviks, and any would-be Russian government. They lost no time in packing it all off to Cheliabinsk.

Obviously the Czechs were in a much stronger position than anyone could have dreamt when Wilson drafted the aide memoire. A major question in the minds of many Americans was whether the Czechs had ever been in as much jeopardy as Wilson had been led to believe.

Czech success in Siberia saved the gold reserves from the Bolsheviks, but its effect on the imperial family was not so salutary. On the night of 16 July the tsar, the tsarina, their children, and members of their household being held in Ekaterinburg were murdered by the local Soviet, which feared that the advancing Czechs might free them. It was a coincidence that while the murders were underway Wilson was composing the aide memoire in Washington. Even as he struggled to define a scrupulously fair and correct policy for the United States in Russia, desperation was forcing both the Czechs and the Bolsheviks to adopt increasingly bloody and ruthless measures.

The Bolsheviks did not subscribe to the honorable code of conduct that bound Wilson, and the Czechs felt they could not afford it. Wilson, far away in Washington, knew nothing of this. Based on the information he had received, he still believed that the conflict was not between the Bolsheviks and the Czechs, but between the Czechs and armed German prisoners of war. These "enemy prisoners" supposedly intended to seize Siberia, complete with the Allied supply dumps at Vladivostok and the western Siberian grain stores.

These prisoners of war, in reality, were never the threat that Wilson believed. Of the prisoners of war interned in Russia, less than half were in Siberia. Those in Siberia were mainly concentrated at several points along the Trans-Siberian railroad at camps in Omsk, Krasnoyarsk, Irkutsk, and Blagoveschensk. The number of prisoners most frequently cited as having been interned in Siberia is 800,000. This is probably a conservative estimate. The majority of these prisoners were technically Austro-Hungarian.[95] But most were not even Austrian—Hungarians comprised the largest group, followed by the Czecho-Slovaks. Only a tenth of all the prisoners in Russia were German, and less than half of these were located in Siberia.[96]

It was widely reported in Europe and the United States, following the Treaty of Brest-Litovsk, that massive groups of miraculously armed "Austrian and German" troops were organizing themselves to take over Siberia, but this was not the case. The German and Austrian governments never sponsored such an undertaking. Such armed prisoners as there were, had been organized and commanded by the Red Army. They were in league with, or subordinate to, the Bolsheviks rather than attempting to overthrow them.

According to the observations of Swedish Red Cross workers in Russia, who had no political axe to grind, no more than 20 percent of the prisoners in Russia ever joined the Bolsheviks. Of this 20 percent, many were forced to join. Of those allied with the Bolshevik cause, only a small percentage were ever armed. The Swedish Red Cross estimated that no more than 15,000 prisoners were armed in all Russia. A third of these were in Turkestan, leaving about 10,000 in European Russia and Siberia. This meant that less than one percent of all the prisoners in Siberia were armed, and only about 5.5 percent of all the prisoners in Russia ever joined the Bolsheviks. Of the prisoners who did join, the Hungarians were the largest group, followed by Czechs and a substantial number of Serbs. The Germans proved more resistant than any other group to Soviet recruitment. Only a negligible number of German prisoners joined the Red Army, mostly in positions of leadership.[97] Nevertheless, the fact remained that the only large, well-organized force of armed former prisoners of war in Siberia when Wilson dispatched the AEF was the Czech Legion itself.

In March 1918 a variety of people attempted to verify the rumors about armed prisoners. William B. Webster, a member of the American Red Cross Commission, and Captain W. L. Hicks, representing the British Mission in Moscow, went to Siberia to investigate. In April they reported that they had found only 931 armed prisoners, whom the Bolsheviks were using to guard supplies and ammunition. They did pass a number of armed Hungarians, however, who were moving east to engage one of the renegade Cossack bands raiding the railway. The Central Siberian Soviet gave Webster and Hicks their written assurance that no more than 1,500 would be armed.[98]

The Soviets did not strictly adhere to the limit. They incorporated some of the former prisoners of war into the Red Army and later used them in attempts to disarm the legion. This action only lent further credence to the Czech belief that the Bolsheviks were acting as the puppets of the Central Powers. It was a common, but erroneous, conclusion. No one seemed to grasp the fact that most of these troops were acting, not at the instigation of their own governments (which strongly disapproved of their soldiers serving in an internationalist revolutionary army), but instead under the direct control of the Bolsheviks. If anyone had understood this, he would have seen that it was impossible to take action against these so-called "enemy prisoners of war" without coming into direct conflict with the Red Army in which they were serving.

The information flooding Washington and the Allied capitals revealed little of this situation. The State Department continued to receive alarming reports. Notable among these were the reports of the American Consul General Ernest Harris, who went so far as to exhume bodies to discover the nationality of various prisoners. He and the French Consul General managed to forward a number of desperate dispatches to Washington, citing large numbers of armed enemy prisoners threatening the city of Irkutsk.[99] When these reports were added to others from a variety of sources they painted an alarming picture of the situation. In fact Harris had some justification for his concern. Irkutsk was near one of the cities where the prisoners of war clashed with Czech soldiers. At Innokentievska, Austro-German prisoners of war attacked a Czech train parked 1.5 miles from a prison camp. The 1000 Czechs quickly defeated their attackers.[100]

Wilson received very little in the way of information contradicting the prevalent view that the Bolsheviks were tools of the Central Powers. Allied representatives told him repeatedly (although they themselves may not have believed it) that the Czechs were under attack from German and Austrian prisoners, to whom they usually vaguely referred as "the enemy."[101]

The Bolsheviks, when they were mentioned at all, usually figured ambiguously as abetting some German plot, not as the principal foe. It is doubtful that Wilson would have dispatched an expeditionary force to Siberia had he known that the Czechs were fighting some of the very "Slavic kinsmen" with whom he wanted them to "get into cooperation." But Wilson did not know this, and perhaps it is unfair to have expected him to realize it. Many other events seemed at the time to be of equal or greater importance. It was natural that Wilson should have believed what the majority of his sources told him. Even if he had had any doubts about the action he was taking, he had so carefully circumscribed the activities of the AEF in Siberia that he believed it would not be used, or perceived, as other than what he intended it—a humanitarian rescue mission.

Unfortunately, he could not know how many other variables entered into the equation. Some of the information he had been given was true after all. In July 1918 someone was attacking the Czechs. Only the most recklessly optimistic military strategist could have hoped that the legion would successfully fight its way 4,000 miles through hostile territory unassisted. Not even the Czech leaders (with a few exceptions) thought that it was possible. Viewing the situation from the ground, they were astounded by their success. Wilson certainly did not know that the Czechs were the best organized and coordinated force in Siberia.

Even while arrangements to organize and transport an American Expeditionary Force to Siberia were underway, Allied troops were landing in Vladivostok. By 3 August, British and French soldiers were disembarking. During the first week in July the precarious position of the Czechs and Wilson's refusal to intervene prompted the British War Office to send a regiment from Hong Kong, and to ask the Canadian government to send troops from British Columbia.[102] The first Japanese units soon followed. The US consul reported to the State Department that the Russians regarded the Japanese with suspicion and hostility.[103]

The number of Japanese troops arriving aggravated the situation. The 25,000–30,000 men of the Japanese 12th Infantry Division began disembarking on 3 August; by 21 August an additional 12,000 men had been unloaded and dispatched to Manchuria and the Far Eastern Province. Ten thousand more arrived in Vladivostok on 26 August. By the time of the European armistice in November, the Japanese had over 75,000 men in Siberia and Manchuria.[104] This was more than seven times the number on which Wilson and the Japanese government had originally agreed.

While Wilson was preparing to put his Siberian policy into action, the very conditions there upon which he based his plans were changing. The president might have thought that he had found a solution to the Siberian problem, but the Czecho-Slovaks, the Bolsheviks, and the Japanese—and even his European Allies—all had other plans.

3

General Graves and the AEF Siberia

ONCE WILSON DECIDED TO DISPATCH TROOPS TO SIBERIA HE HAD TO select a commander. For this position, Wilson wanted an officer with very specific qualities. He was to have his way in this instance; but the very qualities that he sought would produce a conflict between the War and State Departments that would have a devastating impact upon America's policy in Siberia.

Throughout his presidency, Woodrow Wilson's relationship with the American military establishment was a distant one. He respected his military advisors' expertise; he deferred to their decisions on logistics, tactics, and strategy; but he expected that they in turn would abide by his judgment in issues of policy—in short, that they would *obey* him.

Even after the United States entered World War I, Wilson took no interest in the mechanics of running the war. General March recalled that Wilson, although invited, never attended a single weekly meeting of the War Council.[105] Wilson was apparently not only confident in his military officers' abilities; he was sufficiently confident of his own authority over them that he felt no need to oversee them closely.

This attitude was typical of Wilson. At no point in his life did he have any real interest in military affairs. Once, when he was thirteen years old, he went alone to the Planters Hotel in Augusta, Georgia. He wriggled through a large crowd until he reached the front. There he stood gazing in admiration at Robert E. Lee, who was travelling from Virginia to Savannah.[106] Apparently, that was the last time that Wilson went to any pains to seek out a soldier. Although he was reared in the post-war South, Wilson lacked the Southerner's stereotypical interest in things military, even as a historical subject. Government institutions fascinated Wilson, but even as a scholar he paid scant attention to military or war powers.[107]

As President Wilson shunned his constitutional, supervisory power as commander-in-chief, foregoing all but a policy-making role. He did not closely follow the details of military actions; he paid little attention to the appointment of officers, and he rarely, if ever, tried to influence military strategy. During World War I he left Baker in sole charge of the War Department, the General Staff, and eventually the economic mobilization program as well.[108]

Why Wilson acted in this way is unclear. He may simply have wanted to concentrate his energies elsewhere. He may have done it for political reasons; or he may simply have thought it best to leave military matters to the experts. But whatever his reasons, Wilson was the beneficiary of the Root reforms of 1903, the establishment of the General Staff, General March's 1918 reorganization of that body, and the increasing professionalism of the army. Wilson's style of leadership relied heavily on these elements, for what he wanted was trained technicians capable of faithfully translating his statements of policy into military strategy.

When Wilson became president, officers of this sort, trained in the new fashion of the German General Staff system, were beginning to dominate the War Department. But friction between Wilson and the military did occur, especially in the early days of his presidency. Wilson respected his officers' advice, but he expected them to follow his instructions to the letter. This fact, when combined with his use of troops in circumstances that were neither fully peace nor fully war, caused problems. Soldiers accustomed to one or the other often felt uncomfortable in the grey middle ground that Wilson frequently chose for them. In June 1914 General W. W. Witherspoon, writing to his friend Tasker H. Bliss, complained of the restrictions placed on the army during the American intervention at Vera Cruz by the president and the State Department. "I suppose it never will be possible by any means, even if we could get a prolonged interview, to give you an idea of how we are cribbed and confined up here by the attitude of our superiors and an associated Department." He bewailed the fact that even "the most reasonable requests in matters presented in the strongest possible light as necessary are refused."[109]

In May 1915 Wilson clarified his thoughts on the role of the military. "The mission of America," he wrote, "is the only thing that a sailor or a soldier should think about. He has nothing to do with the formulation of her policy. He is to support her policy whatever it is...."[110] Wilson could be severe with those generals he perceived as interfering in his bailiwick, or violating the limits he set for them. In June 1918, for instance, he put a definite end to the War Department controversy as to whether General Leonard Wood would go to France. Wood had made numerous remarks criticizing the Wilson administration. General John J. Pershing, who had received command of the AEF and been promoted over Wood, did not want him there. Wilson wrote an editorial for the *Republican* explaining the situation. He acknowledged that Wood was "a man of unusual ability," but he noted that the general was apparently unable to submit his judgment to those who are superior to him in command."[111] Wilson never published this letter, but it is a fair indication that he felt General Wood had overstepped the acceptable bounds of military conduct.

Wilson played no active role in selecting Pershing to head the AEF, although he approved Newton Baker's choice. Baker based his decision on an interview with Pershing and the recommendation of the General Staff.[112] After Wilson approved Pershing's promotion he met with the general in May 1917. They chatted a few minutes about Mexico and whether Pershing was acquainted with France. To Pershing's astonishment, however, Wilson said nothing about the coming role of the AEF.[113] But when Pershing commented on political affairs, Wilson did not hesitate to bring him to heel.[114]

Although the details of war bored Wilson, he did hold strong opinions on the morality of war. He was not ethically averse to war if the cause justified it. He believed, for example, that the American Revolution was "fought for the plain right of self-government" and that it was therefore justifiable. On the other hand, he believed that the Mexican War was unjustifiable because of the United States's "ruthless aggression." "We were disposed to snatch everything," he wrote of that war, "and concede nothing." As for the Civil War, while he sympathized with the South, he found Northern war aims more morally acceptable.[115]

Wilson would also find acceptable those officers who shared his views and carried them out without question. By 1918, he had secretaries of war and the navy who fulfilled both criteria. As Frederick Calhoun has pointed out, these advisors "shared a general agreement that policy and purpose dictated the use of arms."[116] During his administrations Wilson had two secretaries of war. The first, Lindley Garrison, played only a small role in Wilson's developing military policies. He resigned in 1916 after a dispute with the president over the fundamental principles of army expansion in the wake of the *Lusitania* crisis. Wilson's second secretary of war, a former Cleveland mayor, Newton D. Baker, was a quasi-pacifist. Baker had known Wilson as a lecturer at Johns Hopkins. In Baker, Wilson secured a sympathetic secretary of war, someone who knew and understood his policies, and whom he could trust to carry them out loyally. Only one secretary of the navy served Wilson during his two terms, Josephus Daniels, a North Carolina newspaper publisher. He was a devout Methodist and, like Baker, he had strong pacifist leanings.[117]

Baker and Daniels, continued to be Wilson's trusted advisors and friends long after he broke with Edward House and Robert Lansing.[118] While Baker and Daniels generally opposed the use of force, they agreed with Wilson that it was acceptable in certain circumstances. Under the leadership of these men, the War and Navy Departments adhered closely to the letter of Wilson's decisions. While Baker and Daniels served Wilson, he could maintain the absolute civilian control that he demanded of the armed forces.

Wilson's secretary of state and his department, on the other hand, had different views, not only about the use of force, but also upon the role of presidential subordinates in the policy-making process. These views would early set Lansing and the State Department on a collision course with the military in Siberia.

As is evident in Wilson's consideration of requests for Russian intervention, he accepted advice from a variety of sources while mulling over a problem. Once he made a decision, however, he demanded that his State Department subordinates, like his military officers, loyally adhere to that decision. In the end he, and he alone, determined American foreign policy.[119]

Lansing held different policy views from Wilson, particularly on military action. He was more inclined than the president (and Baker and Daniels) to accept the use of force as a fact of international politics. Colonel House generally supported Wilson's tendency to espouse practical idealism but, like Lansing, he was not opposed to the use of force in the pursuit of peace.

But Wilson jealously guarded presidential policy-making powers. To a great extent he was his own secretary of state, and often he left Lansing at the State Department ignorant of his intentions until he was ready to announce them publicly. If he wanted advice he sometimes turned first to House. House, in fact, frequently briefed Lansing on the status of foreign policy issues.

Wilson's secretiveness frustrated Lansing. To keep himself informed in foreign affairs, the secretary of state hired Gordon Auchinsloss, House's son-in-law (and thus a valuable source of information), to work in the State Department. Wilson's trust in Lansing had so declined by late 1918, because of Lansing's lack of enthusiasm for Wilson's Fourteen Points and their differences over Russian policy, that he came to treat the members of the State Department—including Lansing himself—as mere clerks.[120] The State Department was left to enact Wilson's orders as given, or, in the case of diplomatic representatives isolated in Russia, to tailor them to suit not only changing circumstances, but themselves as well.

In March 1918, Lansing wrote to David Francis, the American ambassador at Petrograd, that "as conditions change so rapidly, Department has issued you only general instructions and relies on your discretion and judgment to direct your movements and matters affecting the policy of this government."[121] Francis took these instructions to heart. On 23

August 1918, he told his military aide, Lieutenant Hugh S. Martin, that he planned to put his "own construction" upon Wilson's guidelines regarding intervention in North Russia.[122] Consequently, while Wilson tightly controlled the making of American foreign policy, State Department officials in Russia felt justified in interpreting it quite loosely. Though the explosion was months in coming, the fuse was already burning.

While Wilson clearly wanted an officer who would follow his instructions exactly to head the Siberian expedition, the selection of a commander was a matter that he left to the War Department. The procedure was much the same as in Pershing's case. On 2 August 1918, Baker called General March into his office to discuss the Siberian command. According to March, Baker was considering two officers. March suggested someone else. "Who is your man?" Baker asked. "General Graves," replied March, and Baker instantly agreed. "Just the man."[123] Baker passed his recommendation on to the president and Wilson approved it.

Major General William Sidney Graves was well known to March; the men had been classmates at West Point. Baker knew him from Graves's second stint as secretary of the General Staff, the post he had occupied when Baker took over the War Department and which he held until 26 June 1918.[124] "I knew him to be a self-reliant, educated, and highly trained soldier," Baker later wrote, "endowed with common sense and self-effacing loyalty, the two qualities most needed to meet the many difficulties I could foresee."[125] When March took over as chief of staff from Tasker Bliss, he asked Graves to stay on at the War Department as assistant chief of staff for approximately four months, after which he would allow Graves to go to France. In May 1918, March told Graves that "If anyone has to go to Russia, you're it."[126] March had apparently made up his mind about a Siberian commander four months before Baker consulted him.

Graves was born in 1865 in Montcalm, Texas, the son of a Baptist minister who had served as a colonel in the Confederate Army. After graduating from the United States Military Academy in 1889 he served in a variety of western posts, mainly in Colorado. In 1899, he secured an assignment with the 20th Infantry in Manila and spent much of the next fifteen years with this regiment. He participated in campaigns against the Filipino insurgents, before serving in a variety of posts back in the United States, and then drew a second Philippine tour in 1903. Graves returned to California in 1906 and did a month's duty coping with the aftermath of the San Francisco earthquake and fire in the spring of that year. He remained in California until April 1909, when he became a member of the General Staff.

Serving in Washington until June 1912, he earned a promotion to major and became secretary of the General Staff in 1911. Upon leaving Washington he rejoined his regiment in Utah and then assumed command of a border patrol in El Paso, Texas. In August 1914 he returned to the General Staff, as a brigadier general. In December 1917 he became assistant chief of staff to General Bliss and remained in that post until June 1918, when he earned promotion to the rank of major general, along with command of the 8th Division in Fremont, California—an intermediate step in his journey to Siberia.[127]

The War Department thought highly of General Graves and felt that he was ideal for the job, but the Secretary of State did not share Baker's enthusiasm. Lansing, who was on holiday when the appointment was made, sent a wire opposing Graves's selection, saying he heard that Graves lacked "the tact and diplomacy...to deal with so delicate a situation where the commanding officer requires other than military ability."[128] But Lansing's protests fell on deaf ears; Wilson approved Graves.

Graves had barely been in his new post in California a fortnight when, on 2 August, he received a coded message directing him to take "the first and fastest train out of San Francisco and proceed to Kansas City, go to the Baltimore Hotel, and ask for the Secretary of War."[129] Upon arriving in Kansas City, Graves sought out Newton Baker, who, due to a scheduling mix-up, had only a few minutes to speak to him. Baker handed Graves a sealed envelope. "This contains the policy of the United States in Russia which you are to follow," he told the general. "Watch your step; you will be walking on eggs loaded with dynamite. God bless you and goodbye."[130]

The envelope contained a copy of the aide memoire. Graves read it through; after a time he believed that he understood it. He wrote later that "I felt there could be no misunderstanding the policy of the United States and I did not feel it was necessary for me to ask for elucidation of any point."[131] Graves had been assigned a delicate mission in the midst of one of modern history's most chaotic military and political situations; his instructions were confining, yet vague, and sometimes contradictory; but he had no qualms about them. His instructions were based on Wilson's faulty intelligence about conditions in Siberia. The situation in Siberia was even more bizarre by the time Graves arrived at Vladivostok. Nevertheless, the aide memoire was the only guideline Graves received during his two years in Siberia. Despite this, to him his orders seemed satisfactory. Throughout his entire stay in Siberia, he tried to adhere to the letter of the aide memoire. In spite of overwhelming pressure to compromise, he never questioned the wisdom of his instructions.

Returning to Camp Fremont, Graves received a memorandum on 6 August informing him of the status of the Philippine regiments, now under his command. The 27th was composed of forty-eight officers and 1,346 enlisted men; the 31st reported forty-three officers and 1,346 men. Both regiments could be dispatched with forty-eight hours' notice. Their auxiliary units, the 9th Cavalry Regiment, a field hospital and ambulance company, a company of engineers, and "D" Company of the 53rd Telegraph Battalion, were also available and could follow within fifteen days.[132]

On 3 August 1918, the 27th Infantry received orders to prepare for immediate service in Siberia, and the regiment, under the command of Colonel Henry D. Styer, departed Manila for Siberia on 7 August. They were to sail to Vladivostok by way of Japan.[133] Five days later the 31st Infantry, commanded by Colonel Frederic Sargarent, left the Philippines aboard the *USAT Sherman*.[134] General Graves and the replacement troops selected from the 8th Division left Camp Fremont for Fort Mason, San Francisco on 14 August. The party consisted of Lieutenant Colonel O. P. Robinson, chief of staff; Assistant Chief of Staff Major R. L. Eichelberger;

forty other officers, assorted Medical and Dental Corps officers, a bakery company officer, and 1,889 men. At the dock at Fort Mason they embarked on to the *USAT Thomas*. At 8:30 P.M. the ship left the harbor and began the 4,754 mile voyage to Vladivostok.[135]

The first American troops arrived in Siberia on 15 August, but General Graves, his staff, and the replacement troops would not dock for more than two weeks, a full month after the British, French, and Japanese. His late arrival on 2 September put General Graves and the AEF at a disadvantage. The absence of an American commander or orders resulted in confusion. Lieutenant Sylvain Kindall described the initial perplexity of the American troops. "On the very first day the astonishing fact developed that there was not a single person among the arriving army who had been entrusted with any information from anywhere as to what the army was expected to do after getting ashore at Vladivostok." Rumors soon took the place of definite orders and directions. Some soldiers believed the AEF would aid the Czechoslovaks. Others had heard that it would be used to recapture numerous bands of German and Austrian prisoners of war. Still others heard that the American forces would move west across Siberia from Vladivostok to attempt the reestablishment of an Eastern Front against the Central Powers. Lastly, Kindall recalled, many heard, and let themselves believe, the Americans had been sent to Siberia to crusade against Bolshevism.[136]

A few days prior to his departure from San Francisco, Graves had received a warning from Washington of difficulties arising from potential Japanese policy in Siberia. He was told that the Japanese strategy would very likely be to "keep the various Russian forces apart and oppose any strong Russian central authority, but to support a number of weak Russian forces which could not form more than a screen for Japanese action."[137] Administration fears concerning Japanese motives were well-founded, but Graves was in no position to take action until he was in Siberia. Before his arrival, however, the Japanese had already begun to act.

By early September the Allies had already taken it upon themselves to make a number of important policy decisions without Graves. They announced that US troops were to be put under the command of General Kikuzo Otani, the highest ranking Allied officer in Siberia, and before Graves arrived, American soldiers had already became involved in a Japanese military operation.

This operation was the only organized Allied military engagement in Siberia in which American troops took ever part. The brief campaign unfolded in the Ussuri Valley north of Vladivostok. General Otani, the acting commander in chief of the Allied forces, persuaded a detachment of the US 27th Infantry to join in an action against Bolsheviks in that area by convincing their officers that it was directed against armed bands of German and Austrian prisoners of war. Although the Americans cooperated in the action, they never had the opportunity to fire a shot, or even to reach the front line.[138]

On 24 August, the Japanese commander sent the US 27th Infantry north to Sviagina en route to Khabarovsk, about 300 miles directly north of Vladivostok. The town was the object of a Japanese and Czech campaign to wrest it from the Bolsheviks. It was an area of strategic importance as the place where the Amur River and the Amur branch of the Trans-Siberian Railway meet. Because of its proximity to the Ussuri River, a branch of the Amur, this area was called the Ussuri front. In reality there was no front as such, only a number of limited skirmishes. The 27th Infantry was ordered to join the Allied forces near Khabarovsk but on 27 August, British, French, and Czecho-Slovak troops withdrew before the Americans arrived. In a communiqué to general headquarters at Vladivostok, the Czechs reported that they had repulsed the enemy after a desperate struggle, and then had relentlessly pursued them along the Beraya River to Kraevski, and that they had captured "much booty and numerous prisoners."[139] The Japanese and Americans were left to continue the campaign. The Japanese forces in the area numbered about 8,000 men, consisting of infantry, cavalry, and artillery.[140]

The 27th Infantry was ordered to the Nikolsk Monastery, by way of Runovka and Uspanka, to cover the right flank of the army on its way to Khabarovsk. A hospital and supply train were organized to follow as soon as the bridges and stretches of track that had been destroyed by retreating partisans could be repaired. On 30 August the 27th Infantry began its march to the Ussuri. They reached the town of Nikotoska, thirteen miles away, that evening. By nightfall of the following day they had marched another fourteen miles to Runovka. It proved to be very hard going. The roads, already in poor condition, were made nearly impassable by persistent rains. Several swamps and marshes presented additional barriers. Logs and brush had to be laid down and then covered with hay in order to get the wagons across marshy areas.[141]

From 1–4 September, the regiment continued its march from Runovka to Ussuri, passing through Aspanka, Ordejefka, and Tikmanova. The total distance from Sviagina to Ussuri was over sixty miles. General Otani later complimented the regiment on its achievement and remarkable endurance. But at no time during this operation did the Americans become involved in any fighting.[142] While all this was happening General Graves and his party were still at sea.

When Graves finally landed in Siberia on 2 September, he found not only that the situation was markedly different from what he expected, but also he faced several unforeseen developments, the most surprising was the new position of the Czech Legion. Graves had orders to rescue it, but when he arrived he learned that the three main Czech groups along the Trans-Siberia Railway had linked forces on 31 August. As a result the Legion controlled the entire railway from Vladivostok to the Volga.

Learning of this strategic development, Graves immediately cabled the War Department on 3 September to inform it that the Czechs in the west had "joined with the Czechs from the east along the Manchurian Railway at Chita. The only resistance," he said, was "at Habarovsk which is slight and will disappear as soon as the destroyed bridges and Siberian Railway are repaired—Railway open from Vladivostok to Samara through Manchuria. Conditions are very satisfactory for Czechs in Siberia."[143]

By the first week of September 1918, the Czech Legion was in a good position, the danger posed by German and Austrian prisoners had evaporated, and the Allies, particularly the Japanese, had established a very

strong foothold in eastern Siberia. Bearing this in mind, it was not surprising that General Graves, reported with genuine astonishment that the
way was clear, and that no further obstacle to the evacuation of the
Czechs remained. What Graves did not yet know was that the nature of
the Czech anabasis had linked the fortunes of the Czech Legion and the
anti-Bolsheviks, particularly the Social Revolutionaries, and that many of
his Allied colleagues were advancing plans to keep the Czechs in Siberia
to exploit that relationship. It would be a long time, in fact, before the
Czechs, or the Americans, left Siberia.

4

America's Siberian Policy Defined

GENERAL GRAVES'S ARRIVAL IN SIBERIA ON 2 SEPTEMBER WAS SUPPOSED to clear up the confusion in the AEF about US policy. But Graves knew little about the actual situation in Siberia. He had received no information from the State or War Departments since his appointment, except the warning about Japanese policy. For the first few days Graves was in Vladivostok he was, as he later said, "not only ignorant as to the discussions which led to intervention, but...ignorant as to the political schemes of the Far East. For a few days, I was disposed to take the statements of prominent Allies at full value and act accordingly."[144] This credulous phase did not last very long.

The War Department had originally chosen Graves for his personal qualities of rigid obedience, unyielding integrity, and common sense. Unlike the English, French, or Japanese military commanders in Siberia, he had no policy of his own to follow, and as a result of his strict interpretation of his duties, American military intervention had a decidedly neutral character, favoring neither the Bolsheviks nor the counter-revolutionary White movement.

Immediately after Graves's arrival, Colonel Henry Styer, the commander of the 27th Infantry, briefed him on the activities of the Philippine regiments since their arrival in Siberia. Part of the 27th and the 31st Infantry, Graves learned, had taken up guard duty along the Ussuri Railroad from Vladivostok to Nikolsk. During August and September the rest of the 27th Infantry had taken part in the Allied offensive to push back Bolshevik forces in the Spasskoe-Ussuri region. Graves recalled that the Allies represented the "enemy" as "Bolsheviks and *German prisoners.*"

He added that he had been satisfied "that the American troops were not departing from the announced policy of the United States Government to refrain from taking part in Russian affairs."[145]

But Graves soon had cause to suspect the accuracy of Japanese reports. An American intelligence officer reported that an inspection of the battlefield at Kraevski indicated that the Japanese had "greatly exaggerated" enemy troop strength. This incident, along with the warning he received from the State Department aroused Graves's suspicion of the Japanese and Allied motives.[146]

On 2 September Graves met General Otani. Otani was a very short, wiry, bald man who affected a monocle. Fortunately he spoke excellent English. Graves found him "a very agreeable man, and disposed to be fair in the handling of questions relating to our respective forces." He later discovered, however, that Otani was a difficult man to get to see. "One had to insist upon seeing him and insist very forcefully," Graves recalled, "before you could get by his staff. The Japanese Staff was very aggressive and would take advantage, or try to do so, at every opportunity to enhance their own prestige...."[147] Otani had posted a notice two weeks earlier that caused General Graves great concern. It stated that Otani was appointed commander of the Japanese Army at Vladivostok and was "entrusted unanimously by the Allied Powers, with the command of their Armies in the Russian Territory of the Far East."[148] A conflict soon developed between the generals over command of the AEF. Otani told Graves that the State Department had notified him that he would have overall command of Allied and American troops.[149] Graves said he had no such orders; on the contrary, the limitations placed upon his use of American troops required him to give all orders for future movements.[150]

Otani shrugged and went on to the next point. The subject never came up again. Otani wanted to order the entire Allied force north to take Khabarovsk, and then, with reinforcements, advance westward to attack the "German prisoners" who were threatening the Czech Legion. Graves asked him where he got his information on the German prisoners. Again

Otani shrugged as if, it seemed to Graves, he did not expect Graves's compliance with his orders.[151]

Graves recalled that he had been deeply impressed by the assurances of his government that they would not intervene in the internal conflicts of the Russian people. He was, therefore anxious to know the composition of the hostile forces the Allies and the United States were operating against. All the Allied commanders assured him that Bolsheviks had been organized and joined by German and Austrian prisoners and that they were plotting to seize the military stores at Vladivostok.[152]

The Wilson administration was concerned about possible Japanese expansion in the Far East, but the president and the State Department believed that they could best maintain the Open Door by taking part in a cooperative venture with Japan, rather than by letting Japan act alone. The administration had warned Graves, before he left the United States, that the Japanese might use a strategy designed to divide any strong forces in Siberia capable of forming a government to foil the attempts of other powers to establish order. Graves suspected that the Japanese planned to do just that by insisting that the Allies must unite under Japanese command, knowing it would be unacceptable to the United States. In this way Japan could keep the Allies apart and encourage the proliferation of weaker groups which it could use to mask its own activities.[153] Although the Japanese had actually received overall command, the fact that they never pressed the point might indicate that Graves's conclusion was correct, even if the information upon which he based his assumption was not.

Wilson was concerned about Japanese territorial ambitions in Manchuria and Siberia and had attempted to guard against it by stating in the aide memoire that none of the governments operating in Siberia had any territorial claims. The State Department feared that the Japanese military party desired to gain control of the Eastern Trans-Siberian and Chinese Eastern Railways, and that Tokyo's civilian government, even if it were to oppose such a plan, lacked the power to stop it. The Japanese military took steps to obstruct the formation of any strong centralized government in Siberia. It particularly opposed the Bolsheviks because they found them politically repugnant and potentially destabilizing. Its most effective tactic in controlling these groups proved to be the subsidizing of the Cossack bands.

The Siberian Cossacks had been established in the Trans-Baikal and Ussuri regions in the mid-nineteenth century by the tsar to develop the economy and natural resources of the area. These Siberian Cossacks were well-known for their prickly independence and were even less easily governed than the Cossacks of central Russia. The two most important Cossack tribes in Siberia were under the control of Grigorii Semenov and Ivan Kalmikov.

Ataman Grigorii Semenov was a member of the Trans-Baikal Cossacks. His father had been a Cossack of no distinction, and his mother a Buriat Mongol. Semenov, one of the most flamboyant personalities in Siberia, was largely self-educated, but was remarkably well-read in philosophy, religion, and military strategy. He always kept a copy of Napoleon's *Maxims* in his pocket, and was often found with his hand thrust in his tunic in an imitation of Bonaparte's classic gesture. In the autumn of 1918 Semenov was only twenty-eight years old, but was already notorious as one of the most ruthless and despicable figures to emerge from the Russian Civil War. He also did more than anyone else in Siberia to bring the White cause into disrepute.[154] During World War I Semenov served in the Imperial Army in Poland; he was later transferred to Dvinsk and Riga on the Baltic Front. He was then sent to Galicia where he, along with his friend Baron Roman von Ungern-Sternberg, served under Baron Peter Wrangel. During the war both Semenov and Ungern-Sternberg received decorations for bravery. After the establishment of the Provisional Government, Semenov approached Aleksander Kerensky, the minister for war proposing that he be allowed to return to Siberia to raise a Buriat detachment. In July, Kerensky agreed and Semenov left for Chita. While he was organizing the Buriat force, Lenin seized power, and Semenov, an ardent anti-Bolshevik, turned his attention to his personal interests. Eventually he mustered a motley assortment of Cossacks, Buriats, other Mongols, and a smattering of Chinese, Koreans, and Japanese into a small army that never numbered more than several thousand men. They were not all volunteers; any able-bodied man who lived in, or traveled through, Semenov's territory was subject to impressment.

By the autumn of 1918 Semenov was the virtual dictator of Chita, where he supported himself lavishly by robbing banks and customs houses. He shipped supplies to Chita on the railroad without paying freight; there he sold goods to civilians in his own stores. Whenever he or his officers required funds, they usually obtained them by robbing Chinese merchants. This supplied Semenov's private fortune. He lived in grand style in Chita with his Jewish mistress, on whom he spent hundreds of thousands of rubles.[155] Semenov also had a wife. Madame Semenov lived in Nagasaki, reportedly travelling to and from Siberia once a month to deposit gold in Japanese banks.[156]

Semenov also attracted foreign support. For a few months in early 1918 the British subsidized him with £10,000 a month to encourage more recruits. They also approached the United States about aiding Semenov, but Wilson declined to do so.[157] Semenov proved a bad investment for the British, he would not do as he was told; neither would he allow the British to train and organize his men. For those reasons, and because of their disgust with his indiscriminate violence, the British struck him from their list.[158]

This left the field open for the Japanese, to whom Semenov had appealed for support in January 1918. With the Japanese his approach had immediate and lasting success. They wanted Semenov to continue to do just what he was already doing—disrupting Central Siberia. His position on the Trans-Siberian Railroad gave him complete control of the direct line between Irkutsk and Vladivostok and put him in the perfect location to obstruct transportation. His uncooperative attitude eliminated the possibility of his collaboration with any other Allied country or Russian faction. Because of his position Semenov effectively blocked Bolshevik expansion in the Trans-Baikal region and kept the Bolsheviks out of eastern Siberia. While doing this he promoted disunity and instability from which Japan hoped to benefit.

The Japanese assigned a liaison officer to Semenov's headquarters and supplied Semenov with money and weapons. They calculated the amount carefully, giving him just enough to keep him independent of other factions, but not enough to allow him to become a rival to Japanese influence in Siberia.[159] In exchange for Japanese aid, Semenov did what he did best. He terrorized the countryside, causing endless hardship to everyone but his Japanese patrons.

Ivan Kalmikov, head of the Ussuri Cossacks, was every bit as evil and corrupt as Semenov. Kalmikov was said to have started out as a captain at Spasskoe Barracks. Being a man of considerable energy and ambition, and no scruples, he was another likely candidate for Japanese largesse. Early in 1918 they supplied him with a boxcar of sugar, a scarce commodity in Siberia. He used it to buy enough votes to have himself declared Ataman of the Ussuri Cossacks.[160]

Graves found Kalmikov particularly revolting. Calling him a "notorious murderer, robber, and cut-throat." After their first meeting, he wrote that Kalmikov "was the worst scoundrel I ever saw or heard of and I seriously doubt, if one could go through the Standard Dictionary looking for words descriptive of crime, if a crime could be found that Kalmikoff had not committed." He added that the only difference between Kalmikov and Semenov was that the former killed with his own hands whereas the latter generally ordered others to do his dirty work.[161]

Semenov, Kalmikov, and their Cossack followers created confusion along the railroad, and resentment among the Allies and their associates. While the AEF was in Siberia, the Cossacks would clash with the Czechs, the Chinese, the Americans, and other White forces as well as the Bolsheviks. But they served the Japanese well, sabotaging the Allied and American efforts admirably by interfering with the railroads and terrorizing the peasantry.

While the Japanese were content to control eastern Siberia, the British and the French never abandoned hope of reestablishing an Eastern Front against the Central Powers. The French played a comparatively small part in the intervention. Their main contribution was several high-ranking officers, sent apparently on the assumption that a general was as good as a regiment, and in the hope that perhaps they might somehow contrive to gain control of the situation.[162] The British military contribution in Siberia was only marginally larger than the French. It consisted of a first-class territorial battalion of Hampshires and a garrison battalion of the Middlesex Regiment. By the end of 1918, the British added a military mission at Omsk and a railway mission.[163]

The head of the British military effort in Siberia was Major-General Alfred Knox. He was in every way the opposite of General Graves. Widely experienced in Russian affairs, he had served as military attaché to St. Petersburg in 1910. Returning to that post in 1914, he followed the activities of the Russian Army on the Eastern Front closely from Tannenburg to the Bolshevik Revolution. He spoke fluent Russian, and he had a wide acquaintance among tsarist civil and military officials. Knox loathed the Bolsheviks, and he did his utmost to destroy them. The disparity between Graves and Knox in their attitudes and experience, and the radical differences in their orders, made it extremely difficult for them to see eye-to-eye on any issue. Within a few weeks of their arrival in Vladivostok the two generals had come to despise each other.[164]

Graves was not alone in his suspicion of Knox. Apparently the United States was concerned about Knox's tsarist leanings even before he arrived in Siberia. Lord Reading informed Lloyd George that while he did not know what military advantage there might be in sending Knox to Siberia "there is an impression here that he has always been against the revolution, and if this is so he would be likely to gather round him in Russia ex-imperial officers and supporters, and this would give the British part of the expedition a reactionary appearance."[165] This is exactly what happened.

Knox's French counterpart was General Maurice Janin. Like Knox he was his government's authority on Russia. He had first visited the country in 1893, while attached to a French military mission, and he had made several tours since then. In 1912 he served as an instructor at the St. Petersburg Military Academy. At the war's beginning he served as a brigade commander on the Marne, and in 1916 he became the head of the French Military Mission to Russia.[166]

The Czech National Council in Paris had given Janin command of the Czech Legion, although this was not a particularly meaningful office. The Czechs deferred to Janin when they found it convenient, but they did not hesitate to ignore his orders when they found them disagreeable. Janin could do nothing about it. The Czech National Council had specified that he would command the legion so long as he did it "in accordance with the general directives of the Japanese Supreme Commander."[167] This proved impossible, as the aims of the British and the French, and those of the Japanese, were completely incompatible. The French and British desired a strong, centralized, pro-Allied, Russian government, and the Japanese did not. They had no desire to reestablish a Russian government that could again rival them in the Far East.

The Supreme War Council, regardless of this contradiction, had decided that the Japanese were to have supreme command of the Allied forces in Siberia. Graves and the War Department, however, did not recognize Japanese authority over American forces. Furthermore, the Japanese had made it abundantly clear that they would not send troops past Irkutsk, 2000 miles east of the Volga front. Japan's Imperial General Staff had estimated that an expedition beyond Irkutsk would have to include every regular soldier in the Japanese Army; it might take over three years to reach Cheliabinsk; it would require 107,000 railroad guards and workmen, ten times the existing rolling stock of the Chinese Eastern Railway; and it would leave other Japanese interests unprotected.[168] Whether this was an accurate estimate or merely a convenient excuse for not extending military activity in Siberia beyond the territory Japan wished to control was debatable. What was not, was that the Japanese had no intention of going far enough west to further any of the other Allies' plans. They would not go into central or western Siberia for any reason. Not only did the Japanese Army have no intention of helping the Czechs, or helping the Allies achieve their goals; they used the Cossacks to thwart these groups at every turn. Thus the Japanese, who were supposed to be commanding the Allied expedition were working at cross purposes with the Allies and their associates from the beginning.

American policy, on the other hand, was to remain neutral in political squabbles. This did not coordinate well with Japanese policy either. The Japanese wanted Siberia to remain unstable and disunited until they could establish a puppet government that would provide them with the territory they desired. In the meantime, they flooded Siberia with troops exceeding the limits agreed upon by the United States and Japan: 38,000 troops guarded the railroad from Vladivostok to Manchouli, 22,000 occupied the Ussuri line from Vladivostok to Khabarovsk, and 20,000 controlled the Amur railroad from Khabarovsk to Chita, forming a triangle around some of Siberia's richest land. In preparation for the eventual administration of Siberia, the Japanese opened a school at Mukden to teach their engineers Russian and the Russian method of railway operation. They sent gun boats and torpedo boats up the navigable rivers in eastern Siberia. The Japanese also introduced their own currency among the local population and made it a capital crime to refuse to honor it.[169]

To complicate the situation further the two major White Russian governments at Omsk and Samara formed a coalition, commonly known as the Directory. It had its own ministry of war which, not surprisingly, believed that it should be responsible for military affairs throughout Siberia. The Directory was not conveniently subordinate to the Japanese or any other Allied power, although all of them tried to influence the new government.

The Directory was better known, but not much more effective than the other ersatz governments which dotted Russia in 1918. These governments ran the gamut from revolutionary to reactionary and had a precarious existence in the shadow of the conflict between Bolshevik and counter-revolutionary forces. In many cases the governments had no armies to speak of. While the White armies, fearing the fragmentation of Russian politics would case disintegration within their midst, scarcely had governments. In 1918 the largest center of White military activity was in South Russia, where General Anton Denikin commanded an army com-

posed of an uneasy alliance of volunteers he had inherited from Generals
Kornilov and Alexeev and a mixture of Don and Kuban Cossacks.[170]

In Siberia the fortunes of the Directory and the Czech Legion were
already entwining. The legion was to some extent linked to the Directory,
inasmuch as the White government had emerged in the wake of the
legion's uprising. Apart from that, the Czechs had done, and continued to
do, the lion's share of the fighting against the Red Army.[171] They had succeeded in gaining control of the Trans-Siberian Railroad, and no physical
impediment remained to their immediate withdrawal from Siberia except
a shortage of shipping.

Many historians have minimized the transportation problem, but
throughout World War I, the Pacific suffered severe shortages of shipping.
In an attempt to send all available soldiers and supplies to the Western
Front, the United States Shipping Control Committee scoured the globe
for all available vessels. The United States chartered ships from twelve
countries, including Japan. Losses to German U-boats exacerbated the
problem. In their rapacity for bottoms the committee seized German and
Austrian vessels and even Great Lakes boats, and it contracted with the
Chinese and Japanese builders for more vessels. All available shipping
went to the Atlantic; the Pacific was stripped to the bare bones.[172]

Apart from the shipping shortage, it soon became apparent that
although the tracks were cleared, the Czechs had become enmeshed in
fighting the Bolsheviks along the Volga on an 800-mile front. Of roughly
66,000 troops in action, 60,000 were Czechs and the rest an assortment
of Cossacks and other anti-Bolshevik forces. Despite the original plans,
the Czechs no longer intended to leave Russia and go to the Western
Front. At the request of the British and the French, they were planning to
remain. The Allies hoped to use the Czechs as the core of a new Eastern
Front, and they wanted to persuade the United States to assist them in
the effort. As early as 23 June, the French ambassador cabled a French
officer in Siberia to "thank the Czecho-Slovaks for their actions." He
added that the Allies had decided to intervene in Siberia at the end of

June and the Czechoslovaks and the French military mission were to form the advance guard of the Allied army.[173]

The State Department, like Graves, was receiving conflicting reports on the events in Siberia. In an effort to resolve these conflicts, the State Department on 4 September, ordered Roland S. Morris, the American ambassador to Japan, to Vladivostok to investigate.[174] Ambassador Morris, a former student of Woodrow Wilson's at Princeton, had been in Tokyo for over a year before American troops were sent to Siberia. During that time he had carried out all the negotiations with the Japanese for joint action in Siberia. Because of the reliability of his reports, and his sound judgment, Wilson and the State Department made him, in effect, their highest civilian authority in Siberia.[175] Morris provided Wilson and Lansing with someone to whom they could refer their questions and from whom they could get credible answers.

When Morris arrived in Siberia shortly after Graves, he reported—accurately, as it turned out—that the Czechs were engaged in the civil war and making no effort to reach Vladivostok. Moreover, said Morris, they could not continue to fight west of the Urals without help. He suggested that American troops be sent to Omsk to work with the British and the French assisting the Czechs and their Russian friends. He believed that the Russian people would welcome them, and that if Graves went to Omsk he would be able to curb impractical plans for reestablishing the Eastern Front. Both Graves and Admiral Knight agreed that Morris should inquire about the possibility of such a move.[176]

Graves was already having difficulties with the Czechs. Soon after setting up headquarters in Vladivostok, Graves met General Gajda. Graves wrote later that he thought it advisable in his discussion with Gajda "to tell him not to expect American troops to go west of Lake Baikal." Graves told Gajda that he was certain Allied representatives were using the Czech leader to get Graves to send troops west.[177] Gajda was bitterly disappointed, and he let it be known. "Why had Allied promises become the promises of women, promises written on water?" he asked. General

Graves responded that he himself was a soldier, and had been sent to Siberia to follow orders, not to keep other people's promises.[178]

Graves soon learned that one of these promises was a cable sent by American Consul General in Archangel, Dewitt C. Poole, in June 1918 which "resulted in a very noticeable resentment against the United States by the Czechs who remained in Western Siberia." This resentment, Graves said, was so palpable, when the Czechs came to Vladivostok, that he took the matter up at Czech headquarters. Poole had apparently led the Czechs to believe that the United States and the Allies were going to intervene in Siberia to help the Czechs against the Bolsheviks. Poole told the Czechs this before Wilson had approved sending any troops at all to Siberia. The result of this cable, and a similar one from the French, was that the Czechs willingly remained in western Siberia for months waiting for help that never came.[179]

But Wilson remained firm in his determination that American troops should not be drawn into western Siberia. After reading a cable from Consul General Harris at Irkutsk citing the orders of British General Poole to send Czech troops from the Perm area to Vologda in Northern Russia to join the Allies, Wilson was furious.[180] He wrote to Lansing a few days later.

> This illustrates in the most striking way the utter disregard of General Poole and all of the Allied governments (at any rate those who are acting for them) of the policy which we express-ly confined ourselves in our statement about our action in Siberia.
>
> It is out of the question to send reinforcements from eastern Siberia (I presume they mean from the forces recently landed at Vladivostok) to Perm; and we have expressly notified those in charge of those forces that the Czecho-Slovaks must (so far as our aid was to be used) to [sic] be brought out eastward, not got out westward. Is there no way—no form of expression—by which we can get this comprehended?[181]

Lansing threatened to remove American forces from Poole's command if he insisted upon using them for purposes contrary to US policy.[182] Although Wilson had made it painfully clear that the Czechs could expect American aid only in the Far East and not in western Siberia, and that the Czech command was told this in early September, it took some time for all parties concerned to accept it. In an interview with the head of the newly formed Provisional Siberia Government at Omsk, P. V. Vologodsky, Ambassador Morris confirmed Graves's statements. He said "that American participation in the establishment of a Russian front should not be counted upon nor expected. That America could not be counted upon to spare troops and material for such purpose in view of her great effort in France." Morris pointed out that the Czechs would receive all possible supplies in assistance but "similar assurance could not be given in the case of Russian troops."[183]

"Allied representatives," Graves recalled, "seemed to know that the principal reason for sending United States troops to Siberia was to help the Czechs." But as Czechs occupied not only Vladivostok but all towns from there to the Urals, the US needed further justification to venture into Western Siberia. On 8 September 1918, Graves had cabled the War Department: "practically all organized resistance, in Siberia, has disappeared." Nevertheless, the Allies had not abandoned their plans for an Eastern Front. In Graves's opinion, they would stop at nothing to get American assistance. Despite Wilson's orders that the United States would take no part in re-opening the Eastern Front, Graves believed that the Allies had brought the AEF to Siberia by misrepresentation, and that they would not hesitate to use the same method to get it into European Russia in order to achieve their purposes by indirect means.[184]

The unexpected success of the Czech Legion caused Lansing to ask the president to review his Siberian policy. On 9 September 1918, he wrote to Wilson that "our confidence in Czech forces has been justified and the fact that now a Russian military force of equal strength has joined them, combined with the gratifying reception given the Czechs by the civilian population of the localities occupied, is strong evidence to prove that the

Russians are entirely satisfied to cooperate with the Czechs in Russia and that assistance to the Czechs is assistance to the Russians." Lansing then outlined plans for getting relief to the Czechs and the Russian civilian population. Lansing's equation of aid to the Czechs with aid to the Russians was the beginning of a slow and subtle shift in his views on the Siberian situation.[185] His definition of "the Russians" was limited to anti-Bolshevik forces.

On 11 September, Graves cabled the War Department that the Czech authorities had told him that the railroad was clear from Vladivostok to Samara and that most of the German and Austrian prisoners of war had been interned, but that the Czech situation west of the Urals demanded immediate Allied attention. If the Czechs did not receive help soon they might suffer military reverses and the Russians would feel that the Allies did not intend to aid the Czechs and would no longer affiliate with them in "rehabilitating Russia."

Graves did not see a need to keep more than 1000 American troops in Vladivostok. "The farther we go [westward]," he declared, "the better the effect will be." As the decision, however, "involves questions other than military the situation as mentioned by Gen. Guida's [sic] representatives is submitted to the Department notwithstanding my instructions." He added that if they decided he should move west of the Urals, and it seemed "that from a military standpoint alone this should be done," then he needed reinforcements—the 9th Cavalry and all field artillery and engineers from the Philippines.[186]

Graves's request shocked the secretary of war. Newton Baker was on an inspection tour of Europe when the request came in. When he returned and read the cables from Siberia, he apparently feared that the Allies were swaying the general, and he recommended to Wilson that he remove Graves.[187]

The request arrived at the very moment when Wilson and the War Department were addressing the question of reinforcements for Russia. On 12 September, General March sent Wilson a letter on the subject from General Bliss with the comment "General Bliss is always interesting and he always talks good sense." [188] Bliss, it seemed, was also getting requests for reinforcements for the North Russian expedition.

"I have no reason to suppose," wrote Bliss, "that the United States would engage in this venture any further than it has done. In previous letters I have stated very plainly my conviction that the Allies think that having made a beginning in Russia and having put the foot in the crack of the door the whole body must follow. I have told my colleagues that I did not believe the United States should send any more troops there and that I individually would not approve it." He added that he thought the Allies were pushing the North Russian expedition because "of their belief that nothing of material value will result from the movement in Siberia from Vladivostok. In regard to the situation in Siberia we are quite in the dark."[189]

Bliss went on to express concern about the ramifications of sending American troops to help the Czechs. The Czechs were, after all, a wild card in the Russian deck. "No one knows what the Czecho-Slovaks will do or want to do if they can once unite. It is one thing to help the Czecho-Slovaks to keep from being wiped out by the Bolsheviks and then march them to Vladivostok and help them to get out of the country." But what would the United States do if the Czechs refused to leave? What if they chose to set up a government of their own there or, if they want to fight their way through Russia to reach the Germans on the Eastern Front? "I certainly do not suppose that we are going to help the Czecho-Slovaks if they want to set up a government of their own; nor do I suppose that we want to face the possibility of having a force of 7,000 Americans wiped out in an attempt to reach Germany's Eastern Front against the will of the Russians." Bliss failed to see how the US could do more in Russia even if it were so inclined. He concluded sharply. "As I have said before, if our Allies have any axes to grind in Russia, let them go and do it."[190]

In mid-September the Czech/Eastern Front question expanded to include the Japanese. On 15 September, General Knox and French President Georges Clemenceau made separate appeals to the Japanese to send an additional force to Siberia to help the Czechs on the Ural front.[191]

Even though the Japanese had already decided not to proceed beyond Lake Baikal, Wilson feared that they would change their minds. He was already greatly disturbed by the fact that the Japanese had 72,000 troops in Siberia, instead of the approximately 10,000 agreed upon. The political as well as military problems of the Siberian expedition were coming home to roost all at once. On 17 September, Wilson asked Lansing with some asperity, "[d]o you not think it would be wise to ask Japan in some courteous but nevertheless plain way, what she is now proposing to do with the large army which she has sent to Siberia?" Wilson pointed out that the railroad is "open and under control of our friends from Vladivostok all the way to Samara, and that the hostile forces which were said to be in the intervening regions are dispersed or cowed under control." What then was the reason for a large Japanese force in Siberia? He instructed Lansing to have its purpose clarified.

Wilson then went on to tackle the problem of the Czechs. He told Lansing that some scheme was afoot to pull the United States away from the mission he had outlined and involve it in new Eastern Front. Perhaps it was necessary to leave some portion of the Czecho-Slovak troops in Western Siberia to prevent the Germans from taking supplies which might be available there, but "by the time the winter closes the country, it is my clear judgment that we should insist that the Czecho-Slovaks be brought out eastward to Vladivostok and conveyed to the Western front in Europe..." He directed Lansing, "we should take no part in attempting to form a new Eastern front and that any attempt to use the Czecho-Slovaks in conjunction with what is being attempted at Archangel would also be walking into the same trap."[192] In a separate letter Wilson asked Lansing to find out what the "so-called Allied Military Council" at Vladivostok was, and who had authorized its formation. Wilson also wanted the secretary of state to make it clear that the US did not recognize the organization and believed that it would only complicate matters further.[193]

Wilson feared he was losing control over the situation in Siberia, if indeed he had had any to begin with. The reply to Lansing's inquiries was small comfort. He said that he understood Wilson's position, but the aide memoire said the United States would not limit the actions or policies of its associates. As a result Lansing was scarcely in a position to insist that the Czechs be brought out of Vladivostok. He suggested, therefore, that the US should make clear that it would not send forces to Western Siberia in support of the Czechs, who Wilson hoped would move east. He concluded that "[i]n view of the statement in the Aide Memoire I do not see how we can go further than to call again to the attention of the Allied governments our policy and say to them that it has not been affected by recent events, particularly emphasizing the fact that we consider the restoration of an eastern front entirely impracticable."[194] Wilson conceded that Lansing was correct that they could not "insist," but he did suggest that Lansing "urge the advisability" of removing the Czechs to Vladivostok.[195]

Wilson's worst fears were confirmed when Graves cabled the War Department on 19 September that the "French and English are, undoubtedly, trying to get the Allied forces committed to some act which will result in the establishment of an Eastern Front."[196] In response Wilson prohibited American participation in those activities of which he disapproved, and left the Allies to do as they saw fit, hoping that they would be bound by their pre-intervention agreements.

Although the United States had announced that it would not attempt to influence the policy of its allies, the Allies never denied that they wished to influence the United States. Graves became increasingly wary of their motives. According to him, one of the Allies' earliest attempts at directing US policy was the formation of the Inter-Allied Board that had concerned Wilson. The Allies insisted that it was advisable to organize an entity that would insure unity of action towards the Russian people and resolve policy disputes. Graves flatly disapproved of this step, stating that there could be no unity of action because the representatives of the Allies and Japan were partisans in the Russian conflicts and he was not. This made cooperation impossible as long as his orders remained unaltered.[197]

The pressure on the United States increased as the Czech military situation soured. On 12 September Czech troops, who had not been relieved, reorganized, or resupplied, withdrew from Kazan, abandoning it to the Red Army to avoid encirclement. On 18 September, General Erwald Paris, the senior French officer in Siberia, reported to Clemenceau that the Czechs could not hold the front much longer without substantial support.[198]

On 21 September, in Washington, Lansing met with Thomas Masaryk to discuss the position of the Czech Legion. In a memorandum to Wilson, Lansing reported that Masaryk "was very emphatic in agreeing with us that the restoration of an Eastern Front was absolutely out of the question." He also agreed that it was wisest for the Czecho-Slovaks on the Volga and in Eastern Russia to retire through Siberia as soon as that could be done with safety." Masaryk added, however, that "it would be most dangerous for the forces at certain points near the Urals to withdraw in their defenseless condition, that the safety of their retirement depended upon getting them arms and ammunition." Lansing ended by telling Wilson that in "every way" Masaryk was "most thoroughly in accord with our policy."[199]

Wilson wanted to entice the Czechs to withdraw from Russia. Secretary Lansing, however, did not entirely favor the policy. Both he and Masaryk were concerned about the effects of withdrawing the Czech Legion, and its impact on the safety of Allied and American citizens living in Russia.[200] This fear carried much weight because of reports of the Bolsheviks' murder of thousands of Russian citizens in Moscow and Petrograd.[201]

The Russian peoples and governments that had allied themselves with Czechs posed another problem. Lansing feared they might become victims of vengeful Red Guards. He confessed to Wilson on 24 September that he sympathized with the Czechs and their plight, particularly when they argued that they could not possibly desert their helpless friends to "certain massacre and pillage." Apart from anything else, Lansing feared the negative effect on public opinion that would result from the US attempting to persuade them to do so, when the Czecho-Slovaks were claiming they would rather die on the Volga than abandon their allies. Consequently Lansing concluded they must expect that the Czechs west of the Urals would remain there. He pointed out that even if they could persuade the Czechs to withdraw, the United States would bear the ignominy if the Bolsheviks destroyed those communities that had been under Czech protection. He went on to express his doubts about the situation. "Yet assuming that we ought to aid these people if we can, what can we do?" The AEF was too small to send supplies, and Lansing was convinced that the Japanese, "even if it were physically possible, would hesitate to enter on so hazardous an adventure." He went on to lay out what he saw as the dilemma. "We cannot abandon the Czecho-Slovaks on the ground that they will not abandon their Russian friends. Of course that would never do. And yet what is the alternative, or is there any?" He pleaded with Wilson to consider what could be done in a situation changed by Bolshevik terrorism and unforeseen when the president wrote the aide memoire.[202]

Lansing was not the only one who felt that the United States ought to give the Czechs more substantial help. Dr. Rudolf Bolling Teusler, the head of the American Red Cross in Vladivostok and a cousin of the First Lady, Edith Bolling Galt Wilson, told Gajda that he felt sure that if the Czechs got into serious trouble Graves would have to come to their rescue. He also told American reporters that although General Graves's response was the official policy of the United States, he was sure that Graves would send troops west if the Czechs needed reinforcements. This statement enraged Graves, who was awaiting instructions from the War Department. He wrote that foreigners attached more significance to Teusler's views than they deserved because he was Mrs. Wilson's cousin.[203]

On 23 September, Ambassador Morris reported to Lansing that Graves thought he should go to Omsk with a substantial portion of his command and form a winter base there, cooperating as necessary with the other Allied forces in supporting the Czechs to the west. Lansing enclosed a copy of Morris's report in his letter to Wilson on 24 September.[204] For his part Graves reported to General March that even though he and Morris agreed that a strict interpretation of his orders would allow his going, he declined to act without the explicit authorization of the War Department.

He believed it would produce charges that the US was going to participate in reviving the Eastern Front, despite all statements to the contrary, and would only encourage Allied representatives who were using every conceivable means to change US policy.[205]

On 26 September, Wilson put an end to any doubts Morris and Graves had on the disposition of American forces. He sent a memorandum to Lansing instructing him to inform Morris that the president was giving Graves authority to establish headquarters at Harbin or some other spot where he could be in touch with an open port during the winter, and where he could make the best use of his force to safeguard the railways and keep them open for the Czechs. But Wilson most definitely rejected the proposal that Graves move to western Siberia. "[S]trongly as our own sympathies constrain to make every possible sacrifice to keep the country on the Volga front out of the hands of the merciless Red Guards, it is the unqualified judgment of our military authorities that to attempt *that* is to attempt the impossible." He promised to send the Czech forces all available supplies, but he could not send them west of the Urals. Therefore, the Czechs should retire east of the Urals, preferably where they would make it "impossible for the Germans to draw supplies of any kind from Western Siberia," but at least where they could secure themselves against attack. Wilson refused to help the legion carry out any other scheme. Wilson further cautioned Lansing to make it clear to Morris that the ideas and purposes of the Allies with respect to what should be done in Siberia and on "'the Volga front' are ideas and purposes with which we have no sympathy and the representatives of the Allies at Vladivostock are trying their best to 'work' General Graves and every other American in sight and should be made to understand that there is absolutely 'nothing doing.'"

Lansing cabled the president's decision to Morris, adding a more refined version of Wilson's "nothing doing" remark. "While we have said that we do not desire to set limits on the actions or to define the policies of our associates," Lansing wrote, "we are not prepared and do not intend to follow their lead and do not desire our representatives to be influenced by their persistent representations as to the facts and as to plans for action which seem to us chimerical and wholly impossible." He instructed Morris to "impress upon the military, naval, and civil authorities of the United States Government at Vladivostok that, notwithstanding any pressure to the contrary, they are expected to be governed wholly and absolutely by the policy of the government expressed herein."[206] A copy of this message was sent to all the Allied representatives in Washington.

The next day General Graves received a cable from the War Department saying that American forces would not go further west than Lake Baikal, and that if the Czechs stayed in the west or moved further westward, General Graves's responsibility to them extended only to keeping the railroad open. He was also informed of Wilson's message concerning the use of American troops in Russia and Siberia. "And this," remarked Graves, "helped me materially in my dealings with the Allied representatives."[207]

These cables ended a month of heated discussions on what course American policy should take. In the end Wilson made clear that if the Czechs wanted American help they must retire to the east. The United States would not reinforce or supply them west of the Urals, and would only undertake to keep their lines of retreat open. The United States would not support Czech military adventures in Russia or Siberia against any foe.

With his responsibilities to the Czechs defined, Graves decided "there was nothing left for the United States troops to do but to help carry out the part of my instructions which stated: 'the only legitimate object for which American troops can be employed, is to guard military stores, which may subsequently be needed by Russian forces.'" Before he could render any aid to the Russians in the organization of their own self-defense a decision had to be made about what faction constituted the Russians referred to in the aide memoire. Only Wilson could make that decision. In the meantime Graves complained that he could not give assistance to any Russian, without throwing overboard the policy of non-intervention in Russia's internal affairs. "I could not give a Russian a shirt without being subjected to the charge of trying to help the side to which the recipient of the shirt belonged."[208]

This being the case, General Graves turned his attention to the more concrete supply question. As far as the supplies were concerned, he had a great deal to look after. During the war, the Russian authorities had constructed scores of warehouses which were filled as quickly as they were completed. Soon it proved impossible to build warehousing as fast as the Allies were shipping supplies to Siberia. Carl Ackerman, a *New York Times* correspondent in Vladivostok, described the appearance of the city overwhelmed by between $750,000,000 and $1,000,000,000 worth of war supplies. "[E]verything from cotton to unassembled motor-lorries, were piled in open fields and lots and covered with tarpaulins." Even outside the city, on the road to Khabarovsk, there were "hills and fields of munitions and materials, rotting, rusting, decaying and wasting. There is a hill of cotton shipped from the United States tacked under mounds of tarpaulins." Ackerman reported there were "37,000 railway track-wheels and heavy steel rails in quantities as to make it possible to build a third track from the Pacific to Petrograd" and "enough barbed-wire to fence Siberia. There are field guns, millions of rounds of ammunition, and a submarine; automobiles, shoes, copper, and lead ingots, and these are only a few of the things which the Tsar's agents purchased from American factories to be used against Germany, but which never came nearer than within 6,000 miles of the front, as near as San Francisco was to the Flanders Battle-line."[209]

Since these supplies were spread over a considerable area, Allied and American troops were posted to protect them from casual looting. But problems arose over what, if anything, the Allies and Americans were entitled to use from these supplies.

General Knox maintained that because he was in Siberia to organize the Russian Army to fight the Bolsheviks he should have all of this property and the control of its distribution. He told Graves that all the supplies had been bought with British money and he proposed to distribute it as he saw fit and that he did not intend for anyone else to have a say in the matter.

General Graves retorted that he had no information about who bought the property, but he felt sure Russia had paid the nation from which she bought it before it was delivered.[210]

The supply problem was further complicated by the French insistence that Graves supply funds to the Czech generals Stanislaus Čeček and Jan Syrový. Graves replied that he had no authority to supply any foreign army with American money.[211] Finally Graves produced a proposal to settle the war stores problem, or at least delay the day of reckoning. On 21 September he pointed out that if each army were permitted to requisition at will Russian arms and supplies, difficulties could well arise in case Russia should demand to be recompensed for them. He recommended that any army which wishes to requisition Russian arms and supplies had to draw up an inventory of the commodities, and have it signed by the person requesting the supplies. The papers were to have a detachable coupon that would be given to those from whom the supplies were requisitioned, to serve as a final receipt.[212] This reasonable suggestion was not adopted, and each country ended up supposedly keeping track of those items which it used. Naturally accounting chaos ensued.

Guarding the Trans-Siberian Railway was one of the chief reasons that American troops were in Siberia. But the men had been dispatched before Graves arrived. After his inspection he reassigned the main body of the 31st Infantry to Vladivostok and its surrounding area to guard the stores there. Company B of that regiment was sent to Harbin for the winter. Companies F and G were dispatched to Spasskoe, Company L to Razdolnoye, and Company M to the Suchan Mines. The 27th Infantry was headquartered at Khabarovsk, with its first battalion at Spasskoe and a platoon at Ussuri. Company E had charge of the POW camp at Khabarovsk. The Americans held these positions throughout the winter of 1918–1919.[213] Graves found he was unable to move any significant number of troops to Harbin because the Japanese would relinquish no quarters to him.[214]

Another practical problem Graves tackled was the disposition of the German and Austrian prisoners of war. Fortunately this proved to be a simple task by Siberian standards, although a few complications arose. Compared to the huge number of German prisoners who had been reported roaming in armed bands around Siberia, the reality proved to be only several thousand hungry men.

Captain Joseph Loughran, a Roman Catholic priest attached to the 17th Infantry, was appointed liaison officer to the prisoners. He recalled that there were about 2,000 at Vladivostok and roughly an equal number interned near Lake Baikal, with some smaller groups scattered in between. These men were far from the ruthless types described in the Allied dispatches. Loughran wrote that "my daily visits to the POW officers and men were a delight…. It was a marvel to me how the POWs retained their musical instruments, which came in mighty handy at Lake Baikal where they provided a choir of 60 voices and an orchestra of 30 pieces and rendered one of Schubert's masses in German."[215]

Lieutenant Sylvain Kindall described the unusual duties of the American troops "guarding" prisoners of war at Spasskoe. When American troops arrived in November they began to round up all the prisoners of war roaming about the neighborhood. "At first only a few of them could be found," he reported, "but these few were not long in discovering that American rations issued to them greatly surpassed the soup and sour black bread which had been their principal food while shifting for themselves." It was not long before word "got about outside the prison barracks that life within it under the new management, with plenty to eat and no labor to be performed, was a much better life at that time than liberty with starvation on the outside." Soon, to his amazement "dozens of other ragged and hungry individuals appeared outside the prison barracks and asked to be placed in confinement." Among these men were several Russians who were claiming to be German or Austrian to get something to eat. The search for prisoners was stopped.[216]

The American commander saw no reason to guard the popular prison. He allowed prisoners to come and go as they pleased. Each prisoner received a pass to identify himself to the sentry on duty when he wanted to get back into the camp.[217]

Other prisoners were used occasionally for labor, but all reports indicate that their relations with their American guards were remarkably good. Russell Swihart, a member of Company "E" of the 31st Infantry, was assigned in mid-October 1918 with twenty other members of his company to supervise 150 German prisoners of war on Russian Island south of Vladivostok. The Czechs had turned these prisoners over to the Americans. They had been housed in a foul camp near Vladivostok. Graves felt the Germans could be more usefully and happily employed elsewhere. Corporal Swihart and his company were to oversee them while they cut wood for the army. Swihart said in retrospect that "I can only admire the high type of men these German prisoners seemed to be. There was no rigid enforcement of rules against talking to the prisoners and, as several of us could speak some German, a spirit of friendliness prevailed." This mutual friendliness extended to including a few of the German prisoners in a party at an orphanage on Russian Island. "True," Swihart admitted, "this was very much against the rules." But he pointed out: "Lest the reader be horrified at what seemed a violation of rules, stop a moment and ask yourself if the goodwill made among the prisoners might not have been paid off in later years."[218]

It paid off sooner than that. Millard Curtis, himself a Siberian veteran, recalled that the "sincere gratitude of these prisoners of war to the American nation and the American Army cannot be appreciated except by those who saw its hundreds of manifestations." A notable example occurred when the 27th Infantry was "stationed at Verkhne-Udinsk, 2,000 miles from Khabarovsk, where 1,000 Austro-Hungarian prisoners of war volunteered to fight for and with the regiment against any and all forces and without asking for pay or clothing" because the United States had done so much for them and their fellow prisoners.[219]

Joseph Loughran recounted a similar incident before his departure from Lake Baikal. He recalled that in January 1920, when the order came to evacuate the Trans-Biakal section of the railroad, a large contingent of Cossacks menaced his camp. "Col. Morrow sent for me to arm my German prisoners with rifles and machine guns in case of any emergency;

the situation was very serious. Had the Cossacks attacked us the German and Austrian prisoners would have been our staunch allies."[220]

The concentration and care of the prisoners turned out to be a much easier task than expected. It also proved to be the task from which the American troops derived the most satisfaction. Other problems were more persistent. Graves discovered at a meeting in early September with Consul John K. Caldwell and Admiral Knight that they had instructed their subordinates not to deal with the Bolsheviks. Graves saw no reason why they should not receive the same treatment as any other Russian faction. This was his first indication that some of the State Department officials and the smaller number of naval representatives did not interpret their instructions the same way he did. It also showed that the State Department and the War Department had adopted different approaches to the situation. Thereafter the difference grew increasingly obvious.

Immediately after Graves arrived in Siberia, the Military Intelligence Office in Washington sent him fifteen officers for work in Siberia. Graves was careful to caution them "not to interfere in political affairs, and not to intervene in internal conflicts." He dispatched them to various parts of Siberia to report on military, political, economic, and social conditions.[221]

Soon after this he received a cable from the War Department stating that the government expected to get its information on conditions in Siberia from State Department sources. Graves was very puzzled. "It seemed clear that the Government wanted me to know that what I said of Siberia or the conditions there, would be ignored." Graves wondered why, "if the State Department wanted to know the real conditions in Siberia, ...did they propose to ignore the information coming from the great majority of United States representatives? The Army was in a much better position to get the facts than the State Department, because of the much larger number of observers and the greater number of places from which reports were received...." In Graves's opinion, the Army reports were "pinching somewhere." The State Department "wanted information along a certain line, as was disclosed by their cable sent to Mr. August Heid, representative of the War Trade Board, that he, Mr. Heid, was not sending the kind of information the State Department wanted him to send out of Siberia."[222]

Graves had a valid point. As a result of the war, the United States had become a full-fledged world power, completing the transformation she had begun in 1898. Its president, partially by virtue of his own personality, had become a world leader. But the machinery of the United States government had not caught up with the country's rise in prominence. The War Department, after years of neglect, had expanded its intelligence arm as a result of the war, but the Diplomatic Corps had not. The army had drawn into its service anyone with an intelligence background, or training in observation or reconnaissance. The army was thus in a better position than was the State Department to evaluate the military viability of the various contending factions in Siberia, as well as their chances of success.[223] By refusing to consider the reports from US Army Intelligence, the State Department deprived itself of a valuable source of information. Army personnel were in a position to report the facts as unaligned observers. The State Department's attitude was particularly unfortunate, as one of the besetting problems in the formulation of American policy was a dearth of accurate intelligence emanating from Siberia. Diplomatic representatives supplied a great deal of information, but very little of it proved to be accurate, or unbiased. The information that they collected for the State Department came from a limited number of highly partial observers. These included American nationals and foreign service officers who had contacts among people closely linked to the tsarist government, and whose opinions and perceptions were unavoidably colored as a result. The basic inaccuracy of much of the State Department information required no further proof than to observe the contrast between the reports sent to Washington describing the Siberian situation before the intervention and the actual situation the Army found when it arrived there.

The Russian Division of the State Department relied for the most part on three representatives: Ernest K. Harris, the consul general at Irkutsk; John C. Caldwell, the consul general at Vladivostok; and Paul S. Reinsch, minister to Peking. These men in turn were only as well informed as their sources. All were quick to see the threat that Bolshevik ideology posed. They believed the defeat of the Bolsheviks to be a pressing necessity.[224]

State Department criticism greatly concerned and annoyed Graves. He cabled the War Department, asking just what the State Department meant. He also told March and Baker that if the State Department wished to depend on the reports of Ernest K. Harris it could do so, but he certainly would not. March reassured Graves that he was sending just the kind of information that the War Department wanted, and told him to carry on.[225] So Graves carried on as directed, clinging to the letter of the aide memoire, and remaining neutral. In the process he rapidly became extremely unpopular in Siberia. In October 1918, he conducted an inspection tour of American troops guarding the Trans-Siberian Railroad. He took along Carl Ackerman, the *New York Times* correspondent, as a member of the party. Ackerman later remarked that it was on this journey with Graves that he had begun to realize "that the United States did not consider the Bolsheviks, everywhere, as enemies of the Allies." [226] In his book *Trailing the Bolsheviki*, Ackerman recounted a typical encounter between Graves and a US soldier. Graves would approach a soldier and ask, "What are you here for?" to which a frequent response was a salute and the statement, "I am here to fight the Bolsheviki."

"Are those your orders?" Graves would ask.

"Yes, sir."

"Where did you get those orders?"

At this point his unfortunate victim was generally showing obvious signs of discomfort. Graves would then press on with the attack.

"Who are the Bolsheviki?"

One particularly intrepid soul replied, "The Bolsheviki are the men who are trying to destroy Russia by killing off the good people and burning the property."

"Have you seen any Bolsheviki around here?" Graves asked.

"Yes, sir."

"Well, what do you do with them?"

"We arrest them, sir."

"Have you any in jail now?"

Ackerman recalled that in one town where there was a prisoner under arrest he and Graves went to see their first Bolshevik. When they arrived at the jail, General Graves asked, "What did this man do?"

"Why nothing, sir," the officer answered.

"Why do you have him under arrest then?"

"Why, he said he was a Bolshevik."

"Do you have orders to arrest the Bolsheviki?"

"Yes, sir."

"Where did you get those orders?"

The officer was then in the quandary the Graves's cross-examination was intended to place him. Graves then continued:

> Whoever gave you those orders must have made them up himself. The United States is not at war with the Bolsheviki or any other faction of Russia. You have no orders to arrest Bolsheviks or anybody else unless they disturb the peace of the community, attack the people or Allied soldiers. The United States is not here to fight Russians or any group or faction in Russia.

He concluded his rebuke by stating that "because a man is a Bolshevik is no reason for his arrest. You are to arrest only those who attack you. The United States is only fighting when American troops are attacked by an armed force."[227]

Thus Graves let it be known throughout his tour that his orders to his officers and men were to remain neutral, and that he expected American troops to obey these instructions.

Following Graves's announcement of a strictly neutral policy for American troops there was a lull in activity. While American troops were all but idle, the Czech troops west of Omsk were falling prey to a devastating Red offensive. In September the Bolsheviks captured the cities of Simbirsk and Volsk; Syran and Samara also fell to them in early October.

On 1 October, General Jan Syrový, the one-eyed commander of the Czecho-Slovak Legion, wrote to Graves from Cheliabinsk. "All the physical and moral forces of the Czecho-Slovak troops have been exhausted by four months of continuous struggle," he reported. "The men are at the end of their strength, the losses from disease and wounds reach a maximum of fifty percent. The units of our eastern detachment are insufficient to hold the front." He emphasized that the situation was very critical and the arrival of Allied reinforcements was an absolute necessity, and the "coming of two or three Allied divisions would instantly change the situation, encouraging, by their presence, both our own troops and the Russian units fighting with us."[228]

Syrový apparently believed that the United States would reinforce him, even though the Americans had stated repeatedly that the Czechs would have to quit the Volga front to receive American aid. The Czechs continued to fight, and they continued to ask Graves for help, because members of the Czech command, along with the British and French military missions, had avoided telling the Czechs at the front that neither the Americans nor the other Allies would be sending them the supplies or reinforcements they needed. This information had been kept from the troops in order to keep them fighting. For a short time the deception was successful. The Czechs fought on, pledging their undying loyalty to the Allied cause and believing that their defeats were temporary and would be reversed quickly when Allied help arrived.[229]

But in October the Czech 4th Regiment mutinied, followed a few days later by the 1st Regiment. The entire 1st Division had collapsed. General Svec committed suicide when his men refused to obey him. Heavy casualties, shortage of supplies, exhaustion, the onset of the Siberian winter, a strong Bolshevik offensive, and the lack of Allied reinforcements all combined to destroy the legion as an effective fighting force.[230]

With the dissolution of the Czech Legion, the *raison d'être* for the AEF seemed to be gone. But at this same moment the State Department was adopting a new position that would make it attempt to redefine the role of the American forces.

The Czech crisis and Graves's tour precipitated a widening of the chasm between the State and War Departments that had begun with the intelligence controversy. It had resulted in the State and War Departments getting their information from completely different sources, and using that information to form two opposing conclusions. By the end of October the State Department was adopting an attitude that was increasingly anti-Bolshevik. Lansing was more moderate in his views than the foreign service officers in Russia or the Russian desk at the State Department, but even he began to show concern over the Bolshevik menace. On 26 October, he wrote that he thought Bolshevism "the most hideous and monstrous thing that the human mind had ever conceived."[231]

Lansing did not see Bolshevism as an improvement over autocracy; in fact he thought it potentially worse. "There are," he wrote, "two implacable enemies of individual liberty and its guardians, Political Equality and Justice. These enemies are Absolutism and Bolshevism. The former is waning. The latter is increasing...."[232] Lansing's anxiety was fueled by reports by American officials in Russia, particularly by Harris, Caldwell, and Reinsch, the minister to Peking, who seemed to find grounds for optimism in the counterrevolutionary cause. They increasingly urged that the United States support the White effort.

Graves, who had seen enough of the White forces to realize that they were not the potential saviours of civilization, objected to the continued interference of the State Department in Russian internal and American military affairs. He feared that continued American presence in Siberia was simply serving to delay and prolong an inevitable clash between the political extremes in Russia. In his judgment the clash would occur even if Allied troops remained in Siberia, but clearly it would occur immediately after the withdrawal of Allied Troops. As he saw it the effect of remaining in Siberia had been to allow a "crowd of Reactionaries headed by General Horvath, supported by former Russian officers, to try to firmly establish themselves while the Allied troops are in Siberia."[233]

Graves was also convinced that the Japanese were using intervention as a mask for their imperialist ambitions in Siberia. He saw no need for so many Japanese troops in Siberia, especially since they did not intend to go past Lake Baikal. Graves reported to the Adjutant-General that the Japanese commanders constantly exaggerated the disorderly conditions in Siberia as an excuse for the large numbers of troops they had stationed along the Trans-Siberian Railroad. Graves was confident that fifty soldiers would be safe in any of these towns and added that he personally would happily station far fewer in most of them.[234]

On 28 October, Basil Miles, acting chief of the Russian Division of the State Department, informed Lansing that the Japanese General Staff had virtually absorbed the Chinese Eastern Railroad, leaving their Foreign Office to make whatever excuses they could.[235] Vance McCormick, chairman of the War Trade Board, told Lansing that he feared that Japanese activities would prevent American economic and railway aid to Siberia. He urged the department to take action to frustrate Japanese imperialism in Siberia.[236] These reports had a very disturbing effect on Secretary of War Newton Baker, who told President Wilson that, for his part, he wished that the United States could arrange to withdraw from the whole Siberian venture.[237] Wilson was also concerned about Japanese activity, but while the War Department saw it as a compelling reason to leave, Wilson found it the most compelling reason to stay. He thought American and Allied presence would provide some insurance that the Japanese could not monopolize the Maritime Province and that the Open Door Policy in the Far East might be salvaged.[238]

Relations with the Japanese, meanwhile, suffered from a number of unpleasant confrontations between American and Japanese troops. In early November a typical incident occurred when a Japanese civilian claimed that an American soldier had struck him. Two American soldiers were falsely accused. A Japanese officer ordered the civilian to strike Sgt. Frank Baelski while Japanese soldiers held him at bayonet point.

Graves, having heard reports of several such incidents lately, requested that General Otani investigate. After the investigation, Otani agreed that the American version of the incident was substantially correct. Otani's solution was to deport the Japanese civilian and to relieve the officer who commanded the guards at Vozhemskaya, returning him to his regiment for punishment or reprimand.[239]

A far more serious problem was the atrocious behavior of the Japanese-supported Cossacks. Graves complained that the Cossack leaders Kalmikov and Semenov, with the protection of Japanese troops, "were roaming the country like wild animals, killing and robbing the people." The Japanese, he believed, could have stopped this at any time. General Graves explained that if "questions arose about these brutal murders, the reply was that the people murdered were Bolsheviks and this explanation, apparently, satisfied the world. Conditions were represented as being horrible in Eastern Siberia, and that life was the cheapest thing there." Ironically, most of the Cossacks' victims were not Bolsheviks at all.[240]

In response to a growing number of reports of Cossack atrocities, Colonel Charles Morrow, commander of the US 27th Infantry, dispatched investigators to report on such incidents along the railroad. The group consisted of Vice Consul Henry Fowler of Chita, the State Department representative; two Japanese lieutenants; two French officers; and Lt. E. Davis of the 27th Infantry. They went to the village of Bobinka to gather evidence of atrocities committed by Semenov's henchmen. Davis reported "a dozen corpses with their hands cut off were lying heaped in a pile half destroyed, all the bodies more or less cut up by saber wounds. The greater part bore many wounds made while living by saber blows, particularly on the face and back." He stated that all the bodies had been burned, many while still alive.[241]

Kalmikov's Cossacks were no better. Another American intelligence officer described a similar scene after a massacre at Gordyevka. "I found that the floor of the room these men were beaten in was covered with blood," he said. "There were loops of rope that were used around the men's necks still hanging from the ceiling and covered with blood. I also found that some of these men had been scalded with boiling water and burned with hot irons, heated in a little stove I found in the room."[242]

Graves found these reports incredible, and he ordered the intelligence officer to report to him in person. He repeated his story and begged,

"General, for God's sake, never send me on another expedition like this. I came within an ace of pulling off my uniform, joining these people [Pro-Bolshevik peasants], and helping them the best I could."[243]

The Cossacks committed many atrocities while searching for weapons the peasants had hidden. The Cossacks argued that the searches were justified because the peasants no longer needed weapons for defense against the Central Powers. The Cossacks entered villages where they seized all weapons that were not surrendered voluntarily. Any peasant found with a rifle was likely to be shot, and if he were lucky enough to avoid execution he was certain to be flogged. Under the pretext of searching for weapons, looting and pillaging went unpunished. The Cossacks succeeded in removing almost all the arms from the peasants in eastern Siberia, leaving the civilian population defenseless against other marauding Cossacks, Japanese soldiers, and Chinese bandits.[244]

In many cases the only protection available to the peasants came from American detachments stationed in or near their villages. In October during the reassignment of American troops, Graves received a request from the village of Alexievsk near Blagovestchensk that was a typical example of many sent to him at that time. The town of Alexievsk thanked Graves for restoring peace and order, and requested that an American detachment remain.[245] The popularity of the American troops led to criticism from General Knox. Graves recalled in his memoir that Knox told him that he "was getting a reputation of being a friend of the poor," and that Graves should know that these people were nothing but "swine."[246]

Graves got into more trouble with his Allied colleagues when he took up the cause of the Bolshevik prisoners in the hands of the Whites. An American officer, Benjamin Dickson, described their treatment at Irkutsk. "Bolshevik prisoners come through here in terrible shape. Wounds are terribly infected, and typhus and dysentery are only too general. The Whites," he claimed, "put fifty prisoners in a long boxcar, lock the doors, feed the prisoners scant bread and water, let the dead lie in the cars, strip the men half naked in a season when nights are chilly. The Russian is a strange bird." Dickson reflected, "he transports these wretches for three thousand miles and then shoots them."[247]

Graves lost no time in reporting these practices to the War Department and making his opinion on this loathsome conduct widely known in Vladivostok. Ultimately it led to charges that he was pro-Bolshevik, not only from Generals Knox and Paris, but also from State Department representatives Harris and Caldwell as well. Nevertheless, Graves felt that he was well within his rights in protesting atrocities and attempting to prevent their commission by any party. He told the Adjutant General that he had been unable to determine what he could do militarily to help the Russians reestablish a civil government. He believed that no military action could have been taken that would have indirectly violated the restrictions against assisting in the reestablishment of the Eastern Front, or meddling in Russian internal affairs.[248]

Graves also worried that by cooperating too closely with the Allies, the United States might lose its moral influence in Siberia. In the same report to the Adjutant General, he pointed out that United States troops, and the American government as well, enjoyed more Russian confidence than did any of the Allies who were operating in Siberia. But Graves also voiced fears that American forces' cooperation with the Japanese on the Ussuri line to the north might tarnish this popularity because of Japanese high-handedness. Ultimately, Graves feared, the Russian peoples would no longer distinguish the Americans from the Japanese. He thus planned to put as much distance between the Japanese and Americans as he could, but moving American troops in any number proved impossible.[249]

Graves also voiced concern over the administration of the railways. He warned that "unless the railroad is opened and put on a business basis, I am unable to see how the people are to get along during the winter. This fact apparently does not worry the Russians and one does not find them making any strenuous or determined efforts to prepare for the winter."[250] The AEF might at least help them by maintaining the railroad.

The railway suffered from a number of persistent problems. It had historically been run at a loss, and had been heavily subsidized by the tsarist government. The Railway Service Corps under Colonel George Emerson encountered a number of difficulties.[251] There was a grave shortage of locomotives, along with a general deterioration of rolling-stock, and the lack of spare parts and lubricating oils had put hundreds of cars out of commission. In addition, low production in the Siberian coal mines caused chronic shortages of fuel. Furthermore, the Railway Service Corps found that the railway workers had not been paid for some time, which led to unrest among the workmen and lengthy delays in both scheduling and repairs.[252]

In the midst of such chaos, corruption and black-marketeering flourished. When American engineers took charge of their sectors of the railroad, they discovered the most astonishing and extensive theft and fraud. Boxcars of guns, ammunition, and other supplies desperately needed by the Czechs at the front were shunted aside to send carloads of more profitable luxury items to Omsk. It was not unusual for entire trainloads of goods simply to disappear in transit.

Early in September 1918 an Allied Railway Committee was organized in Vladivostok, but it soon ran afoul of Graves. On 24 September, he had reported to General March that his investigation of this so-called "Supreme Council of the Railroad Committee" indicated that it was conducted by General Nakajima, who had the committee discuss matters of policy unrelated to the operation of the railway. Graves believed that the Japanese military authorities used the committee as a tool to impress their government by saying that "the committee was of the opinion—so and so—in order to make it more forceful, they spoke of this committee as the 'Superior War Committee.'" The Japanese government, in turn, apparently used these statements in discussion with the Allies.

Graves wrote to General Otani to tell him that matters of any importance would have to be put to him personally. Graves also informed the officers representing him that if a subject came up in the committee over which they had no authority, that they were to repeat that it would have to be submitted to Graves and to take no further part in the discussions.[253] Graves's persistent refusals either to relinquish his authority to the Allies, or expand the limits of his authority to act on issues he felt violated his orders, continued to infuriate both the Allies and his compatriots from the State Department.

The first few months of American intervention had been largely an adjustment period in which Graves investigated the situation, and familiarized himself with the other commanders and their policies. During this time Graves adhered closely to the policy laid down in the aide memoire. Following Wilson's instructions he managed to prevent the United States from being drawn into an attempt to reestablish an Eastern Front. He also avoided any effort to inveigle him into supporting the Czechs against the Bolsheviks. Under more recent orders from Washington he did his best to persuade the Czechs to quit the Urals and withdraw to eastern Siberia for evacuation.

But these actions were essentially negative ones. They merely required a consistent refusal to cooperate with the Allies. Graves was successful because all he had to do to succeed was to say no, and say it repeatedly. It was a practice that was not designed to endear him to the Allied commanders. They strongly criticized his actions as uncooperative at best, and at worst subversive and pro-Bolshevik.

The only problem Graves actually solved was the reinternment of the German and Austro-Hungarian prisoners of war, and that was mainly because it was a unilateral action that required little Allied cooperation. The other two principle problems, railroad management and the distribution of supplies, Graves could not successfully deal with because he could not persuade or compel the Allies to follow his own policy. Therefore, he could only object to their proposals and refuse to cooperate.

Graves was also at odds with a variety of consular representatives, who felt that the best interests of the United States and the Russian people would be served by supporting anti-Bolshevik forces. They were at odds not just with Graves but with Wilson, Lansing, and the War Department as well. They feared that the United States government relied more heavily upon Graves's reports of conditions than upon their own.

The president had relied exclusively on information provided by foreign and State Department sources when making his decision to send troops to Russia, these reports proved to be highly inaccurate. Graves had immediately reported that the situation when he arrived was vastly different from what had been previously described. As Graves had not seen any of the State Department reports or taken direct part in any discussions on intervention, the contrast was all the more embarrassing. All that Graves knew about Siberia when he arrived was found in the aide memoire.

By the beginning of November it was clear to General Graves what sort of action he might expect from his Allies. He also had a better grasp, both of the situation and the motives, of the contending factions in Siberia. He soon had to begin all over again, however, when the entire situation changed dramatically following the declaration of an armistice on the Western Front on 11 November.

5

The Armistice and the Rise of Kolchak

IN NOVEMBER 1918 TWO MAJOR EVENTS RADICALLY CHANGED THE POSITION of the American Expeditionary Force in Siberia. The signing of the armistice on 11 November altered the status of all the Allies and Associated Powers in Siberia. A week later a coup at Omsk turned a relatively obscure figure, Admiral Alexander Kolchak, into the so-called "Supreme Ruler of Russia."

The armistice ended the argument between the United States and the Allies about the reestablishment of an Eastern Front against the Germans. This had been the primary motivation behind British and French policy up to that time. Even if the Bolsheviks had been German puppets, the Allies no longer had any justification for waging a war against them.

These events did not, however, alter Japanese policy. Japan still desired economic and political control of eastern Siberia and sought to prevent the formation of a strong central Russian government. These goals did not change simply because a war, no matter how large and epochal, had ended thousands of miles away.

In spite of the Japanese threat, General Graves felt that the armistice ended the justification for American intervention. The danger that Bolsheviks or escaped prisoners of war would capture the war stores and send them to Germany, or that prisoners of war would take over Siberia, disappeared with the armistice. Graves expected that with the end of the war the Czechs and the German prisoners would be repatriated and that Allied and American troops would soon be leaving Siberia. "All the stated reasons why the United States took part in military actions in Siberia," he later wrote, "entirely disappeared before the Armistice, or at the time of the Armistice."[254] He took the State Department at its word that the United States was not going to take sides in Russian internal affairs. Continued American presence, he feared, would constitute interference in domestic matters. To Graves, this was a moral as well as a political issue.

But the Allied commanders did not share this view. "I seemed to be the only military representative," Graves recalled with irony later, "who was not aware that we had a war of our own in Russia, and that our war was independent and separate from the War in France. The Armistice had absolutely no effect in Siberia."[255] It certainly had no effect on the factional fighting, which was a source of discord between Graves and the English, French, and Japanese commanders. Graves admitted that Americans had taken part in military operations on the premise that German and Austrian prisoners of war comprised at least some of the hostile forces. But the representatives of England, France, and Japan followed a different policy. "It made no difference to them," he observed, "whether the organizations were Bolsheviks, or composed of Bolsheviks and Germans and Austrian prisoners. Therefore, as far as they were concerned, the military was used just the same after the signing of the Armistice as before."[256]

Graves, on the other hand, took the position that "as far as American troops were concerned, the United States was not at war with any part of Russia and we could not take any hostile action except to protect ourselves or the property placed in our charge. This added some of the bitterness of feeling which was already rather intense."[257]

The armistice also helped to bring about the total collapse of the Czech Legion. The deterioration of the legion was already far advanced. Its soldiers no longer obeyed their officers' orders. They had already abandoned large sections of the Ural front, and withdrawn to positions along the railroad. It was fortunate for the White cause (as well as for the Czechs themselves) that military operations had already been suspended because of the onset of winter. During November almost all the Czech units ceased fighting, and began looking for a way home to the newly independent

Czechoslovakia. General Janin reported that the Czechs were no longer a fighting force and would not be again for a long time.[258]

Before Graves received any new orders following the armistice, a coup occurred at Omsk on 18 November, which made Admiral Kolchak the head of the White government in Siberia. Before Kolchak took power, two major governments had operated in Siberia, each seeking Allied support, and each opposing the other. The Samara Government was composed mainly of Social Revolutionaries. The Siberian Provisional Government was a much more conservative organization. The two had merged at the insistence of the British and French to form the Omsk Directory. Neither government had been successful in getting soldiers into the line to help the Czechs against the Bolsheviks. The British and the French, unimpressed, hoped that the Directory would be more stable and more willing to fight the Bolsheviks. But the new government did not meet these early expectations. General Knox made his disdain for the more liberal element of the Directory abundantly clear. Numerous rumors of plots to install a military dictatorship circulated. They gained both credence and support when Kolchak and Knox made their preference for a dictatorship clear. The plotting culminated in the arrest of the Social Revolutionary directors by Ataman Krasilnikov and his Cossacks on the night of 17 November. The three remaining directors met and urged their ministers to offer military and civil powers to Admiral Kolchak. The coup was accomplished with the tacit consent, if not connivance of the British Middlesex Regiment.[259]

On 18 November, Kolchak, who seems to have played no active role in the overthrow of the Directory, became Supreme Ruler. His assumption of power was to have a far greater impact on the Siberian situation than the end of the war in Europe.

Alexander Kolchak was new to the Siberian political scene. He was born in St. Petersburg in 1873, attending the naval academy there. From 1895 to 1899, he served in the Pacific fleet; then in 1900 he took part in a scientific expedition to the North Pole. This work gained him a reputation as a hydrologist. During the Russo-Japanese War he commanded a destroyer, and later a gun battery, where he earned a reputation for extreme personal bravery. He was captured by the Japanese and spent some time as a prisoner of war in Japan. After his release he participated in another expedition to the Arctic and helped to form the Russian Naval General Staff.

When World War I broke out, Kolchak directed the laying of mines in the North Sea against the Germans. In July 1916 he became a vice admiral and assumed command of the Black Sea Fleet. After the February Revolution Kolchak shifted his allegiance to the Provisional Government. He managed to keep his fleet under control and operating until June 1917, when Bolshevik agitation in the fleet caused him to toss his sword overboard in disgust and leave for Petrograd. From there he went to the United States to discuss the possibilities of an American operation in the Dardanelles. Following the Bolshevik Revolution, Kolchak found his way to Japan, where he offered his services to the British ambassador in Tokyo. The British decided to send him to Mesopotamia. He was en route there when they recalled him to take part instead in the Siberian intervention. Kolchak became the paymaster for the White detachments in Manchuria. It was in this capacity that he was serving when he assumed the rank of supreme ruler.[260]

Most observers agreed that Kolchak was a man of the strictest honor, but that he had a fierce temper, and scant knowledge of the art of government. Ambassador Morris reported to Lansing that "Admiral Kolchak is, in my judgment, an honest and courageous man of very limited experience in public affairs, of narrow views and small administrative ability. He is dictator in name but exercises little influence on the Council of Ministers." Morris believed, "his intentions are good, but he seems to have had no appreciation until recently of the political and economic dangers which threaten the government. He has no military knowledge or experience."[261]

Kolchak was a British protégé, and was consequently very popular with them. When he came to power, however, he became a rallying point for thousands of ex-tsarist officers and officials, most of whom shared his shortcomings, a lack of military experience and organizational ability, but not his virtues. The British were unimpressed with his colleagues. "I have absolute confidence in the character of the admiral," Colonel John Ward wrote, "but the pigmies by whom he is surrounded are so many drags on the wheels of state. There is not one that I would trust to manage a whelk stall. They have no idea of the duty of a statesman. Little pettifogging, personal equations and jobs occupy the whole of their time, except when they are engaged upon the congenial task of trying to thwart the Supreme Governor."[262]

Another major problem with the Kolchak administration was its staff, which was ill-chosen, corrupt, bloated, and inefficient. Kolchak had over 4,000 staff officers. The American General Staff in France had only forty-two. Even at the height of the war the German Army had only about 1000 staff officers. It is difficult to believe Kolchak required a larger staff than the kaiser. Kolchak's chief of-staff, Colonel Lebedev, was well-known for his duplicity and sadism. When Knox asked Kolchak why he kept him, Kolchak replied that it was because "I am sure he will not stab me in the back." Knox wrote that "Kolchak forgets the post requires more positive qualities."[263]

In Washington the problem of how to respond to the changes in the Siberian situation remained unanswered throughout 1918 and the spring of 1919. Again, Wilson reviewed the Siberian policy. Again he was besieged with advice. The army made it plain that it wished to withdraw from Russia. The State Department, too, contemplated removing American troops, but its desire to leave centered around the conduct of the Japanese.

Shortly after the armistice Lansing made the first of many representations to the Japanese government protesting Japanese conduct in Manchuria and Siberia. He pointed to the number of Japanese troops there, and the necessity of putting Stevens and his Railway Service Corps in charge of the Siberian railroads. His protests had little effect on the Japanese. Lansing questioned Morris about "the effect of withdrawal from Siberia of all American forces including Stevens and the Russian Railway

Service Corps, as evidence of our unwillingness to be associated with a policy so contrary to our declared purpose regarding Russia."[264]

Morris responded that the Japanese foreign minister had told him that their forces in Siberia had already been reduced, and he felt that those left were necessary to guard 3,400 miles of railroad. Morris strongly advised against removing American troops. He believed this would play into the hands of the Japanese, who, in his opinion, "were not at all disturbed by threats to withdraw American troops."[265]

On 20 November, the Japanese ambassador in Washington, Kikujiro Ishii, sent Wilson a letter confirming Morris's information that the Japanese were withdrawing some troops from Siberia. The ambassador stated that Japanese forces in Siberia and North Manchuria had earlier numbered about 70,000, with a third of these being non-combatants, and that some of these had already been withdrawn. He added that because of the many duties required of them, this number was not at all excessive. He denied charges of any Japanese efforts to obstruct the AEF or monopolize the railroad.[266]

While Morris and Lansing considered keeping the AEF in Siberia to check Japanese expansion, Baker disagreed with their assessment. He believed nothing could be gained by keeping American troops in Siberia. On 22 November, Baker sent Wilson a copy of Graves's report on the situation in Siberia. In the report Graves expressed his view that the foreign military presence in Siberia only benefited the reactionary parties. He believed conditions in Siberia were deteriorating daily. Horvath, the Omsk government representative in Eastern Siberia, and his supporters were, to Graves's way of thinking, either planning to restore the monarchy or establish a dictatorship. This, Graves said, was widely opposed by the majority of Russians, and their government could not survive twenty–four hours without foreign support. Horvath and others were using the Allied presence to entrench themselves in power, hoping to be strong enough to keep it when the Allied troops left. He concluded, "I think some blood will be shed when troops move out but the longer we stay the greater will be the bloodshed when Allied troops do go, as in effect each day we remain here, now that war with Germany is over, we are by our mere presence helping establish a form of autocratic government which the people of Siberia will not stand for," and he pointed out that "our stay is creating some feeling against the Allied governments because of the effect it has. The classes seem to be growing wider apart and the feeling between them more bitter daily."[267]

The next day Baker sent Wilson another cable from Graves in which Graves reported on Cossack atrocities at Khabarovsk. Graves had taken the matter up with the Japanese commander, who promised to prevent future executions by Kalmikoff at Khabarovsk. Graves added, however, that while he thought that the executions would stop at Khabarovsk, Kalmikoff would begin them elsewhere.[268]

Baker, increasingly anxious about American activities in Siberia, wanted Wilson to decide what the War Department should do in that quarter before the president left for the Paris Peace Conference. As far as Baker could see, all justification for the presence of American forces in Russia had evaporated. Intervention in Murmansk and Archangel had been necessary to prevent the Germans from capturing important military stores; Graves had taken the AEF into Siberia to help the Czechs. None of these acts, the secretary of war believed, were hostile to the Russian peoples or any Russian political faction. But the Germans were now withdrawing, and the Czechs seemed to have no need—if they had ever had any—of the American military. American efforts, concluded Baker, should now end. "Our forces in both places," he feared, were now "being used for the purposes for which we would not have sent them in the first instance." The troops in North Russia were frozen in until spring and nothing could be done about them; Siberia was the place that principally worried him. He recounted the remarkable expansion of the Japanese expedition, warning that the Japanese might well continue to send troops to Siberia. Meanwhile they had already seized the Chinese Eastern Railroad, and were reportedly financing the Cossacks against other Russian factions. Baker feared that the Japanese were using the AEF as a cloak for their activities in Siberia, which had nothing to do with repatriating the

Czechs. He discounted the State Department's argument that the AEF could not leave the Japanese forces alone in Siberia. "The longer we stay," he argued, "the more Japaneze [sic] there are and the more difficult it will be to induce Japan to withdraw her forces if we set the example." He also dismissed the idea that a military force was necessary to act, in effect, as a police force for any civil relief efforts that the US undertook in Siberia. "I frankly do not believe this," he said flatly, "nor do I believe we have the right to compel the reception of our relief agencies." Cyrus H. McCormick, the head of the International Harvester Company, who was very active in Russia had already asked Baker to send more troops to Siberia for this purpose.

Baker admitted he did not understand Bolshevism or its appeal and he certainly did not like what he knew about it, but if the Russians did, that was their own business. It was not his place to say "that only ten percent of the Russian people are Bolsheviks and that therefore we will assist the other ninety percent in resisting it...." Baker advocated compelling the withdrawal of the Germans and Austrians and letting the Russians sort out their own mess. The US might not like either the methods or the results, but the imposition of ideas from the outside was clearly not help-ing. Furthermore, Baker was growing increasingly alarmed by the size of Japanese intervention in Siberia, which he described as "growing so rapid-ly and so obviously beyond any interest Japan could have of a humanitarian or philanthropic character that the difficulty of securing Japaneze [sic] withdrawal is growing every hour." He dreaded the growing possibility that the US would "rudely awakened someday to a realization that Japan has gone in under our wing and so completely mastered the country that she cannot be either induced out or forced out by any action either of the Russians or of the Allies."[269]

Baker acknowledged that Wilson might prefer to wait until he arrived in Paris and consult with the Allies, but he ended by opining to Wilson that the United States ought to order the AEF home on the first ship and tell Japan that its mission was accomplished, and that while economic assistance might achieve some further benefit, force of arms could not.[270]

Baker had been particularly alarmed by Graves's 21 November report that the Whites were merely using the Allies' presence as a delaying tactic to entrench themselves in power.

While Baker was urging Wilson to withdraw from Russia, and emphasizing White atrocities, Secretary of State Robert Lansing was taking a very different view. Lansing had no objection to maintaining an American military presence in Siberia; for him, that presence still had an important and much more sweeping purpose than the more conventional one that Baker saw. Specifically, Lansing was growing increasingly impatient with the Bolsheviks in general and the commissar for foreign affairs, G. V. Chicherin, in particular. In October 1918, Chicherin sent Wilson a note that Lansing characterized as a "specious and upstart arraignment" of Wilson's Russian policy.[271] In a second note on 2 November, Chicherin bluntly accused Wilson of trying to overthrow the Bolshevik government. "Give us clear, precise, and businesslike answers," he demanded, firing off a string of questions.

> Do the governments of America, England, and France intend to stop shedding the blood of Russian citizens if the Russian people consent to pay ransom? In that case what payment do the governments of America, England and France expect from the Russian People? Do they demand concessions, delivery of railways on certain conditions, mines, gold mines, etc., or territorial concessions, part of Siberia or the Caucasus, the Murman coast? We expect you, President, to declare decidedly what are your demands and those of your allies.[272]

Chicherin announced that if he did not receive a reply from Wilson he would assume that the Bolsheviks were correct in assuming that the Associated Powers expected payment and he would inform the Russian people. "The Russian people will [then] realize that the demands of your government and those of your allies are so limitless and heavy that you cannot present them to the Russian Government."[273]

Although Lansing did not tell Wilson of the contents of Chicherin's cables until 21 November, Lansing saw them as a definite turning point in US-Bolshevik relations. He told Wilson that "neither of the notes should be dignified by a formal reply." But at the same time he did advocate a public statement that the United States wished by its actions to serve the best interests of the Russian people. Lansing urged Wilson to "call upon all civilized nations to join in expressing their abhorrence of the reign of terror which exists in parts of Russia," by which he meant the areas under Red control. But by now Wilson had learned the contents of Chicherin's notes. Insulted by Chicherin's aspersions, he declined to follow Lansing's advice. Instead he told Lansing to wait until they got to Paris.[274] Caught between conflicting views—the conservative, traditional, and militarily-sound recommendations of Baker and the overtly political and interventionist ideas of Lansing—Wilson wanted to consult the Allies. He was deeply perplexed; on 27 November, he wrote, "My mind is not clear as to what is the immediate proper course in Russia. There are many more elements at work there than I conjecture you are aware of, and it is harder to get out of than it was to go in."[275]

In Siberia, State Department officials had mixed reactions to the Kolchak government. Consul General Harris was particularly enthusiastic about Kolchak. On 19 November 1918, one day after the coup at Omsk, he called on the admiral. Kolchak recalled that Harris "was very friendly and revealed an extremely benevolent attitude. He was one of the few American representatives who sincerely desired to help us, and he did all he could to help our supply troubles. Harris, as far as I remember, was the first to pay me a formal call on the day following [the overthrow]." At this meeting, Harris told Kolchak that "Your basic problem is to lead the nation to the point where it can take the government into its hands, that is, to choose a government according to its desires."

Kolchak promised him that "this is my basic task...I shall not abuse power and I shall not hold on to it a single day after it has become possible to relinquish it." Harris assured him of his sympathy and that if Kolchak stuck to this course, they would work together in the future.[276]

Graves was aware of Harris's promises to Kolchak, and of his belief that Kolchak could resolve the situation in Siberia.[277] But Graves disagreed. He thought that the State Department representatives in Siberia in general, and Harris in particular, were violating Wilson's instructions by interpreting them so loosely as to make them meaningless, and therefore, they were interfering in Russian internal affairs without justification.

Graves had made a similar complaint earlier. On 5 November, he had received an extract of a letter from the State Department to the War Department. This letter stated in no uncertain terms that the State Department felt that consuls general were "authorized, not only to keep in personal touch if possible, with local Governments, but to permit consular officers under them to give aid and advice to these Governments in their effort to improve local conditions." The letter did caution, however, that the United States was not prepared to recognize any government in Russia.[278]

Graves pointed out that the towns in which the consular agents were located were all in White-controlled areas. Consequently, the State Department was giving aid and advice exclusively to the Whites. This caused the Bolsheviks to claim the United States was helping only tsarist adherents. Graves contended that "the instructions opened the door, to some extent, for United States representatives to take sides, if they so desired, and these people had feelings and opinions like everybody else."[279]

These instructions indicated a growing division between the State Department and the War Department representatives in Siberia. But throughout this time, Graves's instructions remained unaltered. The only advantage he could see to pursuing this dual policy was "that it gives an opportunity to easily answer critics, by referring to the action of the State Department or the War Department, as the occasion demands."[280]

The differences between Graves and Harris continued to grow. Harris created particular difficulties for Graves, not only because of his opposition to the general's policy, but also because of his geographic position at Irkutsk. Harris was much nearer to Omsk than Graves, and therefore in an excellent position to give the impression to the Kolchak government and Allied representatives that Graves was deliberately ignoring American policy and acting on his own initiative.

Harris was not the only person who objected to the way Graves performed his duties. The Russian Division of the State Department, now under Dewitt C. Poole (whose promises of aid to the Czechs had created so much ill-feeling), believed that Kolchak and his forces offered the greatest hope for defeating Bolshevism and restoring Russia to some semblance of order. Harris and Poole disagreed strongly with the neutral policy Graves pursued. They wanted him to support Kolchak. Graves refused, maintaining that this would be a blatant breach of American policy. His orders from Wilson instructed him not to interfere in Russian internal affairs, and as far as he was concerned, backing one side in a civil war constituted interference. But because he refused to allow his troops to be used against the Bolsheviks, he laid himself open to charges that he was a Bolshevik sympathizer.[281]

Harris deeply resented the anti-White reports that Graves was sending to Washington; in addition Harris had accused Graves and the army of "playing politics."[282] Graves in turn felt that Harris was largely responsible for a cable he had received from Washington informing him that the United States government expected to get its information from the State Department. Graves wrote Ambassador Morris in Tokyo complaining that he had received a telegram from the chief of staff telling him that the government expected "Consul General Harris at Irkutsk to inform them, not only on civil, but military affairs." Graves was at a loss to understand it. He told Morris that if it meant "that the military is to be withdrawn, I am delighted. On the other hand, if I am to remain here, I shall consider it my duty to continue reporting the situation as I see it."[283]

Graves's influence was further eroded when Frank L. Polk became the acting secretary of state while Lansing attended the peace conference. Polk vigorously opposed Graves's position on a number of issues, particularly more active cooperation between US forces and Kolchak's armies and recognition of the Kolchak government itself. Polk thus gave many observers the impression that Graves was acting on his own initiative.[284] At a particularly low point, an irritated Polk complained that "Graves is a useless old woman...and so the result is that our men are not as effective as park policemen."[285]

Despite the strong criticism leveled at him, Graves had the support of his superiors, including the chief of staff; the secretary of war, who had recovered from his initial fears that Graves might exceed his authority; and the president. In Baker's opinion "General Graves carried out the policy of his Government without deviation, under circumstances always perplexing and often irritating." He recalled that he often heard, both from Allied military attachés and from State Department officials, complaints that Graves was uncooperative. "[B]ut when I asked for a bill of particulars," he noted, "I invariably found that the General's alleged failure was a refusal on his part to depart from the letter and spirit of his instructions."[286] Baker was unable to ascertain either the cause of the conflict between the War and State Department policy, or the State Department's occasional practice of communicating its policy ideas directly to Graves. "Perhaps the State Department," he wrote, "was more impressed than I was with some of the Allied views as to the desirability of cooperation beyond the scope of the Aide Memoire."[287]

Whatever Graves's difficulties with the State Department, he could do nothing but await Wilson's decision on what to do with the AEF in Siberia. The American public had been ambivalent about sending troops to Russia from the outset, and what support there was deteriorated rapidly after the armistice. Wilson, however, was not able to devote much of his attention to the issue throughout the winter of 1918 and spring of 1919. During this time he was largely occupied with preparing for and attending the Paris Peace Conference. In January 1919 the State Department informed the military commanders that Wilson would not make any decision on Siberia until after the conference.

Wilson hoped to negotiate a peace treaty that embodied his Fourteen Points, but he could not hope to achieve this without Allied cooperation. The president hesitated to act independently of the Allies in Russia and

risk losing their goodwill, before the conference began. Instead he preferred to wait until a general Allied policy for Siberia could be discussed
before he attempted to withdraw American troops. Wilson declined to
make a public statement on his policy toward Russia until after the new
year; instead he considered what his policy should be. His thinking centered on two points. The first was that the making of a just peace would
eliminate the menace of the Bolshevik expansion, at least outside Russia,
by eliminating the sources of discontent upon which Bolshevism thrived.
While sailing to Paris aboard the *George Washington*, Wilson told the
Inquiry, his group of policy advisors, that "the only way I can explain sus-
ceptibility of the people of Europe to the prison of Bolshevism, is that their
Governments have been run for wrong purposes, and I am convinced that
if the peace is not made on the highest principles of justice it will be swept
away by the peoples of the world in less than a generation."

Despite his disparagement of Bolshevism (referring to it, for instance, as
a "prison"), Wilson was still disinclined to attempt its destruction. William
C. Bullitt, a friend of Colonel House and an expert in the State
Department's Western European Division, recorded in his diary, "The
President also expressed very strongly several times the conviction that it
was the right of each nation to have the sort of government it desired, and
indicated, I thought, that he was not considering a further advance
against the Bolsheviki."[288]

Wilson's second concern was the threat of Japanese expansion. At the
request of the United States and the Allies, the Japanese had gone into
Siberia, but the civil authorities in Japan, who had agreed to limit the
expedition, had lost control of the military authorities, who were rapidly
taking over much of the Siberian Far East and refusing to cooperate with
the Russian Railway Service Corps.[289] Ambassador Morris hoped to negotiate an agreement with the Japanese for international supervision of the
Trans-Siberian and Chinese Eastern Railway. He hoped, thereby, to ame-
liorate the situation and wrest some control of the railways away from the
Japanese.[290] Wilson, therefore, faced the choice of withdrawing from
Siberia and leaving the Japanese unsupervised or staying and trying to

moderate their policies and thus shield the Russians from Japanese expansion.

Lloyd George, after a conference with Wilson in December 1918, reported to the Imperial War Cabinet that their discussion had begun with the League of Nations. Lloyd George had the impression that the league was the only thing that Wilson really cared about. The prime minister felt that Wilson's thinking was very similar to Lord Robert Cecil's and General Jan Smuts's regarding the form the league should take.[291] Regarding Russia specifically, Lloyd George explained that

> President Wilson, though not pro-Bolshevik, was very much opposed to armed intervention. He disliked the Archangel and Murmansk expeditions, and would, no doubt, withdraw his troops from there. He was not very much in favor of the Siberian expedition, though as regards that his principal anxiety was as to the conduct of the Japanese, who were apparently taking the whole of Eastern Siberia into their own hands, sending sealed wagons into the interior, and generally behaving as if they owned the country. His whole attitude, in fact, was strongly anti-Japanese.[292]

At the same conference Sir Robert Borden, the Canadian prime minister, clearly delineated the problem facing Wilson and the Allies. Sir Robert said that he "did not see how the War could be regarded as terminated if we left the Peace Conference with five or six nations and Governments still fighting away in Russia. There were only two alternatives: one was to go and forcibly intervene in Russia itself; the other, which he preferred, was to get the Governments of the various States in Russia to come and be represented at the Peace Conference."[293]

Lord Robert Cecil agreed with the suggestion. He admitted to certain difficulties in dealing with the Bolshevik government, but he thought they were not insuperable. His principal anxiety was the conduct of the Japanese. He suggested all Russian factions "stand fast where they were till the Peace Conference was over, and that meanwhile Allied Commissions might clear up many disputed points about the situation."[294]

Wilson, meanwhile, was coming under growing pressure from the Senate to explain why American troops remained in Russia and Siberia.[295] Frank L. Polk urged Lansing, on 6 January 1919, to get Wilson to declare his attitude towards the Bolshevik government. Polk warned Lansing, "The reports we receive...show the growing menace of Bolshevism outside Russia."[296] Polk enclosed a cable from Carl Ackerman for Colonel House urging that the US government announce a unified policy in Siberia.

Unlike some others, Ackerman realized that the State and War Departments were at odds in their interpretations of American policy in Siberia. He reported that the contradictory policies of American diplomatic and military representatives were causing confusion and distrust. "I submit," argued Ackerman, "that the United States cannot hope to succeed with any policy in Russia unless the officials representing different departments of the Government speak with unanimity or unless it is absolutely and publicly understood in Russia that such men do not speak with authority." Ackerman urged that the Allies agree upon a policy of either intervening or withdrawing together. He warned that "Russia, the first great reconstruction problem, cannot be solved by divided councils."[297] Polk himself urged Lansing to bring the situation to Wilson's attention.[298]

Lansing duly approached Wilson about Russian policy on 9 January. Wilson replied that he saw no advantage in words and public statements on Bolshevism. He told Lansing, "what I am at present keenly interested in is finding the interior of their minds...."[299] To determine this he asked Lansing to send a representative to Stockholm to confer with Maxim Litvinov, whom the Soviet government had authorized to conduct peace negotiations with the Allied governments.[300]

Wilson ended his note to Lansing with a phrase that became his theme in the following weeks, and summed up his belief that Bolshevism sprang from social dislocation and desperation. "The real thing with which to stop Bolshevism is food."[301] That same day Wilson asked Congress to appropriate money for Herbert Hoover to manage European food relief. "Bolshevism," Wilson argued, "is steadily advancing westward, has overwhelmed Poland, and is poisoning Germany. It cannot be stopped by force but it can be stopped by food...."[302]

At the beginning of January, Wilson remained firmly opposed to the use of force against the Bolsheviks, although he viewed them with increasing distaste. He was sure that they were open to negotiation. He might not like them, but if the Russian people did, he would not interfere. He was determined, however, to discourage the spread of Bolshevism in other countries by sending food relief to Eastern Europe.

The French, meanwhile, were insisting that the Allies take a less pacific course. Marshal Foch requested authority to send Allied troops to Poland to halt the spread of Bolshevism there by force, but in discussions at the Supreme War Council Wilson and Lloyd George repeatedly opposed him.[303]

In January, the Allies began also discussing the problem of Russian representation at the peace conference. Unable to agree on what group should represent Russia at the conference, the delegates finally decided Russia should have no official representation at all.[304] After ten days of discussion, Lloyd George and Wilson persuaded the other representatives, Vittorio Orlando and Georges Clemenceau (over Clemenceau's objections), to invite all Russian factions to a conference on the island of Prinkipo off the coast of Constantinople. All combatants in Russia, they said, should agree to a cease-fire during the conference and select delegates to appear in Paris before the Council of Ten. Wilson and Lloyd George also stated emphatically that the US and Britain would not send any more troops to Russia. Finally the Council of Ten agreed to the proposal, and asked Wilson to draft the invitation to the conference. Wilson's text was adopted and the invitations transmitted.[305]

On 4 February, the Bolshevik government accepted the Prinkipo invitation and announced its willingness to begin negotiations to end hostilities "and even—as it has often said—to purchase such an agreement at the price of important sacrifices."[306] Any hopes for a negotiated settlement in Russia died, however, when all the White governments refused to attend. The Omsk Government replied on 19 February that "we entertain no doubts as to the entire unacceptability of this proposal." The government immediately rejected any possibility of an agreement with the Bolsheviks as well as any negotiations with them.[307]

Allied plans to end the civil war in Russia were foiled, but discussions on Allied Siberian policy continued into February. On 15 February Wilson left Paris to return to Washington. On 17 February the discussions became so bitter that afterward the participants destroyed the minutes. Despite Lloyd George's objections, Winston Churchill, the British secretary for war, asked Allied military officials to consider a coordinated military effort against the Bolsheviks. Colonel House and Arthur Balfour, the British Foreign Secretary, objected. Clemenceau, who supported Churchill, demanded that since the United States refused to furnish men or supplies to fight the Bolsheviks, they should leave and let the Allies get on with the debate. House and Balfour objected strongly, and Clemenceau withdrew the remark. At the end of the meeting each government agreed to consult its own military advisors before taking any further action. That afternoon Clemenceau was wounded by an anarchist and all discussion was suspended.[308]

Wilson was thunderstruck by Churchill's suggestion. He cabled the American commissioners from the *George Washington.*

> Am greatly surprised...I distinctly understood Lloyd George to say there could be no thought of a military action there and what I said at the hurried meeting Friday afternoon was meant only to convey the idea that I would not take any hasty separate action myself but would not be in favor of any course which would not mean the earliest practical withdrawal of military forces. It would be fatal to be led farther into the Russian chaos.[309]

Churchill's proposal was tabled.

In the meantime the State Department had found other duties for the American troops in Siberia. In January 1919 General March had been preparing to withdraw the expedition when State Department officials reached an agreement with the Japanese Foreign Office on a railroad plan for Siberia.[310] The plan stipulated that American troops would stay in Siberia to help Colonel John F. Stevens, chairman of the Advisory Commission of Railway Experts in Russia, and to guard the Trans-Siberian Railway. Secretary Baker did not approve of the arrangement. He made clear to the State Department that "the War Department does not believe that the small force which we now have there is large enough to give Mr. Stevens support with reference to the policing of the Chinese Eastern and Trans-Siberian Railroads, and cannot approve of sending any more troops to Siberia for such a purpose."[311] Thus the decision became Wilson's.

In Paris, Wilson and Lansing reviewed the proposal carefully. On 31 January, 1919 Lansing cabled Polk and instructed him to request a secret hearing before the appropriate Congressional committees. Polk was to tell them frankly about the Siberian situation. Lansing told him to point out the strategic importance of the Trans-Siberian Railway to Russia and the United States. The railway agreement, said Lansing, would mean economic assistance to Siberia, in which anti-Bolshevik feeling was strong, which had a large group of Czechs who needed support, and which had enemy prisoners of war who needed watching. Lansing suggested that Polk might mention the potential value of the railroads in developing American commerce, and then told Polk to describe Japanese activities in the region for the congressmen, as well as to explain how the American presence would keep the railway from falling under Japanese domination. In short, Lansing wanted Polk to explain that the railway agreement was essential to preserve the Open Door Policy in Siberia.[312] But Polk, in view of the restive attitude of the American public, with whom intervention was unpopular, decided not to go to Congress, and Lansing reluctantly agreed.[313]

Not until March 1919 did General Graves receive notification that an agreement had finally been reached on the operation of the Siberian rail-

ways. He reassigned American troops to sections of the railway in eastern
Siberia and a portion just east of Lake Baikal.[314] Otherwise his orders
remained unchanged. Graves continued to recommend the evacuation of
the AEF, while the representatives of the State Department in Siberia
continued to urge that the United States support Kolchak.

Although Wilson had agreed to let American troops remain in Siberia,
neither he nor the War Department saw any reason to alter Graves's
instructions. It is entirely possible that one of the reasons he agreed to let
the troops remain was that he felt confident that his instructions in the
aide memoire would keep them on the sidelines and out of the fray. This
did not, however, keep some State Department representatives from
doing their utmost to alter the situation. They, and not just the Allies,
thoroughly criticized American policy. Graves recalled that "these criticisms were very familiar, as they were almost as common as my meals in
Siberia." He accused the American consul at Vladivostok, John Caldwell,
of cabling the State Department daily with "the libelous, false, and scur-
rilous articles appearing in the Vladivostok press about American troops.
These articles, and the criticism of the American troops in the United
States, were built around the charge of being Bolshevistic." He staunchly
maintained that these charges were utterly groundless and "could not
have been based upon any act of the American troops, because there was
not a single incident where they gave aid or comfort to the Bolsheviks."
He added that this charge was lodged by Kolchak adherents (including
Consul General Harris) against everyone in Siberia who did not support
Kolchak.[315]

The Allied representatives did not hesitate to point out what they considered to be Graves's many shortcomings. Graves received many reports
of widespread dissatisfaction with his conduct; for example, Knox reportedly characterized both Admiral Knight and General Graves as being
"stupid and stubborn."[316] According to General Graves, the British and
French representatives criticized him for his failure to cooperate and
spoke of the Russian faction they supported as "the forces of law and

order," by implication charging other Russian factions as representing law-lessness and chaos. This label, he believed, failed to reflect the facts.[317]

Graves continued, with difficulty, to maintain a neutral position in the midst of varied attacks. The principal reason he resisted adopting a loos-er interpretation of his orders was that he believed that if he succumbed to the British, French, or Japanese, "the American troops would have been used to kill Russians for their political beliefs." Of even more impor-tance, in his opinion, was the possibility "that American troops would also have been used to bring resentment against the United States by the Russian people." He feared that incidents could have been created for this specific purpose.[318]

One of the things that had sparked criticism was Graves's decision to forbid American soldiers from engaging the partisan bands which were beginning to harass the Allied lines of communication.[319] The Americans rarely saw them and the partisans generally left the Americans alone. Graves doubted that the partisans were doing anything more to disrupt and deplete Kolchak's supply lines than the graft of the White army's sup-ply officers had already achieved on a much larger scale. But while the American soldiers kept out of skirmishes, they were stuck in the midst of the storm of controversy that swirled around Graves. They found their sit-uation bewildering. Lieutenant Sylvain Kindall pointed out that "no one seemed to have any better idea as to why American troops were being retained in Siberia, now that the war with Germany was over, than had been brought forth to explain why American troops had been sent to Siberia in the first place." American troops were returning from France as quickly as possible, but in Siberia things were different. "Once a month an Army transport from the States plowed its way into the icy bay at Vladivostok, unloaded another mountain of flour and corned beef and Red Cross sweaters and this done put out to sea again with its hold and troop decks empty. Not a soldier, possibly excepting one who had suffered a frozen leg, was taken aboard the ship for return to the United States."[320]

For American troops the winter was a quiet one. The weather prevent-ed any faction from undertaking extensive military operations, creating the illusion that perhaps things would be settled without too much further trouble.

All was not so peaceful in the Czech camps. The Kolchak coup was unpopular with most of the Czecho-Slovaks, who feared that Kolchak would establish a reactionary dictatorship or restore the tsarist regime. Gustav Becvar recalled Czech commander Jan Syrový's response to the news of the Omsk coup: "[T]he change of government has killed our soldiers," he had lamented. "They say for four years they have been fighting for democracy and now that a dictatorship rules at Omsk they are no longer fighting for democracy."[321] Becvar felt that the installation of the Kolchak government was a deathblow to the Czech efforts. "Filled with indignation and bitter disappointment," he wrote, "the Legionnaires lost the last of their enthusiasm for the anti-Bolshevik cause."[322]

Only Gajda and a few other officers favored the coup. The Russians, Gajda announced, could not "be ruled by kindness or persuasion, but only by the whip and the bayonet." He claimed that a strong dictator was necessary to expel Bolshevism.[323] He made this statement before the Czech National Council had time to comment on the coup. Gajda had ordered his 5th Regiment to attack the Bolsheviks at Perm. They refused. When the National Council did respond, it strongly condemned the coup on the grounds that it violated fundamental principles of law, on which even the Russian government must ultimately rest.[324]

By the end of 1918, a very curious and complicated situation had developed. Despite the Czech government's condemnation of the Osmk coup and the end of the war in Europe, the legion was ordered to remain in Siberia. Under Allied pressure the Czecho-Slovaks, whose new state depended upon Allied support at the peace conference, agreed to keep the legion in Russia. Milan R. Stefanik, the Czech minister of war, who went to Siberia to organize the Czech evacuation, announced to the legion they would not be going home after all. "Brothers," he said, "the date of your return depends upon our unity and faith. We must finish with dignity our task as unselfish Slavs and honest Allies. We will abandon the

Volga Front. But the moral front we cannot forsake. The Allies need us."[325]

An intelligence report received by American headquarters indicated that although the Czechs were worn out and their morale was very low, their orders from Thomas Masaryk, president of the Czecho-Slovak National Council, were to continue the struggle. Colonel Barrows reported that "Colonel Vuchterle informs me that the order is 'to hold the front till every man is dead.' This order of Dr. Masaryk will, in Colonel Vuchterle's opinion, be obeyed by the Czechs." The report also said that the orders came with Allied assurances of help. Apparently the Czech soldiers had never abandoned the expectation that the AEF would come to their aid. "As the matter stands," Barrows warned, "American soldiers are indispensable if support is to be in time.... The American regiments are the strongest and the best equipped element from which early succor might be given."[326] But Graves had refused to allow the use of American troops to support the Czechs during the war, and he certainly was not going to allow it after the armistice.

Stefanik, after consulting with the Allies, began to reorganize the legion. He withdrew the Czechs from the Ural front and posted them as guards along the Trans-Siberian Railroad from Ekaterinburg to Irkutsk; then he went home to Czechoslovakia.[327]

Once the legion left the front, its relationship with the Omsk government grew increasingly intricate. On the one hand the Czech government disapproved of Kolchak. Dr. Vaclav Girsa, representing the Czech National Council in Vladivostok, when asked by his colleagues to conduct an inquiry into the situation, issued a memorandum stating that the Czechs "found the situation intolerable and that if they remained in Siberia they would run the risk of being suspected of supporting a *regime* of assassins." Kolchak was furious.[328] He heartily disliked the Czechs, but they were still the backbone of his army. When the Czech representatives lobbied in Omsk to keep tsarist and extreme conservative elements out of the new government, Kolchak was outraged by what he called "Czech interference in Russian internal affairs." Sir Charles Eliot, British high commissioner in Siberia, was amazed by Kolchak's open contempt for the Czechs.[329]

The extreme antipathy Kolchak displayed towards the Czechs proved to be a grave mistake. Even he was forced to admit that the fate of the White forces in Siberia was, for the foreseeable future, inextricably linked to the fortunes of the Czech Legion. Kolchak soon found that the White Army, such as it was, could not undertake to replace the legion. He was compelled to entice the legion back into White service with promises of high pay and rapid promotion. He was to some extent successful, but within a short time, even Gajda's division was anxious to leave Kolchak's service. Only Gajda and some other like-minded officers remained to take up posts in the new Siberian Army. By 20 January 1919, all Czech troops had left the front. Kolchak nevertheless derived some material advantages from the decision to post the Czechs along the railroad. They were in fact guarding his rear.

The withdrawal of the Czechs from the front was not without incident. General Kappel of the White Army became so angry with General Syrový over what he considered Czech desertion that Kappel challenged him to a duel. General Janin was forced to intervene to prevent them from killing each other.[330]

By the end of March 1919 the friction between the Czech Legion and the Kolchak government had become so intense that an armed clash seemed imminent. Major Homer Slaughter, the US liaison officer to the Kolchak forces, reported to Graves that the Czechs ought not be used to guard the railway because in their present frame of mind they might obstruct the traffic and promote local dissent. In his opinion, the only way to prevent chaos was either to send the Czechs home or at least promise to send them home.[331]

The Czech government's decision to leave its troops in Siberia, like the American government's, seemed to have been motivated by a desire to prove that they were good Allies, rather than by any sound military judgment. The Czechs had already become enmeshed in the Russian Civil War and their attempts to extricate themselves and still remain in Siberia pleased no one—not the Allies whose policies were various and conflicting, not their own men who wanted to go home, and not the Omsk government which wanted their soldiers but not their advice. The Americans, who were supposed to supervise the Czech withdrawal, found this duty once again delayed.

The relocation of American and Czech troops to guard the railways brought the Americans uncomfortably close to the Cossacks. The relationship between the two groups had never been cordial. The Americans had already gotten involved in a Cossack mutiny that began on 27 January 1918. The atrocious behavior of Kalmikov's Cossacks in the Amur Province, the wanton executions, robberies, rapes, and murders, had not endeared them to the American soldiers. After several months apparently even Kalmikov's troops began to feel these rampages were excessive.[332] On the night of 27 January, 700 of Kalmikov's troops deserted. About 300 men hid in nearby villages. Nearly 400 men, complete with mounts, pack animals, and arms which included four field guns and three machine guns, made their way to the headquarters of the US 27th Infantry at Khabarovsk. There they asked the commanding officer, Colonel Styer, for sanctuary from Kalmikov.[333] "We have mutinied against Kalmikov and his officers," they told Styer. "We will fight the Bolsheviks and fight under the Americans, or any proper Russian officers, but we will die fighting in the streets if an attempt is made to force us to return to Kalmikov, or place us under the command of one of his officers."[334]

As the men were threatening to fight it out with the rest of Kalmikov's troops, the commanding officer decided to take them into custody. In his report he stated that "to prevent bloodshed and plunder in garrison, city and vicinity and for the safety of our troops, I placed the deserters under guard and rendered them powerless for plunder and disorder. This was accomplished quietly and at the wish of the mutineers, who were without officials."[335] They were disarmed and marched into the YMCA building. This took place so quietly that the guards in the compound were unaware of it until the Cossacks with their 350 animals reached the YMCA building. During the next two days, desertions from Kalmikov's army increased to a total of 800. Many of the deserters asked to be taken into American custody. Wild rumors circulated that the Americans had enticed the Cossacks to mutiny.[336]

Graves approved of Styer's action, but he was unhappy to have yet another delicate situation forced upon him. Styer suggested turning the men over to Kolchak to reorganize them, but Graves vetoed it. He feared that if these men were turned over to any of Kolchak's representatives "there was considerable chance that they might get into the hands of Kalmikoff and that meant certain death for all of them." Finally Graves told Styer that the disposition of the men was an issue that America had no business deciding. His justification for this was that Kalmikov's Cossacks, as Japanese hirelings, had no recognizable legal status.

The Japanese, not surprisingly, were quite upset by the incident. The Japanese chief of staff called on Graves, asking him what he intended to do with the men. Graves wrote to him later saying that the troops would not be turned over to any other force, but would be released from American custody to do as they pleased. After their release the United States Army would protect them from any groundless persecution by Kalmikov, "charges of desertion, rebellion or mutiny."

Nevertheless, since these Cossacks had been responsible for many atrocities, Graves ordered that if local civil authorities produced warrants for violation of Russian law, together with clear evidence of guilt, then the Americans must hand over the men in question. This, he stated, was the only "reasonable protection to prevent ruthless sacrifice of human lives and for the proper protection of our own soldiers and property."[337]

The Japanese then requested that the prisoners be placed under a joint Japanese and American guard. Graves refused. At that point the Japanese commander at Khabarovsk wrote to Styer demanding to know why, and on whose responsibility, the 27th Infantry had taken in the deserters. He pointed out that this was a matter of military discipline, and as such it was purely Kalmikov's concern. The Japanese thus accused the Americans of interfering with the administration of Kalmikov's forces. Styer sent this note to Vladivostok. Graves told him he would handle it, but not to release any prisoners without his expressed permission.

Meanwhile the Japanese continued to press the case. A colonel of the Japanese General Staff called on Graves to ask that he return the men to Kalmikov. Graves replied that it would never be done. The colonel then requested that Graves surrender the deserters to the Japanese and let them settle the matter. Graves informed him that in his opinion the "suggestion bordered on an insult," and that he had no intention of asking Japanese approval of his actions, and as far as he was concerned the interview was over. The colonel replied that General Inagaki would come to see him about the matter. Graves replied that he would not discuss the question with any representative of Japan.[338]

After these unsuccessful attempts to gain custody of the deserters, representatives of the Japanese Army approached Graves about returning the surrendered horses, arms, and equipment to them. Graves refused. The Japanese then said "all of these things belonged to Japan." Graves told the Japanese chief of staff that if Japan would notify him in writing "that she had armed this murderer, that the property had never been paid for by Kalmikoff, and if they would identify their property and sign a receipt for it, he would let them have it." This was done and receipts sent to the War Department for file with the records.[339]

In February some of the Cossack deserters decided to try to return to their villages. Graves agreed, but he warned they could receive no protection. He allowed the men to take their horses, which he considered personal property.[340] On 22 February, Styer reported the situation regarding the mutineers was working out satisfactorily along the lines approved by General Graves. The large majority were soon to be released.

On 15 March, Styer cabled Graves that only thirty-five men remained and that they would depart in three days.[341] The Americans had thus successfully disposed of the deserters, but Kalmikov was permanently embittered and the Japanese greatly displeased. Graves was concerned that because General Oi had so actively taken Kalmikov's part that if the

Americans and Kalmikov commenced hostilities that the Americans might find themselves fighting the Japanese as well.

The situation at Khabarovsk remained tense. Styer, in disgust, wrote to General Oi that although the Japanese government armed and supported Kalmikov, it was refusing to accept responsibility for him. "On several occasions," he pointed out, "I have reported the conduct of this detachment towards the Americans, and each time you have informed me that you have no authority over Kalmikoff. The mere fact that he is controlled by the Japanese, and supported by them makes you responsible for his acts. I am of the opinion," he concluded ominously, "that unless you control this individual, a clash between his men and our troops is imminent."[342]

While the Americans had their hands full with Kalmikov, Kolchak was having his own problems with Ataman Semenov. After the coup in November, Semenov refused to recognize Kolchak as supreme ruler, and continued to act independently of the Omsk government. He disrupted the railways, interrupted telegraph communications, and killed anyone who interfered with him. Although the Japanese government claimed to be in sympathy with Kolchak, it took no steps to restrain Semenov. As early as 26 November, American headquarters received a report that "a Japanese staff Captain Kureki has been urging Semenoff to declare himself dictator of the Transbaikalia, and to seize the tunnels and the railway; and that Semenoff has recently received 5 million rubles and he plans to issue his own currency."[343]

The Americans were also receiving reports indicating that Kolchak's gaining control over Semenov was the key to his own political survival. In a report to the intelligence officer at AEF headquarters, Capt. Roger W. Straus stressed that if Kolchak could control the outrages of the Cossacks and punish them, he would become enormously popular throughout the region.[344]

On 6 December 1918, Graves had received a report from Chita that Semenov was about to begin a war against Kolchak. Lieutenant Colonel David Barrows wired Graves that it was rumored that General Inagaki would not allow fighting between Kolchak and Semenov because it would interfere with the traffic on the railroad. When asked if Semenov had been arrested by Kolchak's troops, Inagaki said that he "did not believe that Kolchak could arrest Semenoff because the Japanese would not allow Kolchak to use force, because of the Japanese policy to keep railroad communications open." Barrows pointed out that if that policy were carried out Semenov could continue to defy Kolchak so long as the Cossacks did not interfere with the railroads.[345]

On 5 December, Kolchak had dismissed Semenov from his command and ordered his arrest for interference with telegraph service and general disobedience amounting to what Kolchak termed "high treason." For Kolchak to order the arrest was one thing but to effect it was quite another.[346] By 8 December, Kolchak had realized the Japanese might prove an insuperable obstacle to subduing Semenov. Japan, he claimed, was openly siding with Semenov and was preventing him from acting against the ataman. The Japanese generals told Kolchak that no troops could be spared for the suppressing of Semenov's bands.

Kolchak complained, with good cause, that these actions constituted direct Japanese interference in Russian internal affairs, a statement with which most American observers agreed. The situation continued to deteriorate. Omsk troops threatened to blow up railroad tunnels to block Semenov's advance.[347] Rumors circulated that the Japanese would act to stop them. The British and French representatives requested the Japanese disarm Semenov.[348]

As a result, Barrows was sent to find out what Semenov wanted. Semenov told him he would recognize Kolchak only if Kolchak promised to resign in favor of Denikin, another White leader, at the earliest opportunity, and leave Semenov in command of the 5th Siberian Corps. Kolchak would also have to withdraw the arrest order calling him a traitor.

The next day Barrows went to the Japanese general, Oba. In a long conversation, Oba assured Barrows that he would advise Semenov to recognize Kolchak, and that he had already told him that he would not allow hostilities to occur along the Trans-Baikal railways. He also claimed to be completely neutral in the dispute between Kolchak and Semenov.[349] The Omsk government was not convinced of Japanese neutrality. It had already asked the Japanese for a written statement on whether they were supporting Semenov and if so to what extent. It also warned that unless the situation improved, the Omsk government would request an American commission to go to Chita and investigate the problems there.[350]

In the end the dispute between Semenov and the Omsk government remained unsettled. Semenov continued to withhold recognition of Kolchak's government. The Omsk government, occupied in trying to direct operations against the Red Army, was unable to subdue either Kalmikov or Semenov. Kolchak finally admitted that he had no control in eastern Siberia; Japan continued to obstruct Allied efforts to bring Semenov to heel. As a result, Kolchak washed his hands of all responsibility for Cossack activities. A precarious stand-off followed. Kolchak's authority was undermined, and Cossack atrocities continued unchecked.[351]

Meanwhile the AEF concentrated on reorganizing and protecting the railways. The Civilian Railroad Corps had been working under American command to repair and reorganize the railways since 1917. Its performance had impressed even highly critical observers. But while the Railway Corps could tackle the technical problems, the political difficulties were a constant obstacle. Oddly enough, their successes produced further complications. A British colonel, John Ward, observed that while the Japanese, along with all other powers active in the area, had benefited from the Railway Corps, its activities undoubtedly worried the Japanese about the threat that the American presence posed to their own interests.[352] This might well be one explanation for the obstructive policy the Japanese were employing where the Cossacks were concerned.

In March 1919 the Americans took up their duties guarding the railway under the Allied Railway Agreement. Graves issued a proclamation to the towns along the railway in the American sector stating that the sole purpose of the American guards was to protect the railroad and ensure the unobstructed passage of trains, thereby assisting everyone in Russia, "irrespective of persons, nationality, religion or politics. Cooperation is requested and warning given to all persons, whomsoever, that interference with traffic will not be tolerated."[353] This seemingly innocuous statement became the cause of what Graves, himself, termed "an outburst of abuse and vilification," because by implication he had classed the Whites with the Bolsheviks. Dewitt C. Poole, head of the Russian Division of the State Department, criticized Graves to an officer of the War Department, for using the phrase "irrespective of party." This was yet another example of the difference between the State and War Departments' interpretations of "non-intervention in the internal affairs of the Russian people and non-interference with the political sovereignty of Russia."[354]

Upon assuming their duties on the railway the American guards initially had more trouble with the White forces than the few Bolshevik partisans in their sector. The Bolsheviks were mainly occupied in harassing the Japanese. They left the Czechs and Americans largely unmolested. The Americans were initially exempt from attack. Several times American lieutenants met unofficially with Bolshevik guerilla leaders. They agreed that each had their duty; the Americans' was to protect the railroad, and as long as the Bolsheviks stayed away from it, the Americans would not interfere with them elsewhere.[355] This arrangement worked well, but the Allies deeply resented it.

An accommodation of this sort was not possible with the Cossacks, and the American troops used other methods to deal with them. The headquarters and two battalions of the 27th Infantry under Colonel C. H. Morrow were transferred to Trans-Baikal, where Morrow proved an admirable match for Semenov. He soon came in conflict with the Cossacks, who had entered the American sector and arrested several railway workers on the charge of being Bolsheviks. Morrow told Semenov that he would not allow him to arrest these men unless he could produce evidence they had committed a crime. Semenov claimed to be shocked that a foreigner would consider telling him what he could or could not do in his own country. He declared that he fully intended to repeat his action. Morrow made clear that if Semenov entered the American sector "with his armored train he would blow it to perdition or a similar place." Morrow then put thirty-seven millimeter field pieces on each side of the track, piled sandbags around them, and waited. Graves was very worried about the possibility of armed conflict. He feared Morrow lacked sufficient weapons to carry out his threats. Nonetheless, Graves decided to let Morrow handle the matter. The ploy was successful. Semenov did not appear.[356]

This small victory was not sufficient to prevent the railroads from being run for the exclusive benefit of the White forces at Allied expense. Graves claimed that if a "Russian, who was not sympathetic to Kolchak, approached a railroad station with the idea of travelling on the railroad or shipping supplies, he was in grave danger of losing his life or liberty." Anti-Kolchak forces complained that the United States was helping the supreme ruler by safe-guarding his lines of communication. To this Graves could only reply that he was guarding "the railroad for them as well as the other side," and he had no way of knowing what was in the cars they were protecting while in American sections." The Bolshevik partisans remained unsatisfied and toward the end of March began attacking isolated American detachments and the property in their care.[357]

Meanwhile, Kolchak's inability to restore order in eastern Siberia was one of the many issues that caused concern in American circles over his government's viability. The US Army was never confident of the Omsk government's staying power. Graves's reports of growing Bolshevik strength and White weakness irritated the State Department. It dismissed the reports as inaccurate because he was 4,000 miles from the front. But these reports were based on information received from intelligence officers much closer to the action. As early as 27 January 1919, Major Slaughter at Ekaterinburg cabled that "Bolshevik power is growing here, espionage service says any Russian Army will fall to pieces." He also warned, because of mass defections from the White forces, that "the order to mobilize five new classes was the same as organizing an army for the Bolsheviks."[358]

The worst feature of the situation was Kolchak's new mobilization order, which authorized the conscription of large numbers of young men into the White Army. Kolchak was desperate to fill the large gap in the White forces left by the Czech Legion. The White Army enforced the mobilization order with great brutality. The peasants evaded the Whites with greater cunning, and occasionally with the complicity of US troops. Sylvain Kindall recalled that Kolchak's troops would scour one village after another looking for draft evaders who kept one step ahead of them by fleeing from village to village. The town of Sviyagino was located on the railroad, and "was open to the sudden approach of searching parties arriving by train. Because of this danger, the youngsters who lived in this village were forced to seek hiding places during the daytime in villages removed from the railroad. At night, however, Kindall reported, some returned to their houses in Sviyagino. US troops frequently stopped young men crossing their lines, and after making sure they were unarmed, the fugitives were allowed into the village. Kindall explained that, however strained our relations may have been with the Bolshevik peasants at this time, "we had no intention of disclosing the whereabouts of their young men to the Kolchak troops."[359]

Kolchak's fortunes had had one bright spot. In January 1919 his troops had captured the city of Perm, taking about 20,000 prisoners, a large number of railway cars, and 260 locomotives.[360] The State Department hailed this victory with great enthusiasm. But the situation had changed drastically by the end of the month. Consul General Harris reported on 30 January that the Bolsheviks were within ten miles of Kunger. The Seventh Czech Regiment was "reported to have been badly entrapped. Soldiers are suffering intensely from cold weather. Causes of reverse at Kunger are attributed to the refusal of both Czech and Siberian soldiers to obey orders." The Omsk government blamed the Czechs for the deterioration of the front.[361] But the Czechs were not to blame for the massive defection of Kolchak's forces to the Bolsheviks.

By February, General Janin, too, was pessimistic about the state of the Osmk government. In a report to Paris, he insisted that Kolchak's army could not possibly launch an offensive, yet Kolchak would not stop planning one long enough to put his house in order. He persisted in blaming all his troubles on the Allies. Janin described the Omsk government as a political disaster. The reactionaries and progressives displayed signs of vigor only when attacking each other. The General Staff was completely incompetent and incapable of even forming a regiment. Only General Dietrichs had field experience, but he seemed unable to oppose the muddlers on the General Staff. The army lacked discipline. Officers and men behaved like rabble. They had completely sacked Perm. "Admiral Kolchak does not even try to improve the working of the Stavka nor the discipline on the fronts," Janin complained. "He has complete confidence in his officers, and on their advice issues nonsensical military orders from Omsk which will soon have disastrous effects on his personal prestige. The regime as a whole is blind: it does not have even the most elementary intelligence service."[362]

Kolchak had admitted to Harris in March that he was unable to control eastern Siberia or assume responsibility for the actions of the Japanese-sponsored Cossacks. But his declaration, according to Graves, was considered "extremely confidential." No similar statement was issued to the other Allies.[363]

The standard image used to excuse Kolchak was one of the idealistic statesman surrounded by hardened opportunists who used and manipulated him. "Everywhere," Bernard Pares explained, "he found around him a fluid world in which personal character and initiative had almost disappeared."[364] This may have been the case, and Kolchak's supporters touted his personal honesty, but from a military standpoint, he was worse than cruel or corrupt; he was stubborn and inept. He began his rule with little popular support and then allowed the little he had to be systematically destroyed.

Many of the socialist groups opposed Kolchak. The Japanese henchmen, Kalmikov and Semenov, openly defied him. The Japanese plotted to undermine him. The AEF thought he was on the brink of collapse. The Czechs believed his regime was attempting to restore the autocracy to Russia. The French representative was unimpressed with his record. Meanwhile the Bolsheviks were gaining popularity in Siberia, where most of the inhabitants were all too familiar with White excesses, but had not yet experienced life under Red occupation. With such a small basis of support, Kolchak remained unwilling to antagonize his military supporters by putting a stop to their atrocities.[365]

Despite the AEF's deep misgivings about Kolchak's desirability and viability, Consul General Harris remained confident about Kolchak's future. On 29 March, Acting Secretary of State Polk sent a cable to Wilson and Lansing that included Harris's report of meetings with Admiral William Rodgers, General Graves, Charles H. Smith, American representative on the Inter-Allied Railway Committee, and John F. Stevens. Polk attached a note saying that the department fully endorsed Harris's views.

Harris began by criticizing his colleagues: "As I fully expected, practically everyone in Harbin and Vladivostok knows but little about the true state of affairs in Central and Western Siberia. They are continually misled by false rumors and misstatements in the press." He then said he believed "things brighter than ever before.... The campaign of the Siberian Army against the Bolsheviks is progressing favorably. Kolchak's government is stronger than ever before and growing in power. This power is practically absolute in Central and Western Siberia, and while Kolchak is not a strong man he is at least a good man and a Russian patriot of the best type." Harris added that Kolchak was supported by zemstvos (local assemblies) in those areas and that the cities and villages were beginning to pay regular taxes to Omsk. He stressed that Kolchak was *not* supported by monarchists and reactionaries. Harris claimed Kolchak's "chief advisers in all civil matters are right Social Revolutionaries."

According to Harris, the only problem was the Cossack atamans who "have devised every possible difficulty by their intrigues with Japan and their treatment of Zemstvo members and people." He ended his report with a request for aid, claiming that Kolchak was not asking for "foreign soldiers to assist him in fighting Bolsheviks. He can do that himself and is doing so successfully. He does need clothes, and munitions and economic assistance." But what he "wants above all things is protection in his rear against Semenoff.... Kalmikoff and Japanese intrigue. He can do nothing towards this of his own accord. He depends on the Allies to do it. Japan must play fair with Allied and Omsk governments. The disturbing influence of Cossack Atamans...[must] be completely eliminated." Harris claimed, " Now is the time for plain talk, honest methods and firm decision. Russia is now a fair way to mastering Bolshevism with her own resources, but at this moment success practically depends upon our decisive policy as adopted right here in Eastern Siberia."[366] Harris's report directly contradicted Graves's reports to the War Department.

While the relationship between Graves and Harris and the Russian section of the State Department became increasingly bitter, Graves also faced opposition from Allied military representatives. In March 1919 the situation worsened. Generals Knox and Graves, never the best of friends, had another disagreement when Knox again attempted to secure Graves's support for Kolchak. On 2 March, Knox wrote Graves that he wished that they "could see more eye-to-eye," that their "objects were undoubtedly very similar but we are falling into different ruts." It was British policy to support Kolchak. Knox assured Graves, "I believe in that policy, for if he goes there will be chaos. I don't for a moment pretend that Kolchak is the Angel Gabriel, but he has energy, patriotism and honesty and my eight years in Russia has taught me that when you get these qualities combined in one man, he is a man to keep." He warned Graves that considerable propaganda declared that the AEF was pro-Bolshevik, and that Graves should try to counter it "in the interest of Allied solidarity."[367] Much of this propaganda was the product of White newspapers which had offered to stop it in exchange for large sums of money, an offer Graves refused to consider.

Graves responded to Knox's letter by denying any intention on his part to interfere in Russian internal affairs. He became more pointed on the subject of Kolchak. "I fear you think I consider Admiral Kolchak has monarchial tendencies," he told Knox. "I consider it none of my affair as to what the tendencies of the contending factions in Russian affairs are." As far as anti-American propaganda was concerned, Graves said that he was certain it sprang from the anti-Bolsheviks rather than from the Bolsheviks. "It is hopeless or useless to try to contradict such misrepresentations as appear in these papers," he stated. "They emanate not from a desire to do justice, but from what they foolishly think they can force Americans to do by such misrepresentations."[368]

This exchange was General Knox's last direct appeal to Graves to come into line with British policy. He henceforth directed his efforts to London and the State Department. Shortly after this exchange he reportedly approached the American consul general in Vladivostok, Caldwell, and suggested that he cable the State Department that Graves did not correctly interpret America's Siberian policy, and did not follow the real will of the United States government or the American people.[369] This was a highly irregular action under any circumstances. Needless to say, Graves resented Knox's attempt to have him relieved of his command by approaching the State Department.[370]

While Knox wanted Graves removed from his command, Kolchak wanted the Americans removed from Russia. He wrote in a widely circulated memorandum: "the American troops, consisting of the off-scouring of the American Army, Jewish emigrants, with a corresponding commanding staff, are only a factor of disintegration and disorders. I consider their removal from Russian territory necessary because their further presence will lead only to a final discrediting of America and to extremely serious consequences." Similar attacks appeared almost daily throughout Siberia.[371] At one point a White newspaper alleged that "all Americans are degenerate" and made other remarks that, according to Graves, "common decency made it impossible to repeat." Graves threatened the Omsk foreign minister that if such reports were not stopped, he would arrest an editor and padlock the newspaper building.[372] In mid-March Graves wrote to the War Department about the great bitterness prevalent in Siberia. He reported "each faction claims that if you are not with them you are against them."

The Japanese had by this time begun a campaign to put down a Bolshevik uprising in the Amur Province. Graves had not allowed American troops to participate. He observed that his refusal to use American troops in the war between Russian factions had drawn fire from each side: Whites accused the AEF of being pro-Bolshevik, while the Bolsheviks claimed that the Americans were siding with the Whites.

Graves pointed out that the United States and Japan had come to Siberia with the same announced purpose and now were taking opposite courses. As a result he found it advisable to ask whether his policy of viewing "the Bolshevik trouble in Siberia, entirely an internal trouble, in which I should take no part, is the policy the Department desires me to follow?"[373]

Polk recommended to Lansing that Graves be allowed to urge modera-tion. He could use his influence to prevent factional conflict and even to use force to protect communications and AEF security. The people along the railroads, he argued, should have some protection from arbitrary acts. But Polk was concerned about Graves's competence. "In my opinion," he told Lansing, "the situation is somewhat beyond General Graves, and I think he will be required to be told specifically how far he can go, as his inclination is to interpret his instructions very conservatively. This will no doubt require your discussing the question with the President."[374]

The Japanese were very agitated over Graves's refusal to send troops to the Amur campaign. Graves staunchly maintained that if he sent American troops with Japanese troops as General Oi requested, "Americans would no longer have been pacific observers of the atrocities being committed in Siberia, but we would have been participants in them."

In a legalist vein, Graves asked Oi exactly what these Bolsheviks had done to justify sending Japanese soldiers to destroy them. Graves pointed out that they "were Russians, in Russian territory against whom no nation had declared War, minding their own business and not endangering life, limb or property of any Ally." Oi's answer was not recorded.[375]

Bolshevism was at that time a relatively unknown quantity to Americans. Graves was the first to admit he did not understand it. During his entire service in Siberia he was completely cut off from any part of Soviet-controlled Russia. He could not conceive of the menace that the Russian Division of the State Department seemed to see so clearly. What he could see were the innumerable atrocities that the Whites were committing.[376] Moreover, Graves, as a War Department officer, took his orders from his commander-in-chief, in the form of the aide memoire. Thus he frequently ignored the State Department, whose members were not above him in the chain of command.

Even if Graves had been inclined to follow State Department policy, he would have faced some practical problems. "To those of our people who were impressed with the necessity of fighting Bolshevism regardless of American policy," he admitted, "I was never able to determine who was a Bolshevik or why he was a Bolshevik." The definition of the Japanese and the Cossacks in Graves's experience was that "all Russians were Bolsheviks if they were not willing to take up arms and fight for the Semeonoffs, the Kalmikoffs, the Rozanoffs, the Ivanoff-Rinoffs, and the annals of crime in the United States will not show worse characters than these."

The British and French had a slightly different criterion. To them "all Russians who were not willing to take up arms and fight for Kolchak were Bolsheviks." And, as Graves was always quick to point out, "[a]t this time no nation was willing to recognize any of these men or any other as the de facto or de jure head of any Russian Government, not even Admiral Kolchak."[377]

Knox cabled the War Office complaining about Graves. He mentioned that the Bolsheviks were claiming that they had the support of the AEF, and that this was endangering both Allied solidarity and Allied safety. Knox also stated that Graves's attitude was cultivating the hatred of the educated classes in Russia and consequently increasing the popularity of the Japanese.[378]

The British, in particular, remained angry over the attitude of the American troops. On 19 May 1919, they informed the State Department of nine incidents, the most recent only a month old, in which Graves had taken a stand against the Omsk government.[379] Knox was unhappy with the reports that Graves was sending to Washington. He claimed that Graves was totally ignorant of the real situation outside of Vladivostok, and unsupportive of Kolchak and the British government. Knox also said cases that involved the mistreatment of peasants often hypnotized Graves.

For his part Graves thought Knox an autocratic snob who "could not, if he had desired to do so, give sympathetic consideration to the aspirations of the peasant class in Russia whom he characterized as swine."[380] The only point that Knox made on which everyone could agree was that the split between the Americans and the British gave Japan a clear field in Siberia.

Relations with the British had not been substantially improved by an interview between Graves and Sir Charles Eliot, British high commissioner to Siberia. The day before, Graves had received a warning from the wives of four men who had been arrested by White troops under orders from Ivanov-Rinov, the Cossack commander. They told Graves "there will be an uprising and all we want you and the other Allies to do is continue your policy of non-interference." Sir Charles got wind of the warning and came to see Graves. He had heard that Graves had promised American troops would not be used to suppress an uprising. Graves had not said this, and he told Sir Charles so. Sir Charles asked if American troops would be used in such a situation. Graves said that it was impossible to say before the causes and circumstances were known to him. Sir Charles became insistent and pointed out that the lives and property of British subjects were at risk and that he must know.

After further discussion, Graves told Sir Charles that he was fully cognizant of the fact that he wanted to know Graves's attitude towards protecting Ivanov-Rinov and Horvath. Sir Charles, said Graves, knew that Ivanov-Rinov "was a cold blooded murderer and that the United States had never been in the habit of protecting murderers, and I did not intend doing so now and, so far as I was concerned, they could bring Ivanoff-Rinoff opposite American headquarters and hang him to that telegraph pole until he was dead, and not an American soldier would turn his hand." Sir Charles immediately left Graves's office.[381]

Shortly after this incident, Ambassador Morris conferred with General Graves, Consul Caldwell, and Admiral Knight about the situation in Siberia. The question was whether the United States could maintain its presence in Siberia while allowing reactionary groups to suppress representative institutions.

They ultimately agreed that the United States, in initiating and acquiescing to the expedition, had thereby tacitly consented to Czech and Japanese actions in wresting control of the railway. American forces, therefore, were obliged to stay and see it out. But, they agreed civilians should be shielded from the excesses of any faction. They feared, however, that Japan would not accept such a policy.[382]

Because of the precarious nature of the situation, Admiral Rodgers wanted to put a battleship fleet in the northern Pacific. He thought that this would have a salutary effect on diplomacy. Both he and Graves were concerned about potential clashes between the AEF and Japanese troops. But the suggestion was vetoed by Lansing, who feared it would only make matters worse.[383]

The American troops were in an anomalous position. The Cossacks were trying to convince anyone who would listen that the Americans were the cause of all the trouble in eastern Siberia. At the same time the Cossacks were trying to convince Bolshevik groups to attack American detachments to force the Americans to cooperate in the Japanese campaigns against the Bolsheviks.

Graves was more apprehensive about the Cossacks than he was about the Bolsheviks. Admiral Rodgers and several American consuls in Siberia shared his anxiety. Lansing confessed to Wilson that reports from

American consuls in the region bolstered Graves's assessment that the Japanese were endeavoring to aid the reactionaries, with an ultimate eye to dominating eastern Siberia.[384] If Lansing was concerned, Baker was growing increasingly disturbed over reports which more than fulfilled his dire predictions of the results of sending troops to Siberia.[385]

Graves, meanwhile, continued to adhere to the aide memoire, and criticism of him was rampant. The State Department was keeping up an almost constant stream of criticism, an example of which was written by Basil Miles, head of the State Department's Russian Division, on one of Graves's reports. "I consider this report of little real value...it is entirely out of perspective and written with little real knowledge of Russia and Russian ways of doing things."[386]

Graves himself became increasingly aware of opposition in Washington. He had been posted in Washington shortly before leaving for Siberia, and still had many friends there. Graves undertook to discover the source of opposition to his reports. He then found out "in what offices my actions would receive sympathetic consideration, and where they would be criticized." In one instance, Graves received a sharp reprimand for his poor supervision of censorship. Graves examined all the communications from his office and could not find any violation of regulations. He decided as a result that Brigadier General Marlborough Churchill, head of the Military Information Division (which handled such matters), was being overly critical. Apart from General Churchill, however, Graves seemed to have no quarrel with the War Department. He avoided difficulties with Churchill by sending some of his communications directly to the chief of staff instead of to the adjutant general, where they would first pass in review before General Churchill. After the cable criticizing his handling of censorship, Graves cabled General March to explain the situation. March replied that Graves's views on censorship were absolutely correct, and that he would make sure that Graves received no more such communications.[387]

Graves felt that the vast majority of the criticism directed against him was the result of his refusal to permit the use of American troops against the Bolsheviks. He argued that he simply could not allow it: "No one above me in authority had given me any such orders," he stated flatly. The contents of his orders were not widely understood. When Graves returned from the Far East in December 1920, after the Red Scare had swept the United States, he was told by General Leonard Wood that if Graves had not had copies of his papers, he would have been "torn limb from limb in the United States" because he did not take part in fighting Bolshevism.[388]

Baker and March were both aware of the difficulty of Graves's position, and they supported him fully. Graves had dispelled any doubts that Baker once had about his conduct. He wrote to Wilson that all his recent reports showed Graves was conducting himself with "discretion and good judgment," and that he had the approval of various State Department officials in the Far East.[389] On 28 March 1919, March wrote to Graves in reply to a cable asking for confirmation of his instructions. The answer had been some time in coming. The State Department had passed it along to the president, March explained; the president's failure to reply thus far had been the source of the delay. "Your action as reported in the cablegram was in accordance with your original instructions and is approved," March confirmed, "and you will be guided by those instructions until they are modified by the President."

In a personal note attached to the cable, March said "Keep a stiff upper lip. I am going to stand by you until _____ freezes over."[390]

While State Department officials in Washington and eastern Russia endeavored to use the AEF to combat Bolshevism, and Graves stubbornly refused to involve his troops in Russian internal politics, Woodrow Wilson was developing still another policy in France.

When Wilson returned to Paris in March 1919, he was encouraged by reports from William C. Bullitt that Lenin, Litvinov, and Chicherin were anxious to reach a settlement with the Allies.[391] Wilson was inclined to offer the Bolshevik authorities at least de facto recognition, and he expressed some sympathy with their cause.[392] He was still anxious to prevent Bolshevik influence from spreading to Central Europe. At a meeting of the Council of Four he declared that all he had heard "confirms in me my policy, which is to leave Russia to the Bolsheviks—they will stew in their own juice until circumstances have made the Russians wiser—and confine our efforts to keeping Bolshevism from invading the other parts of Europe."[393]

Marshal Foch, meanwhile, urged the Allies to combat the spread of Bolshevism through force.[394] Both Wilson and Lloyd George opposed him. "I combat Bolshevism, not by force," Lloyd George declared, "but by searching for a means to satisfy legitimate aspirations which have given birth to it."[395]

Wilson took a similar stand against military measures or the *cordon sanitaire* against the Bolsheviks.

> The word "Bolshevik" covers many different things. In my opinion, to try to stop a revolutionary movement with ordinary armies is like using a broom to sweep back a great sea. The armies, moreover, can be impregnated by the very Bolshevism which they would be charged to combat. A germ of sympathy exists between the forces that one would wish to oppose one against the other. The sole means of acting against Bolshevism is to make its causes disappear. Moreover, it is a formidable enterprise; we do not even quite know what the causes are…. The only way to kill Bolshevism is to establish frontiers and to open all the doors to commerce.[396]

When the French pressed Wilson to act against the Soviets in Eastern Europe, he absolutely refused. "To send troops," he maintained, "would create a state of War, into which the United States could not enter without a formal declaration, by Congress, so, I could not send a man, even if I wanted to, which I do not."[397]

The French could point to the AEF in Siberia as precedent for their request. But to justify his use of troops in Siberia, Wilson could argue that he originally sent the AEF there as an extension of the congressionally-declared war with Germany. The troops were to rescue the Czechs and to provide humanitarian assistance, congressional approval for the latter objective presumably being unnecessary. Compliance with French requests to use troops against the Bolsheviks in Eastern Europe would be, according to this view, an act of an entirely different character.

Colonel House, meanwhile, was working on a plan to send food to Russia and cooperate with the Soviets.[398] But Herbert Hoover, America's relief expert, opposed deals with or recognition of the Bolsheviks; instead he recommended that a respected neutral country of high reputation undertake a relief mission for Russia.[399]

In the beginning of April news of possible de facto recognition of the Soviets leaked to the press creating an uproar in the United States. The *Washington Post* in particular expressed alarm that "twisted brains in American skulls are giving Lenine [sic] aid and comfort. Certain treacherous Americans are doing their best to forward this arch-murderer's cause. They have not hesitated to prostitute their own reputation in serving Lenine."[400]

This outburst indicated a strength of anti-Bolshevik feeling in the United States of which Wilson had been unaware. In an attempt to find a less controversial method of dealing with Moscow, Wilson leaned toward the creation of a relief commission under the Norwegian humanitarian and explorer Fridstjof Nansen, who had a great deal of familiarity with Russia. This commission would be apolitical, and it could work in cooperation with the Bolsheviks.[401]

House, meanwhile, complained that nothing was being done toward settling the Russian question. In the Nansen plan he saw a way to end the fighting in Russia, the spread of Bolshevism, and the conservative criticism at home.[402] On 7 April, Wilson drafted a letter to Nansen, saying that the Allies would gladly cooperate in Russian relief, providing that Nansen's commission would supervise food distribution by the Russians. Wilson also added that

> such a course would invoke cessation of all hostilities within the territory of *Russia*.... And the cessation of hostilities would necessarily involve a complete suspension of the transfer of troops and military material of all sorts to and within *Russian*

Territory. Indeed relief to Russia which did not mean return to a state of peace would be futile, and would be impossible to consider.

If these conditions could be met Nansen would have full support from the Associated Powers. On 17 April, Nansen sent Wilson's conditions to Lenin.[403]

On 19 April, Herbert Hoover drafted a press statement that threatened to sabotage the Nansen Plan by its scathing denunciation of Bolshevik Russia. House and Wilson acted quickly to suppress it.[404] A new wrinkle appeared on 21 April, when the State Department proposed once again that the United States recognize the Omsk government. Reports indicated that government was growing stronger each day.

Wilson was deep in conflict with the other delegates. The Italians were demanding the port of Fiume on the Serbian coast, and the Japanese were demanding Germany's former rights over Shantung. Both issues, Wilson believed, were ones of self-determination. The Italians stood firm, and Britain and France, bound by wartime treaties, supported some of Italy's demands. The Japanese refused to join the League of Nations unless they received Shantung. Wilson, distraught, finally decided it was better to have Japan under league supervision than running amok in the Far East. As a result of this strain, Wilson suffered what was probably a small stroke on 28 April, which affected him until 10 May. After that date, he seemed to recover quickly.[405]

During these turbulent spring days, Wilson considered the problem of what to do with the northern Russian and Siberian expeditions. In early April, Baker cabled Paris about Graves's proposed instructions for guarding the railway. The inter-Allied agreement assumed that guards would protect a strip six miles wide along the railroad. To do this, Baker said, would require an enormous force of over half a million men. He feared that "such definite control would inevitably mean very large additions to the Japanese forces or additions to our own." At any rate it would sanction Japanese control of a large section penetrating Siberia. Baker pointed out the conflicts that already existed between inter-Allied forces and various elements of the native population. "Would not the establishment of this long zone," he asked, "increase the frequency of such conflicts and so make possible local disturbances which would appear to justify assumption of civil control and perhaps military repression which in effect would mean occupation and administration of Siberia by Japan?" [406]

Baker recommended that the State Department discuss with the Allies a policy to limit the duties of military forces to preserving order about the railroad, the stations, and trains. Baker also thought that the State Department should make it clear that the United States would not add any more troops to those in Siberia, and that it had no wish to see any other nation add troops. According to Baker, such a policy would limit military operations to the areas along the railroad, thus providing no excuses for any nation to increase its political activity or troop strength in Siberia. William Phillips of the State Department supported Baker's view that establishment of a six-mile zone would lead the people of Siberia to think foreign governments had taken control for political and commercial rather than altruistic purposes. [407]

The next day Wilson received word from Ambassador Morris that he felt the Japanese were willing to moderate their policy in Siberia. In an interview with General Tanaka, the minister of war, Morris learned that it was Tanaka's personal conviction that Japanese military action be limited to guarding the railway. This revelation led Morris to believe that the Japanese were now prepared to cooperate with Graves and modify their old policy of supporting the Cossacks. [408] Wilson saw Tanaka's discussions with Morris as making Baker's suggestions feasible, and he accordingly ordered that the State Department should formulate a policy "to limit the use of the military forces to the preservation of order in the immediate vicinity of the railway, its stations and trains when those in charge so request…" Inter-Allied forces could be used "to suppress local violence by conflicting Russian forces only when such conflicts affect the despatch of trains or operation of the railway and even then only to the extent necessary to protect the railway and those engaged in its operation."[409] These instructions did not alter Graves's existing orders.

On 16 April, Wilson authorized the release of Russian assets for use in maintaining the railroads, as long as they would go to some productive and non-partisan use that would not imply American recognition of any Russian faction. Wilson also permitted Russian diplomats to continue to function in America as long as they complied with this statement.[410]

On 18 April, General Bliss warned Wilson that things were getting out of control in North Russia, and that General William Ironside, the British commander, was going to advance on Kotlas to try to join with the White Siberian armies. Bliss was anxious because he and Wilson had already decided to withdraw American forces from North Russia as soon as the ice broke.[411] Wilson, in short, persisted in following a very restricted course in Siberia, withdrawing from North Russia, limiting Graves's duties in Siberia, and advocating relief instead of military action in Eastern and Central Europe. As president, he was free to make these decisions, to determine his nation's foreign policy—or at least to resist other nations' efforts to determine that policy. His subordinate in Siberia, however, was in a more difficult position.

From the time of the signing of the armistice and Kolchak's coming to power, General Graves was under increasing pressure to alter his interpretation of his orders to favor the White cause. This he steadfastly refused to do without specific instruction from his superiors. Despite the enormous criticism by other governments and the State Department, there is little doubt that Graves's interpretation of the aide memoire was the one Wilson intended. Graves made several applications to the War Department for confirmation of his actions, each time his decisions were upheld, not only by the War Department, but by Wilson himself.

The dispute between the State and War Departments was an unforeseen, but not unforeseeable, development. It was the result of the tension between the State Department, which was accustomed to evaluating and making changes in foreign policy, and the War Department, whose function was to carry out policy as instructed, until higher authority changed that policy. In this case, with Wilson and Lansing both in Paris awaiting the decision of the peace conference, no one was in a position to order a change, regardless of whether or not it was justified. This state of affairs not only confounded the Allies, who were unsure about what American policy really was, but it created confusion and dissension among American diplomatic and military representatives. This situation was to grow markedly worse before it got better.

6

Wilson, Russia, and the Peace Conference

IN MAY 1919 THE COUNCIL OF FOUR APPROACHED THE RUSSIAN PROBLEM
from a new angle. Now, for the first time, the council's deliberations
included consideration of diplomatic recognition of the Kolchak government. Heretofore the council had centered its discussion around either
reaching an accommodation with the Bolshevik government, or waiting
for its overthrow by its internal enemies. But in May the reported disintegration of the Red Army and the military victories of the Whites caused
the council to shift its focus away from Moscow and towards Omsk. The
issue was essentially twofold. First, should the Omsk government be recognized as the provisional government of Russia, or, at least that part of
Russia which it occupied? Second, should the Associated Powers support
and supply this government?

Woodrow Wilson was under increasing pressure from Frank Polk and
the Russian Division of the State Department to grant Kolchak de facto
recognition at the very least. On 6 May, Polk cabled the American commissioners in Paris, using selected statements by Morris, Stevens, Caldwell
and even Graves, to urge Wilson to recognize Kolchak in exchange for his
promise to install a democratic government in Russia, complete with a
constituent assembly and a program of civil liberties. Polk also recommended that Kolchak pledge to fulfill "foreign obligation and
undertakings." Recognition, he concluded, would depend on Kolchak's
agreeing to make such a declaration.[412] Polk suggested attacking the
Russian problem from a new direction. Instead of attempting to moderate
the radical policy of the Bolsheviks, which had been notably unsuccessful,

he argued, the council should try to moderate the reactionary tendencies of the White governments.

The "curious collapse of the Bolsheviks," as Lloyd George called it, raised both the possibility of a total defeat of Bolshevism, and the frightening specter of a powerful military dictatorship in Russia. Lloyd George pointed out that the time to impose conditions on Kolchak was before he seized Moscow. He feared that thus far Kolchak's political program was "vague and indefinite." Wilson advanced Polk's suggestion that the Associated Powers demand reforms in exchange for support which would otherwise be cut off by the signing of the peace treaty.

The council also feared the establishment of a reactionary military government in Russia. Likewise, the council was concerned that Germany would gain economic control of Russia by forming an industrial and commercial union with her. This prospect was as frightening, if not more so, than continued Bolshevik rule.[413]

In May, Wilson, still suffering from the after effects of his stroke of 28 April, approached the council with his Siberian problem.[414] According to the account of Sir Maurice Hankey, Wilson reminded the council that the US and Allies had agreed to send supplies to the Siberian civilian population from Vladivostok. At the request of the Allies and John F. Stevens, the head of the Railroad Commission, the United States had agreed to police sections of the railroad east of Irkutsk. The difficulty, Wilson explained, was that "the United States did not believe in Koltchak."[415] The British and French military representatives did, and they actively supported him. The presence along the railway of "neutral" United States soldiers, furthermore, was starting to irritate Kolchak, because the impression among the peasants of Siberia was that the United States was the standard of a free government which they ought to imitate. When they saw the neutral attitude of American soldiers, the peasants thought that something must be wrong with the Kolchak government. To make matters worse, Wilson added, "the Cossacks were out of sympathy with United States soldiers and he suspected that the Japanese would be glad to have a collision between the Cossacks and American soldiers." Wilson believed that he had two choices. He could side with Kolchak and send more troops to Siberia, or he could withdraw American forces completely. If the US increased its commitment Wilson believed, the Japanese would certainly increase theirs even more. If American troops remained just to guard the railroad, and maintained a neutral policy, then confrontations were inevitable. If American troops were attacked, they would respond. If the AEF were withdrawn, "Siberia would be left to the Japanese and the Allied-backed Kolchak."[416]

Lloyd George, in reply, underscored the need for a united policy towards Russia. Wilson reiterated his belief that "the proper policy of the Allied and Associated Powers was to clear out of Russia and leave it to the Russians to fight it out among themselves." Lloyd George, however, persuaded Wilson to delay his decision until the council had heard the opinion of a liberal Russian expert, Nikolai V. Tchiakowsky. He suggested that Wilson cable Graves to advise him that the matter was under consideration, and to take no action in the meantime. Wilson feared a potential clash between the AEF and the Cossacks, but finally agreed to delay his decisions if the Allies undertook to discover what Kolchak's program really was.[417]

The account of Professor Paul Mantoux, another witness to this meeting, differs from that of Hankey on two points. According to the personal stenographic notes of Mantoux, official translator of the conference, Wilson was growing more concerned about the difficulty in attempting to impose liberal conditions on Kolchak. He was also concerned with how Kolchak might be compelled to keep his promises. "We will be able to obtain promises from him," said Wilson: The problem was "how to force him to keep them." Lloyd George explained, "The fact that Bolshevism will have finally failed because it encountered the opposition of the world will be a lesson for Kolchak." Kolchak, Lloyd George added, needed the Allies to supply him with railroad equipment without which he could not rule Russia, even if victorious. Besides, he added, by all reports Kolchak was a trustworthy man. He concluded, "I think we can impose conditions upon Kolchak if we do it now."[418] Mantoux then recorded that the prime minister asked if the council should send troops to Archangel to meet Kolchak, if he succeeded in taking Moscow.

Wilson, who had already authorized the removal of US troops from North Russia, remarked that the American troops in Archangel were not secure. "It is always dangerous to interfere in foreign revolutions," he observed. The Russians were taking the initiative, Lloyd George explained; the role of the Allies was merely to provide support. This, to Lloyd George's way of thinking, was not interference.

Wilson, skeptical thus far, suddenly seemed to tire of the matter, and—uncharacteristically—he capitulated, perhaps because of illness, exhaustion, frustration, or bewilderment. To Lloyd George he replied, "You have more experience than we in far-flung expeditions. You have an officer corps which has a long tradition in this respect. As for ourselves, except in the Philippines, we have never had the same reason to act at a great distance, and the American officer remains first and foremost a citizen. In accordance with your request, I am postponing my decision on the subject of Siberia."[419]

The council's interview of Tchaikowsky on 10 May dealt mainly with Kolchak's character. Wilson explained the council's fear that a Kolchak victory would result in "a policy of reaction and military power."[420] Tchaikowsky explained at length that, in his opinion, these fears were groundless.

Lloyd George told him two things were essential if Kolchak wanted the council's support. First he must summon a bona fide constituent assembly and entrust the problem of land distribution to it. Second, the council must know Kolchak's attitude towards the new border states, Finland and the Baltic countries.

Tchaikowsky assured the council that Kolchak had promised to resign immediately once there was a chance of getting a constituent assembly. "No one," Tchaikowsky said, "could ask more of him than that." About the border states he was more evasive, but in the end said Russia would deal with them as equals. When Lloyd George questioned him about a Foreign Office memorandum, which reported Cossack atrocities, and

Kolchak's lack of popular support, Tchaikowsky dismissed the report as exaggerated.

Wilson was worried about Kolchak's supporters and counselors. He wanted to know their political views. Tchaikowsky could not tell him, but at the end of the discussion he predicted Russia would eventually become a federal republic like the United States.[421] Wilson remained concerned about the admiral's advisers. He remarked in the afternoon session that he had the impression Kolchak's government would incline to the right as soon as it attained power. Lloyd George agreed, but added that public opinion would not permit Kolchak's abandonment no matter what he did; the world, he said, was interested mainly in order at this point. He admitted, however, that "it would be awkward to be placed in position of supporting a government that we did not believe in."[422]

Wilson then decided that the council must get another opinion of Kolchak and his entourage. He was not satisfied to rely only on the opinions of Allied military men, and he suggested that the council send Ambassador Morris to Omsk to report on the situation there.[423]

A few days later, Lloyd George raised the issue of a possible conflict between the AEF and the Siberian Cossacks. He told Wilson that British military representatives reported that Ivanov-Rinov "had done his best to smooth matters," and that Graves was the source of the trouble. Wilson took issue with the latter statement. The British representatives, he pressed further, were friendly to Kolchak, if not actually partisan. Lloyd George agreed that one might fairly call them partisan.[424]

That same day, Wilson ordered Morris to Omsk, instructing him to consult Graves on his way. Morris was to obtain official assurances of the future policy of Kolchak's government and determine the methods it would use in setting up a new regime. Morris was to ask for promises regarding a constituent assembly, land distribution, and security of suffrage. "My object," Wilson wrote, "is to satisfy myself as to whether the Kolchak government deserves recognition or at least the countenance, if not the support, of our government."[425] Within a few days Wilson authorized Vance McCormick to inform Kolchak that his government was

under scrutiny, and that the US was not disposed to recognize any government in Russia that assumed power without the open and free support
of the Russian people. Wilson suggested that the time might be right for
an election, and indicated that if the results were favorable the US would
consider recognizing Kolchak's government as the de facto government of
the area it controlled, or came to control.[426]

That Wilson wanted Russia to establish a constitutional democracy was
no secret. He greatly feared the establishment of a dictatorship there,
whether by the proletariat or by military junta. As Kolchak's fortunes rose,
the latter threat seemed more immediate. Wilson and Lloyd George wanted to gain some form of moral influence over whatever government might
control Russia to insure that the Russian people retained some measure of
personal and political liberty. To Wilson the establishment of democracy
in Russia would mean that she would pose no military or political threat
to Europe. In this way not only the Russians, but the rest of the world,
would benefit. No lasting peace would come to Europe, he believed, without peace in Russia. Wilson was sure that the majority of Russians wanted
a constitutional democracy, and that a free election would prove it. He
remained oblivious to the polarization of Russian political factions that
had occurred since the fall of the Provisional Government. Wilson's hopes
lay in the Russian middle ground, but it was a no man's land uninhabited
by the living.

On 16 May, while the Council of Four awaited Morris's report on
Kolchak, it received the Bolsheviks' answer to Nansen's aid proposal. In a
lengthy reply, Chicherin turned down the council's conditions, but he
proposed Nansen send aid nonetheless, while the Soviets opened peace
negations with the Associated Powers. Chicherin's tone was accusatory,
suspicious, and polemical, but not unjustified. He declared that the
Soviets had every reason to expect military success and could not cease
military operations. The Bolshevik government, furthermore, did not
intend to be the "objects of foul play." Chicherin accused the council of
supporting Denikin and Kolchak whose forces, he said, committed
numerous atrocities, and were reactionary and monarchical. The

Associated Powers were, Chicherin wrote, "carrying on the most reckless intervention policy and even the American Government...seems at present to be wholly dominated by the implacable hostility of the Clemenceau Ministry against Soviet Russia."[427]

The reply perplexed Lloyd George. It was, he said, another instance of extraordinary difficulty of getting the facts about Russia. Chicherin indicated that the Bolsheviks were winning but all the information in British hands indicated they were collapsing.

The Council of Four submitted Chicherin's reply to a committee, which included Robert Cecil and Herbert Hoover. The committee told the council it had only two choices left in Russia. First, it could decide that Soviet rule was inimical to peace and smash the Bolsheviks, but it must spare no effort to support opposition to the Soviets, and it must completely sever relations with the Bolshevik government. Cecil cautioned that such a policy would no doubt involve greater bloodshed and destruction of material wealth. The alternative was to propose a cease-fire supervised by international commissions. The Associated Powers would then supply all complying factions with food and clothing, while the Russian problem was submitted to the League of Nations, which would supervise free elections. Cecil concluded his report by saying that while either approach might work, a combination of the two was indefensible. The council must not ask Lenin to stop fighting while it supplied Kolchak or Denikin, nor should the council encourage Kolchak and Denikin while negotiating with Lenin to give him economic assistance. That sort of policy would only prolong hostilities and spread the belief in Russia that the Associated Powers could not be trusted.[428]

Unfortunately, the council ignored Cecil's advice. Clemenceau believed Bolshevism was clearly on the decline, and if the Bolsheviks did not want humanitarian aid that was an end to it.[429] Wilson argued that Lenin had been correct in claiming that the Allies were supporting Kolchak and Denikin, and were not pressing them to stop fighting. Lenin's position was that to stop fighting was to sign his own death warrant.[430] Clemenceau responded that the council could enjoin Kolchak and Denikin to stop

fighting but they would not do so. Wilson suggested the Allies stop sending them arms. Clemenceau countered by saying even if they stopped
Denikin and Kolchak, that would not stop Lenin. "Can we not try to sway
Lenin morally?" Wilson asked, to which Clemenceau answered "I have no
hope of this kind." Frustrated, Wilson declared that he no longer regret-
ted not having a fixed policy in Russia. "It seems to me impossible to
define one in such conditions," he remarked.[431]

The council was caught in a dilemma. Lloyd George pointed out on one
hand were "violent revolutionaries without scruples" while on the other
were "people who claim to act in the interest of order, but whose intentions are suspect to us." Nevertheless, he continued to worry about the
effects of abandoning the White forces, now that the Allies no longer
needed them. Wilson again said they must ask both groups to agree to
elections and let matters be settled by a constituent assembly. All factions
must assure the council they would work to restore the Russian Republic.
Meanwhile each group should be asked to guarantee a local regime based
"on individual liberty and universal suffrage." Lloyd George feared this
would prolong the division of Russia. If Kolchak took Moscow, he argued,
a national assembly for all Russia could be elected immediately.[432]

Once again the council delayed its decision. News of White victories
helped Kolchak's case. Wilson also received word that the Omsk government had recalled Ivanov-Rinov, one of the most obstructive Cossack
leaders.[433]

General Graves, meanwhile, had come under additional criticism.
McCormick suggested to Wilson that a number of sources indicated that
Graves's removal from Siberia might reduce friction there and restore har-
mony.[434] Acting Secretary of State Polk had suggested the same thing. He
also warned the Omsk government that its military authorities must
remain on friendly terms with Graves and the AEF or face a collapse of
the railway agreement and, consequently, of the Omsk government. At
the same time Polk warned McCormick and Lansing that the situation in
Eastern Siberia was dangerous, but that he believed that "[t]his has been
due primarily to the character of the instructions issued to General Graves

which he has interpreted as requiring a rigid and aloof neutrality on his part." The British, said Polk, were distressed by Graves's claim that he was only responsible to the US government, and his refusal to consider orders from the Japanese or the Railway Commission on how to guard his section of the railway. The British complained that Graves considered himself bound to keep aloof from Kolchak's commanders.

Graves's cables to the War Department, Polk thought, showed "that he had been, to say the least, tactless in his dealings with the Japanese military commander, and further that his views of the situation in some instances seem based entirely upon the opinion he had formed as a result of the arbitrary and stupid conduct of General Ivanoff[-Rinoff] and the buc[c]aneering of the Cossack leaders Kalmikoff and Semenoff." As a result, said Polk, the British believed that Graves sympathized with the Bolsheviks rather than the Whites. "The American command in Siberia," he added, "has always required a high degree of tact and large experience in affairs. I cannot help thinking that in spite of the narrow limitations set by his instructions General Graves has proved lacking in both these qualifications." If the US did not decide to support Kolchak, Polk said, Graves could not retain his command "without open rupture either with the Russians or the Japanese or possibly with both."[435] Polk again stressed the need for a common Anglo-American policy. "If we do not somehow relieve the situation in which General Graves finds himself," he warned, "our policy in Siberia will prove a total failure when it seems to promise real success."[436]

In reply to Polk's entreaties Wilson cabled Newton Baker asking him to tell Roland Morris to decide if Graves ought to be replaced.[437] On 22 May, Baker reported compliance with Wilson's orders, but he also rose to Graves's defense. "I feel from all the information we have," he said, "that General Graves is carefully and intelligently carrying out orders under trying circumstances, and that the efforts made to involve him in hostile operations against some part of the Russian population are insidious and baffling. He seems to have displayed firmness and good judgement." Polk, Baker pointed out, felt that Graves had followed his instructions too rigidly and that he had been too tactless. But Baker was not at all sure that Polk was in a position to judge this matter from his vantage point, and anyway, Baker admitted, he himself may have been to blame for any rigidity in light of the orders he had given Graves.[438]

Baker went on to say that both he and Polk felt that Morris's views would be invaluable. "The dispatches made it clear that there is a wide difference of policy among the nations represented in Siberia. [But] Polk and I both feel that Graves's removal at this time would create the impression that the United States Government was dissatisfied with his conduct and would be used to show our approval of other policies with which we are not in sympathy."[439]

Baker had apparently succeeded in modifying Polk's opinion of the situation. He concluded that if Wilson wanted the US to cooperate with the Omsk government, Graves would comply with such orders instantly upon receipt. "Up to the present time," Baker reminded the president, Graves's only orders had been to guard the railroad and preserve local order without getting involved or taking sides in the factional warfare in Siberia. "Such clashes as have occurred between him and others," Baker assured Wilson, "have for the most part been caused by violence toward the local population."[440] The next day Wilson cabled Washington that he entirely agreed with Baker's message, and felt they must all await Morris's report.[441]

In May 1919 the Japanese were putting additional pressure on the Council of Four to recognize Kolchak. Clemenceau warned that Japan was about to propose recognition and that he thought that the council should anticipate this. Wilson asked if the Japanese wanted the Omsk government recognized as a local or national government. When Clemenceau indicated the latter, Wilson refused to agree to such a step.[442]

That afternoon, the council considered a draft despatch to Kolchak. Wilson asked for clarification of one point. He asked if recognition of Kolchak would depend on his meeting the conditions of the despatch. Lloyd George assured him that Kolchak's acceptance would only mean that he would continue to receive assistance, not recognition. In that case, Wilson pointed out, the despatch only applied to the British government, which alone had supplied the Russians with munitions and supplies. The United States, he said, had supported the Czechs, but this had stopped, and it had never supplied Kolchak. Wilson told the council that he was in an awkward position. The Allies dealt with Kolchak as a de facto government. The United States, he said, had only looked on, and helped to guard the railway under international supervision. He called his position anomalous, and he insisted on consulting Lansing before associating himself with the despatch to prevent that position from becoming even more so.[443] Still uncertain after conferring with Lansing, Wilson told the council that his secretary of state approved the despatch to Kolchak, although he personally would prefer to delay sending it until they had Morris's report; he finally agreed, however, to send it at once.[444]

The council then turned to the problem of supplying Kolchak in the event his reply was satisfactory. Lloyd George wished to divide the burden among the governments according to their abilities to pay. This would shift the bulk of the responsibility to the United States. Wilson pointed out that the Congress would have to consent and that up to this point it had opposed the idea of Russian intervention. He added this attitude might change if Kolchak replied satisfactorily.[445] Meanwhile Wilson anxiously awaited Morris's report, but on 28 May, Lansing informed him that they could not expect the report until 20 June. Morris was still in Japan.[446] The next day Lansing sent Wilson a report of Consul General Harris's recent conversation with Kolchak. Kolchak asked for economic aid, saying it was "a great necessity." He professed goodwill toward the United States, and he pointed out that he had recalled Ivanov-Rinov to reduce friction with the Americans. He did not ask for diplomatic recognition, saying that he was leaving the matter entirely to the Allies.[447]

By the beginning of June, Kolchak's forces suffered a serious setback. The westernmost point of his advance was about 65 miles southeast of Kazan. The Red Army had attacked in late April, and by early June it had pushed the White forces back to Ufa, taking the city on 9 June.[448] While Kolchak's military situation worsened, Lloyd George had Kolchak warned specifically that the British would withdraw all support if he did not guarantee the reforms mentioned in the despatch.[449]

The Council of Four now sent Kolchak a virtual ultimatum, which it was impossible for him to refuse. To secure the means to continue the war, he had to give the council the assurances it demanded regardless of whether he intended or was able to fulfill them. On 4 June, Kolchak wrote to Clemenceau, giving the council the assurances it requested and promising not to retain power after "the Bolsheviks are definitely crushed." He did, however, decline to recall the 1917 assembly, claiming that the majority of its members were now in the Soviet ranks.[450]

On 7 June, the council received the complete text of Kolchak's letter promising amnesty to those forced to join the Bolsheviks and giving the constituent assembly full powers to determine the future Russian government. Clemenceau, Lloyd George, and Wilson were all satisfied with Kolchak's reply. Military aid continued.[451] Nevertheless, the council declined to recognize the Kolchak government. "It is impossible to recognize his government as the one of all Russia," Lloyd George explained. "We do not know what will happen after the fall of the Bolsheviks. A new situation can arise, and all we can do is promise Admiral Kolchak to support him."[452] Thus the details of what kind of support, and who would supply it, remained undecided. Wilson showed no desire to make specific arrangements, and indeed, as he pointed out, could not do so without congressional approval.

The council was distracted in mid-June, moreover, by another crisis in the continuing saga of the Czech Legion. John F. Stevens reported that the Czechs, by now dissatisfied, wanted to go home. Their commander, General Syrový, claimed that he could not keep them under control for more than three months. Four regiments had already refused to fight the Bolsheviks any longer. Stevens feared that the men would defy their officers and make arrangements with the Bolsheviks to go home through European Russia. He thought the result would be war between the Kolchak forces and the Czechs. He speculated that the White forces would lose, that Kolchak would be overthrown, and that the result would be "anarchy under the Bolsheviks."

Stevens wanted the Allies to send 50,000 to 76,000 troops to relieve the Czechs. He warned that action must be taken at once or "all Allied work here will go to naught and we may as well give up our efforts and leave the Russians to whatever might come.... I tell you frankly that the situation is an impossible one and cannot continue. I have no hopes of ultimate success unless the Allies realize exactly what the situation is and take necessary steps without delay." [453]

Acting Secretary of State Phillips also urged the immediate repatriation of the Czechs, advocating the immediate formulation of a statement of the exact aid to be given to Kolchak, the amount of it, and whether it was financial, military and/or economic. This statement, he emphasized, must then be followed "by prompt and direct action." [454]

Prompt action was not forthcoming. Wilson and the Council of Four, uncertain of what to do about the Czechs, concentrated on whether to continue the naval blockade against Russia after the signing of the peace treaty. Lloyd George believed that the only result would be to insure that Germany would have a monopoly on Russian trade.

Wilson objected on other grounds. "It is impossible from the legal point of view to maintain the blockade after the signing of peace. I do not see how we could do it. We fought for international law; it is not for us to violate it." Wilson remained firm on this point despite repeated requests in the following months to approve a blockade, which was, after all, an act of war under international law.

The kaleidoscopic changes in Russia perplexed Lloyd George and Wilson, and they were skeptical about Kolchak even as they agreed to support him. "If I believed we could crush the Bolsheviks this year, I would favor making a great effort in which the English and French fleets would participate," Lloyd George declared. "But Admiral Kolchak has just been pushed back 300 kilometers. One of his armies is destroyed. In this strange war taking place in Russia, each time one of the two adversaries is defeated part of his troops goes over to the other side." To Wilson this indicated that "the population did not have much faith in either party."[455]

The council discussed pessimistic reports on the condition of Kolchak's army by Generals Bliss and Janin, but Lloyd George, like Wilson, clung to the belief that democracy would eventually evolve in Russia. "Admiral Kolchak will not beat Lenin," Lloyd George predicted. "Instead there will come a time when the adversaries will get together to put an end to the anarchy. It seems that the military affairs of the Bolsheviks are well managed. But the observers who inform us say that pure Bolshevik doctrine is increasingly abandoned and what is being constituted over there is a state that does not differ noticeably from a bourgeois state."[456]

Wilson agreed that Russia was bound to turn to democracy in the end. Clemenceau, however, quickly reminded his colleagues that they must keep the commitment they had recently made to Kolchak. But Wilson was just as swift to point out that "we committed ourselves only to help him by furnishing him with materiel." This was Wilson's understanding. The question as he saw it was "Are we at war with Bolshevik Russia?" This question he answered by stating "the operations in which the Allied troops participated in Russia do not constitute a state of war in the legal sense of the word. There has been no declaration of war." Therefore, he believed there was, and could be, no war. A blockade was an act of war; and because there was no declaration of war, Wilson was not prepared to blockade Russia.[457]

During the last half of June, Wilson was largely occupied with the struggle to get Germany to sign the peace treaty. During the same time his health continued to deteriorate. He did, however, discuss Russian policy with Vance McCormick on 23 June. Wilson said he had no intention of recognizing Kolchak. The despatch to Omsk only outlined conditions under which Kolchak could continue to receive supplies and munitions. McCormick argued that it was most difficult to send money, to an unrecognized government, particularly to Siberia for railroad development.

Wilson assured McCormick that he would ask Congress for funds. He told McCormick that he saw the opportunity for "a great constructive program" in aiding Russia through the Siberian railroad. He also thought this program would protect the Open Door Policy and prevent Japan from monopolizing Siberia and jeopardizing Chinese interests. Wilson believed that Russia had to have economic aid to get back on its feet, and that it should receive such aid without the Allies interfering in its internal politics. The problem was that political interference would be inevitable. McCormick agreed that this was true, in light of the Allies' policies. "The Russian people," Wilson again stressed, "must solve their own problems without outside interference and Europe had made a great mistake when they attempted to interfere in the French Revolution." This situation, he owned, was "hard on the present Russian generation, but in the long run it means less distress for Russia."[458]

Away from the influence of the Allies, Wilson reverted almost completely to his former policy of espousing economic aid and non-interference in Russian affairs. He remained vague about the extent of the support he felt obliged to give Kolchak, beyond his plan to seek funds for the railroad. It was not even clear if he intended the British to continue sending munitions and supplies to Omsk, or whether the US was now to provide all, or some, of his support.

When Wilson learned that Morris could not report from Omsk until the end of June, he had cancelled the mission. Now once again, he felt the need of Morris's opinion, and once again he ordered Morris to Omsk. The Council of Four's decision to support Kolchak still left unresolved the questions of diplomatic recognition and the extent and nature of its support. Wilson wanted Morris to make recommendations on both points.[459]

While Wilson awaited word from Morris, Kolchak's military situation continued to deteriorate. Winston Churchill submitted a proposal to the Council of Four to solve Kolchak's military problems and the Czech crisis. Churchill, a vehement anti-Bolshevik, wanted to attach the Czechs to the right wing of Kolchak's forces in order to prop up the latter. Churchill asked for immediate action, but the council referred the matter to the Supreme War Council for consideration.[460]

The situation by the end of June was growing steadily worse in Siberia. Edward Beneš wrote to the council requesting the immediate repatriation of the Czech Legion.[461] The council began inquiries about available shipping for this purpose.[462] The next day, however, it cabled Kolchak to ask if he would accept Churchill's scheme for the cooperation of the legion with the right wing of his forces.[463] The council remained sure of its course in Russia. The members were tentatively committed to Kolchak, and they were no longer seeking a settlement with Bolsheviks, but they remained less than enthusiastic about the Omsk government.

On 27 June, when Wilson was asked about the problem of recognizing a Russian government at a press conference, he replied "My own principles of recognition are two: First—it's absolutely none of my business what kind of government another country has. Second—I am entitled to wait until they have time to find one that suits them and until it has held power for a time…. We haven't found a Russian government yet. We are looking for it. The one we bet on is being chased eastward just now."[464]

On 28 June, Wilson left Paris to return to America. He learned en route that the Senate had requested that he immediately explain his reasons for sending US troops to Siberia, outlining what their duties were, how long he intended to keep them there, and what his policy in Siberia was.[465] Wilson would not reply to this request until he had returned to Washington.

The Paris Peace Conference was at an end. Wilson had agreed to "support" Kolchak in exchange for Kolchak's guarantee that he would establish a democratic government as soon as possible. In this way Wilson could justify some short-term diplomatic and political interference in Russia, on the grounds that he was supporting the only faction that ultimately promised a government elected by universal suffrage. Once this government was set in place, self-determination would be secured.

After scrutinizing all sides in the civil war, Wilson had decided that Kolchak was the only immediate hope for establishing a democracy in Russia. He was willing, therefore, to consider backing one side against the other financially, as he had in Mexico. He still refused, however, to consent to military intervention on any grounds.

Wilson had needed, and still needed, time to determine the outcome of events in Russia, and the best way to help the civilian population and Kolchak. He needed time to approach Congress and to form an aid package. Meanwhile in Washington aid to Kolchak was held up by the State Department's inability to establish a credit system for the Omsk government.[466] During this time Wilson left General Graves in the same quandary which he had been in for over six months—sitting in Vladivostok with his orders unchanged. What Wilson did not realize was he had even less time left in which to maneuver than General Graves.

The voyage home offered the exhausted Wilson a much needed rest. During his final days in Paris he had displayed increasing signs of strain on his nerves and his health. As a result he was unable to complete his address to the Senate presenting the Treaty of Versailles.[467] On 8 July, Wilson returned to Washington, but he refrained from public comment on Russian policy. On 10 June, he was asked if he wished to give his opinion of the Kolchak government or any of the other Russian governments. Wilson answered, "No sir. That is an athletic feat, to adjust one's mind to those things."[468]

On 12 July, Polk asked Wilson if he approved of selling to Kolchak, on a credit basis, any available surplus materials from the War Department, provided that it carried no implied recognition of the Omsk government. Polk hoped Wilson would authorize such a transaction, and he added that Harris hoped the United States "would take the same liberal attitude toward Kolchak that the French and British had adopted."[469]

A few days later Baker warned Wilson of an impending crisis. General Bliss expected the Council of Four to ask Wilson to send more troops to Siberia "to replace 50,000–60,000 Czechoslovaks in case the latter are repatriated." Bliss urged Wilson to take the first opportunity "to plainly declare that Europe can expect no troops from America unless Germany should renew the war."[470]

The next day Polk reported that Roland Morris was finally in Siberia and on his way to Omsk. Polk also mentioned the need to replace Czech troops, and added he had reports the Japanese were sending troops to the front to engage the Bolsheviks.[471]

But before Wilson could make a decision based upon this new information, he suffered another small stroke, which affected his temperament, judgement, and memory for some time.[472] The stroke came at a particularly bad time, for two days later, on 20 July, Ambassador Morris's first long-awaited report arrived. Morris described railway conditions east of Irkutsk. He found Allied inspectors "struggling with serious difficulties." Except for the two American sectors, the military control of the railway was in the hands of Japan, which was "subsidizing and using the Cossacks to discredit Allied operations." In Morris's opinion "Kolchak is powerless to withstand this influence which has gone so far as to the appointment of the bandit Kalmikoff as the representatives of Dutoff, the Kolchak commander of all military operations in the east."

To Morris the Japanese plan was perfectly clear. Japan's attempt to take possession of the Chinese Eastern and Trans-Siberian railways and dominate Eastern Siberia and northern Manchuria was frustrated by the railway agreement. Therefore, the Japanese government was supporting "a less obvious, but a more insidious scheme" of using the Cossacks who were the only substantial support Kolchak had east of Chita as proxies. Morris predicted it would "not be difficult for Japan to dispose of the Eastern Cossacks when they have served their purpose."[473]

On 22 July, Wilson replied to the Senate's request for information on Siberia. His answer was essentially a restatement of the aide memoire. He also explained the Inter-Allied Railway Agreement and the role of the Stevens Commission.

> The instruction[s] to General Graves direct him not to interfere in Russian affairs, but to support Mr. Stevens wherever necessary. The Siberian railway is not only the main artery for transportation in Siberia, but is the only open access to European Russia today. The population of Siberia, whose

resources have been almost exhausted by the long years of war and the chaotic conditions which have existed there can be protected from a further period of chaos and anarchy only by the restoration and maintenance of traffic on the Siberian railway.[474]

Wilson told the Senate that partisan bands "having no settled connection with an organized government, and bands under leaders whose allegiance to any settled authority is apparently temporary and transitory, are constantly menacing the operation of the railway, and the safety of its permanent structures." He stressed that "the population of Western Siberia and the forces of Admiral Kolchak are entirely dependent upon these railways."

Wilson then addressed the situation of the Siberian civilian population. He described them as lacking shoes, clothing, agricultural machinery, and a multitude of other items basic to a sound economy. He pointed out that "having contributed their quota to the Russian armies which fought the Central Empires for three and one-half years, they now look to the Allies and the United States for economic assistance."[475]

Wilson reported that the Russian authorities in the United States had shipped large amounts of supplies to Siberia, and that Baker was working with both European and Russian agencies to send still more. Kolchak's government was working to buy medical supplies from America, and the American Red Cross was making relief efforts. "All elements of the population in Siberia look to the United States for assistance," Wilson said, and "assistance can not be given to the population of Siberia, and ultimately to Russia, if the purpose entertained for two years to restore railway traffic is abandoned." He assured the Senate that the presence of the AEF was crucial. The Stevens Railway Commission could not survive without it.[476]

Wilson concluded that the purpose of keeping American troops in Siberia was to hold open a necessary artery of trade, and extend to Siberia economic aid which would be essential in peace-time, but indispensable under the conditions which had followed Russia's prolonged and exhausting participation in the war against the Central Powers. He added that this participation "was obviously of incalculable value to the Allied cause, and in a very particular way commends the exhausted people who suffered from it to such assistance as we can render to bring about their industrial and economic rehabilitation."[477] Despite the discouraging reports on the condition of the Trans-Siberian Railway, Wilson clung to the hope of using it as a conduit for American aid to Russia; apparently he felt that the Senate would be receptive to such a scheme.

Even as Wilson was assuring the Senate of the importance of the Steven's Railway Commission in Siberia, Lansing sent him a copy of a cable from the members of the Inter-Allied Railway Committee to the Kolchak government. The cable reported that the committee's mission had met with little success, due to interference by Russian military authorities. For the railway work to succeed, interference by Semenov and his ilk had to be stopped, and the supervision of the railroads left to the civil railway committee authorities. The committee emphasized that it was anxious to aid Russia and had the means to do so, but could not unless its requirements were met.[478] Indications were that support of Kolchak and the railway committee might be mutually exclusive, but Wilson did not seem to acknowledge this contradiction, for by late July he was consumed with the fight for ratification of the peace treaty.

On 25 July, Wilson discussed the evacuation of the Czech Legion with Lansing. Wilson was considering sending the Czechs through Bolshevik Russia. Lansing told him that if they tried that route "they would be murdered." Wilson then apparently abandoned the notion.[479]

On 31 July, Baker informed Wilson that they had been deceived about the plight of the Czechs the summer before. Baker had just read an intelligence report of over 100 pages, by Lawrence Packard, a captain attached to General Graves's headquarters, which Lansing said demonstrated that the Czechs could have gotten out of Siberia during the summer of 1918, "but that influence was brought to bear (perhaps by the French who were interested in having them remain in Russia) and that at least part of their difficulties with the Russians grew out of this changed desire on their part." It appeared the United States had been misled into "rescuing" the Czechs.[480]

Baker also sent Wilson another report by General Graves, already one month old. Graves described his proclamation on the duties of American troops along the railroad. "Where there is interference with the railroad, I contemplate inflicting punishment on the party or parties interfering with the railroad." Graves stated, "This is not difficult where bodies of armed troops interfere with the road, because we go to their villages and inflict punishment there or anywhere we can find them. This seems to have the effect of making them respect our duties and obligations." [481]

Graves reported that the Japanese had been having more trouble than the Americans lately. The Bolsheviks had taken one American soldier prisoner; Graves hoped to get him back. As far as Bolshevik prisoners were concerned, he reported that the "Japanese and Russians undoubtedly kill some of their prisoners." He added, "the general belief is that a mere statement that a man is a Bolshevik is, generally speaking, enough to cause him to disappear. The Russian soldiers are very bitter and the so-called 'Intelligentzia' are launching a campaign against Americans because we put two Bolshevik wounded in our hospital and have eleven prisoners. They claim we are feeding Bolsheviks and looking out for their sick."[482]

On the subject of the railroads, Graves reported that the White Army control led the transportation of people and supplies. He explained that this "means the Army officer class is depriving the peasants in various sections of the country of the absolute necessities of life." They have established what they call passport control stations and check all passengers to determine whether they are authorized to travel on the train. In the peasant villages there is no one with authority to give them permission to travel. If they are caught on the train without passports they are put in jail. Graves claimed that there "are thousands and thousands of peasants who have no means to prevent so-called Bolsheviks from coming into their country" and "who have not been permitted to have one pound of food shipped to them since the Allies took over guarding the railway." When peasants in the Olga District sent two representatives to Vladivostok to complain about their plight, they were immediately arrested and, Graves reported, were still in jail, on the charge of being Bolsheviks.[483]

Graves was increasingly concerned that the American presence was having a very different effect from the one Wilson intended. "As I see this question, we become a party, by guarding the railroad, to the action of this governmental class in depriving the peasants of food. This naturally causes resentment not only against Koltchak and his representatives but against all the Allies." Two days before Graves had been told by the representatives of the peasants of the Olga District that "they did not believe the President of the United States knew the result of the action of US troops in this country." Graves himself was convinced "that there is no possibility of settling this trouble by such oppressive, unjust and inhumane actions as are being committed by the Koltchak representatives here in Eastern Siberia,...."[484] Graves then reiterated the necessity of removing Semenov from the Siberian scene, and he also took the opportunity to express his views on General Knox. Knox was "very anti-American and has no hesitancy in expressing openly his antagonism to President Wilson's views...General Knox evidently thinks that the Ambassador in Tokio [sic] and I are responsible for the policy of the United States in Siberia." Graves believed this because Knox had asked Caldwell, the US consul, to send a "cablegram requesting that both of us be removed, as we were not representing the views of the United States." Graves also suspected that as "General Knox is so closely associated with Admiral Koltchak and the Omsk Government, it is possible that he had something to do with the anti-American feeling which exists in the Government class. He, however, apparently denies this...." Graves's patience with Knox was wearing thin. He reported that he had told Colonel Summerville, representing the British Mission, "that I was getting tired of this pin-pricking from Britishers here in Vladivostok and if they desire to fight the United States' representatives to come out in the open, like I expected Anglo-Saxons to do, and we could have a show down, then I felt we would have a better understanding."[485]

Graves was clearly beginning to feel the strain of his anomalous position.

On 7 August, Lansing sent Wilson a memorandum from Dewitt C. Poole urging him to issue a statement attacking the Bolshevik government.[486] Poole warned Wilson of the danger of Bolshevik subversion in the United States. He stressed that Bolshevism was international, not national, in nature. He referred to the duplicity of the Bolshevik leadership and its willingness to agree to any terms, but, Poole assured Wilson, that it had no intention of being bound by its promises once they no longer suited their purpose. The Bolsheviks, he said, were "in essence a small coterie of men who are seeking to profit by the existing unrest to impose upon the world, by any means whatsoever, a preconceived order of existence." The only reason why the Bolsheviks were able to continue "their work of destruction at home and their subversive propaganda abroad," was that the progressive leaders of the world, especially Wilson, had not condemned Lenin and his government publicly. He urged Wilson to make such a statement as soon as possible.[487]

On 16 August, Lansing sent a draft of a statement by Poole to Wilson. Poole believed that a statement by Wilson coupled with the promise of economic assistance would not only warn people in general against "the evil fatuity of Bolshevism," but might help in resolving the situation in Russia. "Seeming uncertainty in the attitude of the United States has long been a reliance of the Bolsheviki and a source of confusion to their opponents." He added that a statement from Wilson would carry great moral weight.

Poole then launched into a chronological account of Bolshevik "offenses" against the Allies and the Russian people. He claimed Lenin had been in collusion with the Germans during and after the war. Lenin himself overthrew the democratically elected constituent assembly; he overthrew the more representative Provisional Government; and he took forcible control of Russia. Poole also claimed that the Bolsheviks, at

Germany's behest, had moved to destroy the Czech Legion in the spring of 1918, although Baker had recently questioned the truth of this interpretation of events. Poole further accused the Soviets of conducting an extensive reign of terror against the Russian people. Most of its victims, he said, were liberal rivals of the Soviets. Finally he accused the Bolsheviks of using food distribution to build up the Red Army and starve the opposition.

Poole wanted Wilson to promise that the United States would seek, on the one hand, to relieve the economic distress of the Russians, and, on the other, "to hasten the end of the Bolshevik regime in Central Russia." Wilson should also promise continued support for those working to establish a democratic government—presumably the Kolchak regime.[488]

While Poole was pressing Wilson to take a public stand against the Bolsheviks, Wilson was also coming under pressure from family members of the AEF troops to withdraw the force from Siberia. On 21 August, Wilson was visited by members of the 27th and 31st Infantry Siberian Expedition Auxiliary, who requested the return of their relations to the United States. "I shall look forward to consulting you about this matter," Wilson wrote to Baker afterwards, "because it involves the whole question of the maintenance of American forces in Siberia. I am a good deal perplexed in judgment about it."[489]

Because of information on the Bolsheviks reaching Washington, Wilson and Baker apparently came to some agreement concerning the AEF. A week later Lansing wrote to Wilson his understanding that the decision was for the withdrawal of the force from Siberia. He voiced concerns over the Japanese reaction. At any rate, he noted, "there will certainly not remain time for them to [manifest] by their actions in Siberia a change of heart before Vladivostok shall be frozen in."

Lansing recommended that Wilson give Baker definite orders to send transports to Vladivostok immediately. It might be a month before the transports could arrive. If the port iced up in the interval, the AEF would have to use the Manchurian railroad to reach an ice-free port. This railroad was exclusively in the hands of the Japanese: That fact, observed

Lansing, ruled it out as a means of exit. He took this opportunity to advise that the withdrawal take place as soon as possible.[490]

Lansing enclosed a copy of the cable he had sent the Japanese government protesting their actions in Siberia. He restated America's policy as outlined in the aide memoire, and he pointed out that the Japanese government had agreed to follow this policy in the summer of 1918. But since then a radical divergence of interpretation of that policy had appeared. This had caused great problems with the railway commission. He reminded the Japanese of their duty to support and protect John F. Stevens and his men. Lansing stressed that the "engineers are to be protected as a vital element in the protection of the railways."[491]

The Japanese forces, however, seemed to interpret the protection of the railway as "limited strictly to safeguarding railway property and keeping the line open," and to believe that it entailed no obligation whatever for cooperation on the part of Japanese forces in furthering the general operation of the plan itself." The result was that the Japanese commander refused to protect the lives and property of the railway inspectors in the area controlled by Semenov.

This, Lansing said, was unacceptable. Moreover, the Japanese were treating the Omsk government as an officially recognized authority. Lansing observed that neither the United States nor Japan recognized the Kolchak government. The Japanese plan for organizing the railway made no mention of that government, and it was only "by a later development of circumstances that the Russian Chairman had a connection to Admiral Kolchak." Even so, he argued, Kolchak favored the railway agreement; all hostile "action of Russian authorities acting in the name of the Omsk authorities can, therefore, only be in disobedience to express instructions." Nevertheless, the Japanese had allowed the situation to become so dangerous that the Allied engineers might have to be withdrawn, because of the Japanese refusal to protect them, even though they were attempting to carry out their duties under a plan that Japan itself had proposed.

This was a source of grave concern to the United States. Lansing concluded that his government could not "be held responsible for that for which it is not in fact responsible." American-Japanese cooperation was essential to the smooth execution of the railway agreement. Since Japanese officials were failing to guard the Railway Service Corps, the United States was prepared to place the blame for the agreement's failure squarely on Japan. Now the United States, warned Lansing, had to decide what choices it had other than to end its efforts in Siberia.[492]

Wilson never had the opportunity to follow Lansing's recommendation. On 25 August, his health rapidly deteriorating, Wilson left Washington in a fit of anger to undertake a national speaking tour to rally support for the Treaty of Versailles. Throughout the tour Wilson repeatedly referred to Russia. Probably influenced by Poole, he consistently characterized the Bolsheviks as a minority government. In Kansas City, he remarked that the tyranny of the minority was at the heart of the Russian tragedy: "The men who are now largely in control of the affairs of Russia represent nobody but themselves." Wilson argued that there "is a closer monopoly of power in Petrograd and Moscow than there ever was in Berlin, and the thing that is intolerable is not that the Russian people are having their way, but that another group of men more cruel than the Czar himself is controlling the destinies of that great people."[493]

Wilson continued to make similar remarks throughout his tour. On 17 September 1919, Lansing wrote to Wilson about William C. Bullitt's statement to the Foreign Relations Committee. Bullitt testified that Lansing was highly critical of Wilson and the peace treaty. Lansing acknowledged Bullitt's conduct as "despicable and outrageous." He claimed Bullitt had used the opportunity to avenge himself on the Wilson administration for failing to accept his report on Russia.[494]

Wilson was outraged by what he considered final proof of Lansing's duplicity. His private secretary, Joseph P. Tumulty, believed that if Wilson had not fallen ill that same day he would have demanded Lansing's immediate resignation.[495] That morning, however, the president's doctor observed the first signs of distress in Wilson: he was pale, his lips trembled and he was beginning to drool.[496] Wilson was never to acknowledge Lansing's telegram.

On 19 September, Phillips wired Wilson about aid to Kolchak. "Latest reports show that unless Kolchak forces are provided with clothing at an early date they will face rigors of a Siberia winter unequipped and will scarcely survive the ordeal." Phillips urged Wilson to authorize Baker to sell military surplus shoes and clothing to Kolchak. He warned that a failure to do this would weaken Kolchak and possibly benefit Japan. Recent reports, he added, said Kolchak had resumed the offensive and was pushing the Bolsheviks back towards the Urals.[497]

Phillips also alerted Wilson to the "urgent necessity" of repatriating the Czecho-Slovaks. He warned "their retention might be a source of danger rather than a protection" to the Omsk government. Moreover, their return had become a "burning political question" in Czechoslovakia and threatened the overthrow of the Czech government.[498] Wilson was not to act on either of these suggestions.

When Wilson left on his Western tour he was already seriously ill. He had suffered for years from untreated malignant hypertension. As early as 1900 he had been afflicted by a series of minor strokes which affected his right arm. In 1906 he had a retinal hemorrhage which impaired his sight in one eye. By 1916 he was apparently suffering significant kidney malfunction as a result of the disease, and in the spring of 1919 in Paris he was victim to episodes of heart failure, at least one other stroke, and a host of cognitive disturbances which, during the following summer, were most noticeable during his testimony before the Senate Foreign Relations Committee on 19 August.[499] The degree to which Wilson was impaired physically and mentally has been the subject of extensive historical debate, but the debate is only over the degree of impairment. It was a tribute to Wilson's considerable intellect that he functioned as well as he did for as long as he did. But by the end of his Western tour many of his speeches had become repetitive and rambling. He displayed increasing rigidity in his thinking and reluctance to weigh any new facts.[500] This made policy-making almost impossible for him, and his life-long unwillingness to delegate authority only exacerbated the problem.

On 25 September, Wilson collapsed in Pueblo, Colorado, his blood pressure running out of control. Dr. Cary Grayson, Wilson's personal physician, ordered his return to Washington. At the White House on 2 October, Wilson suffered a major stroke. This was not made known to the public. His doctor claimed that Wilson was suffering from "nervous exhaustion" and later "functional fatigue neurosis."[501] Wilson was seriously disabled in both a medical and constitutional sense; his thought processes and ability to perform his presidential duties were never again to be the same.[502] Irwin H. (Ike) Hoover, the head usher at the White House, and one of the very few people with daily access to the president, described Wilson as "looking dead" on the day of his stroke. "It was three weeks or more before a change seemed to come over things," Hoover recalled. In his words, Wilson was "a wreck of his former self."[503]

In time the president improved, but not by much. During his early illness all presidential business came to a stop; for a month and more, nothing came before him. Hoover reported later that "matters of importance requiring his signature were read to him and with a pencil, his hand steadied and pointed, he would sign there where the hand had been placed. I saw many of these signatures and they were but mere scribbles compared to his normal signature. All a sort of mechanical process which even seemed to exhaust him withal."

"If there was ever a man in bad shape," Hoover said,

> he was. There was no comparison with the president that went to Paris and before. He was changed in every way and everyone about him recognized and understood it to be so. He could not talk plain, mumbled more than he articulated, was helpless and looked awful. Everybody tried to help him, realizing he was so dependent for everything. The stories in the papers from day to day may have been true in their way but never was deception so universally practiced in the White House as it was in those statements being given out from time to time. And the strange part to me was that the President in his feeble way entered into the scheme.

During the winter of 1919–1920, Edith Bolling Wilson controlled access to the president. According to Hoover, Wilson heard only the papers which his wife chose to read to him. Grayson or Tumulty would brief her on a subject and she would tell the president. Apparently, Wilson's Annual Message to Congress on 2 December 1919 was written by Tumulty and a stenographer, with the help of some cabinet members, but was represented as having been written by Wilson.[504]

Wilson's stroke also left his Russian policy paralyzed. It remained frozen as he had described it in the aide memoire. He had not authorized aid to Kolchak, or the repatriation of the Czechs, or the withdrawal of the AEF from Siberia. For the next few months a decision on Siberian policy was once again delayed. By October 1919, Graves had been waiting for a definitive statement of policy for over ten months. Now he would have to wait a few more.

7

Kolchak's Defeat and American Withdrawal

THE SPRING OF 1919 BROUGHT AN END TO THE LULL IN FIGHTING THAT the weather had imposed on all Russian factions. The American forces' main concern became the Bolshevik campaign to gain control of the Ussuri Valley. Until now, US troops had had little contact with Bolshevik forces, except for their very limited involvement in the Allied campaign in August 1918. But the AEF's new duties under the Inter-Allied Railway Agreement placed Americans at strategic points along the Trans-Siberian Railway just as the Bolsheviks were planning to wrest control of the railroad from the Allies and the Omsk government.

The main duty of the AEF had now changed. The railway agreement drastically altered the nature of American participation. Heretofore, the primary duty of American troops, according to the aide memoire, had been to assist the Czech Legion in leaving Siberia; now they were to protect and maintain the Trans-Siberian Railway. In theory this was a non-partisan act of benevolence, but in practice it aided only the White cause.

The Inter-Allied Railway Agreement provided for the stationing of American troops at three specific locations along the railroad. Three sectors were assigned to the United States: An area north of Spasskoe, near Lake Khanka; a second position just north of Vladivostok in the vicinity of Nikolsk-Ussuriski; and a third in the Lake Baikal District, west of Verkhne-Udinsk.

In April, General Graves issued a proclamation assigning the sectors and reiterating the neutral policy of the United States. In this proclamation, Graves stressed that his goal was simply to protect the railway and its traffic in his sectors. "All will be equally benefitted and all shall be treated alike by our forces irrespective of persons, nationality, religion, or politics," he emphasized. "Cooperation is requested and warning given to all persons whomsoever that interference with traffic will not be tolerated."[505]

Graves's implementation of this policy faced real and immediate obstacles. It was impossible that all could be "equally benefitted" when much of the railroad remained in the hands of the Japanese and at the mercy of their Cossack henchmen. Neither of these two groups had shown any scruples about arresting and summarily executing anyone whom it suspected of being a Bolshevik, or of harboring Bolshevik sympathies. Not only were such people unable to use the railways, but the numerous partisan bands were fully aware that the railroad was being used primarily by Kolchak to transport conscripts and supplies to the Ural front. It was naive to imagine that the Bolsheviks would long refrain from attempting to disrupt an arrangement so convenient to Kolchak.

The Siberian peasantry did not seem to place much confidence in General Graves's proclamation. Lieutenant Sylvain Kindall wrote of an incident in which a literate peasant read a posted copy of the documents to his comrades in the village of Uspenska. Kindall recalled that "a shower of sunflower seed juice upon the bulletins was their reply." The peasants then "made prisoners of two railroad officials, kicked over a few chairs about the place, and then went out a mile north of the station and set fire to a bridge."[506]

The number of cases of vandalism and sabotage increased as part of a deliberate Bolshevik campaign to disrupt traffic in the Ussuri Valley. These incidents generally occurred at dawn. "The Bolsheviks usually worked at destroying small bridges, tearing up stretches of track, chopping down a few telephone poles and slashing the fallen telegraph wire to pieces," Kindall reported. At other times "they would pull spikes from a rail along a bad curve of road, or prepare a pair of rails by turning their bottom flanges upward and spiking them down again in this inverted position." Any train which came upon one of these sections was certain to be wrecked.[507] Estimates indicate that in the course of the Civil War 826 bridges were blown up, fourteen water supply depots and at least twenty railroad stations leveled, and thousands of miles of track destroyed. Much of this damage was attributable to Bolshevik partisan activity.[508]

The number of Bolshevik partisans and their supporters grew substantially in Eastern Siberia during the winter of 1918–1919. The peasantry had grown increasingly hostile to Kolchak as a result of his harsh recruiting and requisitioning practices. Punitive expeditions against the partisans only served to swell the ranks of Bolshevik supporters, and undermined American support for Kolchak. "All over Siberia," Ambassador Roland Morris wrote, "there is an orgy of arrest without charges; of executions without even the pretense of a trial; and of confiscation without the color of authority. Fear, panic, fear has seized everyone. Men suspect each other, and live in constant terror that some spy or enemy will cry 'Bolshevik' and condemn them to instant death."[509]

Even in the absence of violent opposition to the Omsk government, there was little support and much indifference. Increased oppression stimulated resistance. Men hiding in the countryside to avoid conscription into Kolchak's armies formed partisan bands. As these bands came under Bolshevik control, they were incorporated into the campaign to immobilize the Ussuri Valley.

Up until the beginning of this campaign American troops had had little difficulty with the Bolsheviks. Cossacks and the Japanese had been the principal danger. Relatively few Bolsheviks had operated near American positions and they had refrained from attacking American troops directly. Many American soldiers, revolted by White atrocities, sympathized with the partisans. The Americans' status as guardians of the railroad and the mines, however, made them targets of Bolshevik hostility. Within a few weeks the Bolsheviks were kidnapping American soldiers and interfering with rail traffic in American sectors.

As if the situation were not complicated enough, trouble also broke out in the Suchan mining district in April. The Suchan mines, seventy-five miles from Vladivostok, were a long-term source of anxiety for the Allies.

Supplying the city, the Maritime Province, and the Eastern Trans-Siberian Railway with coal, they were of great importance to the region.

When General Graves arrived in Siberia in August 1918, mining operations were at a halt, but political squabbling continued uninterrupted. At this point, as Graves put it, "Allied commanders unselfishly decided that the United States should look after this section." Graves consented and dispatched a company of 250 soldiers. Colonel O. P. Robinson went with them to evaluate the situation for Graves.

Robinson found that Bolshevik agitators had forced the manager of the mines, Mr. Egeroff, to flee the area, but that the Allied commanders had brought him back to run the mines. They reasoned that he was familiar with the operation of the mines and, as Graves sarcastically remarked, they probably thought that besides producing more coal, he would also cause more trouble for the AEF. Colonel Robinson, however, was doubtful about the wisdom of reinstating the manager. But Egeroff assured Robinson that he was an engineer who never factored politics into his calculations.[510] Egeroff wanted the Americans to arrest several men who had been responsible for running him out of town, but Robinson declined to do this, suggesting that they be asked to leave the district of their own accord. Seven were transported, but three had already fled, possibly to join partisan bands in the area. Colonel Robinson then approached the miners. He told them that the United States wanted the coal only for use by the Russian people.[511]

Operations went well for a time but soon General Graves began receiving reports that Egeroff was advocating a return to "Czarist methods" at the mines and that Allied guards were being used to suppress the political activity of the miners. Disturbed by this information, Graves dispatched a telegram to the commanding officer at Suchan, ordering him that "troops must take no part in arresting people because of their political affiliations, they have no authority to arrest and confine citizens unless they commit some illegal act. I cannot hold in confinement a Russian citizen because he has taken part in some meeting."[512]

For nearly seven months following this announcement relative peace reigned. The miners worked without incident. By mid-1919 the Bolsheviks had succeeded in infiltrating the work force and had begun a series of strikes that substantially lowered coal production in the Suchan sector. In the spring of 1919 miners and peasants in the Suchan Mining District were objecting to the continued mining of coal there. The coal was vital to maintaining the railroads, and the railroad was being used to support the Omsk government. Rumors circulated that the miners would quit and the partisans in the area might attack the Americans stationed there to destroy the mines. The feelings against the mines became increasingly severe when an impressment expedition of White Army officers swept through the area drafting peasants to serve in Kolchak's Army. Many young men of draft age fled, and in retaliation the impressment gang tortured and killed their fathers.

General Graves warned the Kolchak authorities that if any more of these expeditions entered the mining district, he would withdraw American troops and no longer protect the Suchan Mines. The White forces agreed that they would send no more expeditions to the vicinity of the mines.

A group of officers from the impressment expedition was besieged by irate peasants at Vladimir-Alexandrovskoya—near the mouth of the Suchan River on Amerika Bay. In April, the White Army sent an expedition ostensibly to rescue them, but in fact they launched a punitive expedition up the Suchan Valley and were fighting partisans and peasants at the town of Pirytin.[513]

Graves sent Lieutenant Colonel Robert Eichelberger to investigate conditions at the Suchan Mines. While on his way to visit the nearby partisan headquarters, to determine their attitude toward American troops, he encountered a stream of refugees from a nearby village. The villagers reported that the town of Pirytin had been destroyed by shelling and that Novitskaya would soon follow. Novitskaya was on mine property and under American jurisdiction. Eichelberger sent a message to the mine commander, Colonel Pendleton, to send forces to protect the village.

Eichelberger and another officer went into the village, walking through the battle in search of the partisan leaders. They finally ended up in a school house drinking tea with the teacher while the building was raked by machine gun fire. The partisan leader never appeared, but a patrol of Kolchak troops from the British-run officers training school on Russian Island did. Eichelberger and his companion were arrested. "We were insulted by both officers and soldiers," Eichelberger reported. "We were called 'Bolsheviki' and the attitude of a large part of them apparently was to shoot us at sight." Eichelberger had a very uneasy night in which he was given every opportunity to escape. He declined to attempt this as he was certain his captors merely wanted this excuse to kill him.[514]

Meanwhile, Lieutenant Rumans, Eichelberger's interpreter who had been left behind at Novitskaya, grew alarmed when Eichelberger did not return. Rumans sought help from the partisan forces. He had an unarmed partisan drive a droshky flying an American flag down the road toward Pyratin to find the missing officers. The droshky returned shortly; the dashboard was shot away and the driver lay across the seat, shot twice by Kolchak troops. Rumans sent the driver to the American hospital at Suchan, with a report for Colonel Pendleton, but he received no reply.

At 9:30 P.M. a partisan general told Rumans that Eichelberger and Winnigstad were being held prisoner at Pirytin and would surely be killed. The general offered to raid the village and release them. Rumans declined his offer but decided he would try to rescue Eichelberger and Winnigstad himself. He took five partisans with him to distract the Kolchak forces. Rumans planned to sneak into the village and release the Americans. Before he could reach the village, however, his group was ambushed and two of the partisans were wounded. When Rumans returned to Novitskaya he found the town full of partisans, who had orders from their commander to hold it for the Americans. As the town was on mine property, Rumans asked them to leave and they did. He reported his impression later that "they showed every evidence of being well disciplined. They occupied no rooms that were normally occupied by the villagers, and they accepted no food nor tea from the inhabitants, although it was offered. They conducted themselves in a quiet and peaceful manner." This behavior was a marked contrast to the practices of the White forces. As he left, the partisan commander told Rumans that he expected Kolchak's forces to attack Novitskaya at dawn and assured Rumans that if American troops failed to arrive or did not arrive in sufficient numbers, the partisan forces would be at his disposal.[515] The next morning Colonel Rubets, who was in charge of the White forces, authorized the release of the Americans, and Eichelberger and Winnigstad walked back to Novitskaya. Since the White forces had already killed some villagers and set fire to a building, Eichelberger believed his presence at Pirytin prevented the destruction of the town. The peasants also believed it, so they were very grateful to Eichelberger. The significance of this incident as Eichelberger perceived it was not just the intention of Kolchak troops to attack the mine property, but the fact that these were not renegade Cossack bands, rather British backed and equipped forces.[516]

The actions of the White Army did nothing to convince the American headquarters of the need to take the field against the "Bolsheviks." Eichelberger, head of the Intelligence Section, and the person on whom Graves relied most heavily for information, believed firmly that most of the partisan groups were not truly Bolsheviks. "All the Allied forces here except the Americans are out against the so-called Bolsheviki," Eichelberger wrote, even before visiting the mines. "The particular band of Bolsheviki here are almost all simple peasants who have been stirred up by the murderous actions of the punitive expeditions sent out from Vladivostok. It is quite a victory for one of our allies, to get the other allies to assist them in burning a few villages and killing some peasants."[517]

Eichelberger saw nothing at Pirytin to alter his conclusion. After his release he returned to Vladivostok to report to General Graves. The general was furious that Colonel Pendleton had made no effort to rescue Eichelberger. Eichelberger wrote later to his wife that Graves said little, other than to tell him that he would have Pendleton relieved and sent back to the United States. Graves also ordered Pendleton to leave the peasants, who were wounded trying to rescue Eichelberger, in the

American hospital; apparently Pendleton had tried to remove them. General Graves also remarked that in "Pendleton's place he would have thrown a company into Novitskaya and had American patrols all the way down the road to Pyratin."[518] Graves expected his officers to remain neutral in Russian internal disputes, but not inactive when their fellow countrymen were attacked.

Graves then took up the matter of the White Russian presence in the Suchan District. He wrote Ivanov-Rinov demanding to know why the troops were in Pyratin and by whose orders. He asked "if Eichelberger and Winnigstad were threatened and insulted because they were American officers."[519] Graves also considered, and may have issued, an order for the arrest of Colonel Rubets or his chief of staff (the men who arrested Eichelberger) if they entered the American sector.[520]

Lieutenant Colonel Eichelberger came to admire Graves greatly, especially his implacability in the face of the many pressures he felt.[521] Nearly thirty years later General Eichelberger, who by then had served with many of America's most famous commanders, wrote of Graves, "He was a man whom I admired extravagantly and his character made a very definite impression upon me—probably more so than any officer with whom I have served."[522]

Once Eichelberger reported to Graves, he returned to the Suchan sector and followed the White retreat down the valley. He found that Kolchak forces had killed peasants and burned villages on their return trip before evacuating Vladimir-Alexandrovskoya. Eichelberger and Captain William McChapman, aide to General Graves, found the partisans in charge of the town. Eichelberger spent two days trying to convince them not to attack the Allied guard at Suchan. The partisans were outraged by the fact that peasants had been tortured to death in the town during the White occupation. Eichelberger exhumed the bodies and took photographs. They showed men who had been kept alive for days and burned with red hot irons.[523]

From April through June 1919, relations between the peasantry and the mine guards became increasingly tense.[524] Throughout this period Graves reported frequently to Ambassador Morris. Before the Suchan incident, describing the diplomatic tightrope he was walking, he complained that there was a constant effort by the English, French, and Japanese to pull him into the Kolchak camp and force him to take "some action which will nullify what I have done heretofore. They tell me that Russians have no use for Americans and it is because I am helping the Bolsheviks. They claim my help consists in doing nothing, which enables the Bolsheviks to say to the peasants that Americans are with them and in this way the peasants are joining the Bolsheviks." He concluded it "seems peculiar reasoning to me, but I am still skating along on thin ice and have not broken through yet."[525]

He also warned Morris of impending difficulties with the peasantry. "Undoubtedly, the peasants will not submit to draft for service in the Kolchak Army. Representatives of the peasants have been to me and stated frankly that they would not support any government that did not permit them to vote and while Kolchak professed to be in favor of the peasants exercising the right of suffrage his every act indicated that he was not, and they cited as examples his treatment of the Zemstvos and Cooperatives." The peasants assured Graves that they would not interfere with the railroads or the mines.[526]

Within a fortnight things had changed. Graves reported to Morris that the situation was getting worse. The peasants were leaving their villages to form organizations opposed to the Omsk government. Many of these were undoubtedly under some measure of Bolshevik influence. Graves was also concerned the Japanese had just agreed to give Ivanov-Rinov money and arms to equip 2,000 more Cossacks, and he feared they would cause further trouble for US troops. Graves also charged Japanese General Inakagi with spreading deliberate lies against the American forces.

In light of the Eichelberger incident, Graves told Morris, "the Cossacks have recently become very insulting to Americans and it is sure to bring on a conflict with them very soon." He had told Ivanoff-Rinoff and Horvat that he would consider their troops' actions an act against the uniform of the United States, and that he would no longer tolerate it. "I have also told the commanding officers," continued the General, "to try to avoid a quarrel with the Cossacks but to maintain the dignity of the uniform of the United States and if necessary to use force for this purpose."

Graves also informed Morris of a report that 4 million rubles had been allocated for anti-American propaganda in England, France, Japan, and the United States. The object of the propaganda, Graves believed, was to secure his own removal. "They seem convinced that I am responsible for the United States' policy. These men also state that they expect to attack me on the streets some day when the opportunity presents itself with the idea of telegraphing to the world that I am personally so obnoxious to the Russians that I cannot go out of my office without being attacked. I personally do not think they have the sand to do it."[527] By the end of April, Graves could see the various Russian and Allied factions arraying themselves against him. Starting in May he would begin to feel pressure from the Bolsheviks.

General Graves was concerned about the Bolshevik activity, but he was also deeply troubled by the White response to it. On 25 May 1919, General Sergei Rozanov, Kolchak's governor in Yenisei and Irkutsk, published a declaration stating that the gravity of Bolshevik interference with the railway compelled him "to abandon those general moral principles which are applied in relation to the enemy in war. The prisons are full of the chiefs of these murderers." Therefore, he ordered his subordinates "to regard the Bolsheviks and bandits who are kept in prison as hostages," and for each crime committed they were to "shoot from three to twenty local hostages."[528]

The prospect of these reprisals appalled Graves, especially as the "crimes" of many of these prisoners were dubious anyway. But under the provisions of the aide memoire, Graves was limited to protesting these measures on humanitarian grounds, and he was unable to intervene to stop them outside American sectors.

In Graves's own area of jurisdiction the aide memoire also limited his available courses of action in coping with the partisans. Ultimately Graves decided that American troops could and would be used to protect not only the railroads, but also the towns along the railway and their inhabitants, from destruction.[529] This was not a new policy. It was merely an extension of the one already in effect regarding Cossack pillaging to include Bolshevik partisans.

In the wake of Eichelberger's adventures at the mines, Graves believed that the White Army initiated at least some of the trouble there. "The Koltchak Government has practically thrown down the gauntlet to me," he told Roland Morris in a letter dated 7 May, "and has practically said they would not let United States soldiers perform their duty on the railway unless we came in wholeheartedly against Bolshevism." This obstructive attitude apparently extended to the operation of the Suchan Mines as well. Ivanov-Rinov, Graves wrote, was trying to starve the entire area, mines and all; empty stomachs were about to produce a labor strike. If the mines shut down, the Whites would use the fact as propaganda about American ineffectiveness. As for the White atrocities, Graves forwarded Eichelberger's reports and photographs. "Every time I try to get evidence they counter with a tirade of abuse about Americans favoring Bolshevism," he fumed. Half a world away, Wilson was considering recognition of Kolchak's government: Graves's perspective was very different. Although the AEF's refusal to support Kolchak threatened his government, if the US recognized it other complications would arise. "United States troops can never take part in such atrocities as those being committed by Kolchak and Japanese troops," he advised Morris.[530]

Regardless of the role they might have had in provoking the strike, White commanders at Vladivostok were incensed and wanted to put an end to the unrest by typically ruthless means. Graves, still the appointed commander of the district, forbade any military action against the strikers except in cases of criminal activity. A strike, he pointed out to his White counterparts, might be inconvenient and disruptive, but it was scarcely a crime. This observation convinced no one and only served to direct at General Graves a stream of protest and abuse by the Allies, the Omsk government, and officials of the State Department.

On 17 May, Graves reported to the War Department that Ivanov-Rinov had been removed as head of the White Army in Eastern Siberia, possibly to placate the United States while the Council of Four was considering support for Kolchak. In Graves's opinion Ivanov-Rinov's recall was window dressing. His replacement, Chreschatitsky, Graves reported, had been "the Japanese paymaster and is a man with no more principle that Ivanoff-Rinoff, but not such a forceful character and will not cause quite so much trouble in the East. He is undoubtedly a grafter and will take anything he can get from any source." Some time before, Chreschatitsky had sent a member of his staff to AEF headquarters to say that the abuse of the US in the local papers could be stopped. The key was food or bribery. "The United States ought to furnish supplies for their soldiers," Graves reported him as saying, "but if we did not see fit to do so that twenty to twenty-five thousand dollars per month would be satisfactory to them."

Graves also reported that the American Red Cross had taken the side of the White forces in the Civil War and was supplying them exclusively, and that this made his position more difficult. While the Red Cross was not a government agency, Dr. Teusler's attitude made it harder to convince the White commander and Allies that America's policy was really one of non-interference.

The White commanders, Graves felt, would use any means at hand to push the US into the anti-Bolshevik fold. He also believed that the great majority of the Whites were absolutely opposed to any form of democratic government in Siberia. Graves said that what information he could gather led him to conclude that Admiral Kolchak might be sincere in his promises to institute democratic reform. Nevertheless, he warned, Kolchak was very different from most of the men who surrounded him, which made predicting the course of his government difficult.[531]

While Graves was informing Morris and the War Department of these new wrinkles, the strike at Suchan continued. Partisans now occupied many of the surrounding towns. White punitive expeditions into the area did nothing but produce new recruits for the partisans. On 22 May 1919, Suchan miners proclaimed a general strike in the Maritime Province. The next day Triapitsyn, the Bolshevik leader in that area, threatened to use force to remove Allied and American troops from the district.

Tension mounted. Army intelligence reports estimated that 2000 Red partisans were in the area. The American forces at Suchan, along with the few Japanese and Chinese troops there, totaled only about 300.[532] An uneasy interval passed during which coal production dwindled and skirmishes with the Bolsheviks attacking the railroad in the American sector became more frequent. On 22 June, fighting broke out between US troops and Bolshevik partisans as the result of the kidnapping of five American soldiers while they were fishing. Fighting also began between the two groups at dusk in the village of Novitskaya, when an American detachment was ambushed. When the skirmish ended, five Americans and several more Bolsheviks had been killed, and the American hostages had been spirited away to the nearby village of Frolovka. In the meantime, Colonel G. H. Williams, the commander of the Allied mine guard, was negotiating with the Bolsheviks to exchange the Americans for three partisans.[533] Colonel Eichelberger undertook the actual exchange of prisoners with the same partisan commander who had offered to rescue him in April from the White officers.[534]

General Graves decided to act. He informed Ambassador Morris that he was sending reinforcements to clear the area that surrounded the mines.[535] But the engagement at Novitskaya and its aftermath were soon overshadowed by events that took place at Romanovka two days later. At dawn on 25 June, bands of partisans from the villages of Petrovk and Novo Rosskaya attacked a small detachment of Company A of the 31st Infantry, which was guarding the railroad at Romanovka. The partisans' objectives were: to capture the town, organize its Red sympathizers, destroy the American contingent, and seize its arms and supplies.[536]

The American camp at Romanovka, unfortunately, was in an extremely vulnerable position. It stood beneath a 60-feet-high bank created when a spur of hills had been cut away to build the railroad. This bank was completely barren, but a thick stand of scrub forest concealed the top. The railroad ran along the foot of the bank, with the American camp directly opposite.

To compensate for this unfortunate position, the Americans had built a small redoubt on a hill a short distance from the edge of the bank. Each night several men occupied the redoubt, under orders to stay there to guard the camp until morning. A misunderstanding emerged over what constituted morning. In June at that latitude the sun rose about 4:00 A.M.—long before reveille. This was the time when the men returned to camp. The Bolsheviks, therefore, planned to begin their attack shortly after 4:00 A.M. As dawn approached, the partisans waited until the men left the outpost and allowed them time to get to bed. When everyone in the camp except the cook and the internal guard were asleep, the attack began, the Bolsheviks firing on the camp below.

The Americans suffered heavy casualties in the first few minutes. Those soldiers still able ran into the log houses of the village and conducted their defense of the town from there. A messenger was dispatched to summon help from Company E at Oovo Nezhino, some six or eight miles from Romanovka. About three miles from Romanovka the messenger intercepted a train. The American soldiers on board reversed the train to Novo-Nezhino, where half of Company E was assembled and sent to Romanovka. The battle had been going on for four hours when the reinforcements arrived. Of the seventy-six Americans stationed at Romanovka, twenty-six were dead and twenty-five wounded.[537] Other attacks soon followed. The next morning Novo-Nezhino itself was assaulted. But this time the Americans were prepared: only two US soldiers were wounded, and more than twenty Bolsheviks were killed.

General Graves, outraged by these attacks, gave orders for US troops "to proceed with force and vigor" to rid the Suchan area of the Bolshevik partisans.[538] But the campaign to suppress the insurgents proved more difficult than was initially anticipated. The partisans had severed all communications in the Suchan area and destroyed the railway line. Trains from Vladivostok could not resupply the American units that were now converging on Suchan Mine Number 1. Colonel G. W. Williams had been given the command of the operation and, unable to obtain help from the Army, he turned to the Navy. By 1 July, the crew of the cruiser USS *Albany*, with help from British and Russian merchant marines, construct-ed a wharf in Amerika Bay, about 20 miles from Suchan. There they unloaded food, ammunition, pack mules, horses, and 37-millimeter can-non, and transported them overland to the Suchan area.

The American campaign plan was three-pronged. On 2 July, Company C of the 31st Infantry, under the command of General Graves's son, Major Sidney Graves, began the attack from Suchan by swinging west-ward and then moving in an arc to the northeast. Colonel Williams, with Company M and a detachment of Japanese soldiers, left two days later, moving in a counterclockwise direction to form a pincer movement. On 5 July, Colonel Eichelberger headed north to attack the Bolsheviks head-on. Their objective was to drive every Bolshevik and partisan out of the area.

The campaign unfolded in extremely messy conditions. Rain soaked the ground and left the roads a sea of mud. Progress was steady but slow. Each encounter followed the same pattern. The American forces would envel-op a village and the partisans would retreat to the surrounding countryside. Town after town was occupied. Novitskaya, Godryevka, Movrosia, Olga, and Tethune were taken and then garrisoned by sailors and marines from the *Albany* and a second cruiser, the USS *New Orleans*. By 7 August, the partisans had completely withdrawn from the sector.539

In a limited military sense, the campaign was a success. The Suchan District was no longer at the mercy of saboteurs. The mines were restored to American control, and production resumed. The railroad was now secure, but the partisans had destroyed much of the track before retreat-ing. It took months to repair the damage.

The damage to American prestige, however, was even greater. Technically the Americans had in no way violated their neutral policy. Partisans had kidnapped and ambushed American soldiers. The railway, which they were to protect, had been repeatedly attacked. Clearly the Americans were acting in self-defense and within the limits of the Inter-

Allied Railway Agreement, not in any politically motivated campaign. Nevertheless, the tacit understanding between the Bolsheviks and US forces that had prevented armed conflict hitherto had been destroyed. The fact that the American forces had had the assistance of Japanese troops and British and White Russian merchantmen helped to obscure the line that had kept the United States aloof from the Allied policy of support for the Omsk government. It also led to an increase in anti-American sentiment and propaganda by the Bolsheviks.[540]

The Ussuri campaign also disillusioned many American soldiers who previously had sympathized with the partisans' plight. Lieutenant John W. Blue, the commander of the headquarters company of the 31st Infantry, writing to his sister in the summer of 1919, displayed some of the first strong anti-Bolshevik sentiment. "The Bolsheviks are very quiet just now on this front. I certainly hope they will soon be stamped out all over Russia, they have just about completely ruined this poor country as it is, the things they have done over here are far worse than the things the Germans did in France and Belgium, and that is saying a lot, nothing is too horrible or cruel for them to do."[541]

The Americans soldiers were now thoroughly fed up with all Russian factions. They were fully aware that while they held the Suchan sector for the present, it would quickly revert to a state of chaos if they left it. Intelligence reports estimated that at least five hundred Bolshevik partisans had been killed in the Suchan campaign. But even though partisan casualties were much higher than those of the American forces, the War Department was not sanguine about the results. General Tasker Bliss wrote to Secretary Baker, stating his opinion that killing Bolsheviks was not a solution to the Russian problem. "The trouble is that we are trying to kill Bolsheviks and not Bolshevism. The latter can be killed but not by force of arms...most thinking men have come to the conclusion that a way must and can be found to combat Bolshevism otherwise than by armies." He then added, "I am sorry to see statements in the American press that our government has decided to lend aid to the Kolchak

Government. The real trouble in Russia will begin after the Kolchak Government wins out."[542]

The battles were not all on the military front. Diplomatic skirmishes abounded. The Ussuri campaign raised Allied hopes that Graves might abandon his strict interpretation and support Kolchak. Wilson hoped that Graves's and Morris's trip to Omsk might settle matters between the War and State Departments. The Omsk government, its supporters in the State Department, and the British delegation had been vehement in their protests that Graves's information on Siberia was inaccurate because he had remained in the Far East and had no conception of conditions west of Irkutsk. But Graves had dozens of intelligence officers reporting to him from Western Siberia.[543]

The primary objects of the visit was to form an opinion of Kolchak's viability and to assess his worthiness as a recipient of American aid. On the journey to Omsk, both Graves and Morris sent their interpreters out at each station to conduct discreet interviews with the people there. "You and I have been much criticized because of our attitude toward the Kolchak regime," Morris remarked to Graves at the end of their trip. "It has been repeatedly said we have a Far Eastern orientation and that if we would come West, we would find an entirely different situation after we left Irkutsk." But during their journey, he observed, "we have not found a single individual who spoke a good word for the Kolchak regime."[544] The comment goes far to show the Kolchak government's unpopularity, since those who were most opposed to Kolchak dared not come any where near a railway station.

The outlook was not promising for Kolchak. By the end of June 1919, even Harris was concerned. He reported to Polk that the situation on both the Ufa and Perm fronts was critical.[545] On 3 July, after the city of Perm fell to the advancing Bolsheviks, a series of unpleasant scenes followed. Gajda, who commanded the front and who was very unpopular with the White generals, demanded that the White terror come to an end. Kolchak claimed that he had no control over White atrocities. Gajda also exposed extensive bribery and corruption. He wanted Kolchak to cashier a number of officers to achieve some level of efficiency in the chain of command. Instead, Kolchak fired Gajda.

The basis of Kolchak and Gajda's final disagreement was Gajda's demand that Kolchak withdraw his Northern Army to Omsk and prepare to defend the city. Gajda informed Kolchak that it was high time he put Siberia in some sort of acceptable order. He needed to establish a decent land policy and a republican form of government with civil and criminal courts to try the political riffraff. In the course of the interview, Kolchak threw an inkwell at Gajda and broke several pens. "What can I expect of you?" Kolchak shouted at Gajda. "You have no military education!" "And you," Gajda sneered, "you commanded three ships in the Black Sea. Does that qualify you to govern an empire?" There was nothing to say to this. Amateurs were definitely running this war.[546]

Gajda, stripped of his command, now began a dangerous journey eastward. Kolchak replaced him with General Milo K. Dietrichs, who told him that the White Army had received a fatal series of blows at Ufa, Perm, Tobol, and Ekaterinburg. He explained to Kolchak that the only hope the Whites had was to withdraw to Omsk. Dietrichs believed that the only way to gain support was to portray their struggle as a holy war against atheistic communism. Kolchak refused to entertain either suggestion.

The United States had agreed to supply Kolchak just as his cause was losing whatever chance of success it might have had. By mid-July Harris was reporting a string of mutinies, courts-martial, and executions in the White Army.[547] The strongest criticism of the Omsk regime came from Ambassador Morris. He painted a depressing picture of the situation at Omsk. The situation there was "extremely critical" and Kolchak's Army was completely demoralized. Morris felt this situation was sufficiently dangerous to order the evacuation of the American Red Cross nurses.[548] He had expected to find either pro-Kolchak or at least anti-Bolshevik sentiments in Omsk, but instead he found that "the Kolchak government has failed to command the confidence of anybody in Siberia except a small discredited group of reactionaries, Monarchists, and former military officials…. [T]he withdrawal of the Czechs," he concluded, along with every-one else, "would be a signal for a formidable anti-Kolchak if not pro-Bolshevik uprising in every town on the railway from Irkutsk to Omsk."

Morris believed that several factors lay behind Kolchak's lack of support. First was the distrust of the Cossack atamans representing him in eastern Siberia. Second was the inability of his military and civil officials to comprehend changing popular sentiments in the wake of the war and the revolution. A third factor was the lack of any constructive program to solve the serious financial and economic problems of the region. Instead, Morris heard of widespread corruption. Still another element was resent-ment against conscription efforts that took boys from the towns and villages, placed them under "inefficient and criminal officers, and led them, untrained, unequipped and ill-fed, to mutilation and death at the front." Finally, the Kolchak government had acted to suppress all attempts at local self-government in the larger cities and towns.[549]

Despite Morris's reports confirming Graves's estimate of the situation, the gulf between the policy of the War Department and the desires of the State Department continued to widen. Ambassador Morris and General Graves had maintained a harmonious relationship up to this point. Soon after their July arrival, however, Morris received a telegram from the State Department that probably informed him of the Council of Four's decision to support the Omsk government. After reading it he turned to Graves and said, "Now, General, you will have to support Kolchak."

Graves answered that he had received no orders from the War Department to support Kolchak. "The State Department is running this, not the War Department," Morris replied with some asperity. "The State Department is not running me," Graves retorted. The general clung to his neutrality. Wilson had assured the Senate that Graves would be neutral, and neutral he intended to remain, until his superiors told him other-wise.[550]

The disagreement was nearly academic by now, for the situation in Siberia was degenerating. In August, Graves reported to the War

Department that Kolchak's forces were so demoralized that any hope of reforming his army and renewing the offensive rested not on Kolchak's strength, but on Bolshevik weakness and a lack of desire to take Omsk, a circumstance, Graves noted ominously, "which I cannot assume to be the case."[551] General Gajda seconded Graves's opinion. After arriving in Vladivostok on 8 August, he announced that the Kolchak government could not last. "If the Allies support him," Gajda warned, "they will make the greatest mistake in history." He also stated that the Omsk government's promises of a liberal reform were insincere and designed for foreign consumption.[552] By 16 August, American headquarters was reporting that Gajda and the representatives of the Eastern Siberian Zemstvos in Vladivostok were planning a coup d'état to overthrow Kolchak with the intention of establishing a representative government.[553]

On 8 August, Morris reported that the United States and the Supreme Council in Paris should consider two questions before deciding to continue their policy of "sympathy and assistance to Kolchak." First, he asked, "Is the Kolchak government, as it now exists, sufficiently strong to rescue Russia from the grip of Bolshevikism?" Morris then answered his own question, saying that in his opinion it was not and no amount of Allied support in its present state could make it so. The government was corrupt and bankrupt of popular support, and unwilling even to attempt the steps necessary to remedy the situation.[554]

The second question Morris posed was this: "Would it be possible with the assistance of the Allies to affect changes in personnel and methods?" The answer he gave was equivocal at best. "The Kolchak government might," he said, "with the exercise of tact and judgement and above all patience, be shaped into an instrument with which to combat Bolshevism. But," he cautioned, "it would be a long and at times a most discouraging task. For the moment we can only await the outcome of the present crisis. Should the Government survive," he emphasized for good measure, "it can continue only provided it receives immediate help from the Allies."[555]

Stevens was even more pessimistic. "Unless a miracle occurs," he told Lansing flatly, "before winter the Reds will have control as far as Irkutsk if they want to." The only hope he saw lay in the deployment of a strong Allied army exclusive of the Japanese. Otherwise he feared that the "Reds and Japanese will divide Siberia and northern Manchuria and the Baikal." He seemed to understand the remote chance for American reinforcements, and he advised Lansing not to push for any. "None of us can stay here very long," he said. "I think if the real Allies want to keep the Chinese Eastern out of Japanese hands they must strike quickly and decisively."[556]

On the strength of Morris's appeal and a similar one by Clemenceau, Wilson considered sending additional troops to Siberia. He was deterred, however, by the pessimistic reports he received from an assortment of sources as well as his own reluctance to expand the American commitment in Russia which could easily lead to war. In early August, Wilson stated "with the utmost regret" that the United States would be unable to furnish additional American troops to replace the Czechs.[557]

Once again Wilson had refused to take the final step that would lead the United States into war. Nevertheless, the pleas for aid to Kolchak continued. Morris, failing to realize that the tide had now turned in Washington as well as in Omsk, wrote to Lansing in mid-August. Obviously, Morris argued, it was risky to aid the Kolchak government in the "hour of discouragement and defeat" but "if by our timely and active service Kolchak should survive, we should be in a pre-eminent position to assist and even to lead in the reconstruction of Russia, to maintain the 'open door' now in imminent peril of being closed, and to preserve the integrity of Siberia."[558]

Morris's recommendations did not fall on receptive ears. Lansing cabled him on 25 August that the State Department would not recognize Kolchak because it could not give him the amount of support Morris believed necessary to keep him in power, let alone to ensure his success. The United States was not able to assist Kolchak with credits for military supplies unless he was a recognized co-belligerent against the Central Powers. As Kolchak had not come to power until a week after the armistice, he could not meet that criterion. Therefore, unless Congress made specific allocation for that purpose, which it would not do, Kolchak could not receive commercial credits. The State Department could expect no action from Congress until after the ratification of the peace treaty. The only aid Kolchak could expect was a shipment of rifles, increased contracts for goods from Siberian co-operatives, and fifty million dollars in private loans from British and American banks. Wilson was discussing an assistance plan to help build up the Siberian social and economic structure, but was apparently not considering military aid.[559] None of this was enough to shore up Kolchak's declining fortunes.

In view of these unfavorable reports, the War Department once again began to press for the withdrawal of the Americans from Siberia. Graves maintained that Kolchak's cause was hopeless, and that the Railway Service Corps could no longer do any good under the circumstances.[560] Baker was not only concerned about withdrawing the troops; he was also anxious that it should be done as discreetly as possible and under the stipulations of the aide memoire. He wanted the troops to be withdrawn "to the last man" before anything was said that might cause the Japanese to prevent the American withdrawal. Explanations and recriminations could wait until the AEF was clear of the Japanese grasp.[561]

Relations between the American and Japanese forces were severely strained. There were a number of incidents involving the Japanese and more clashes between American troops and Japanese-sponsored Cossacks. In early September an American Army captain and an enlisted man were arrested by Cossacks in Iman in front of Japanese troops for not having proper passports. It was a completely spurious offense as no serviceman was required to have a passport. Graves sent Colonel Robinson to General Rozanov to demand their return. Rozanov refused. In the interval, American troops were sent to Iman to secure the release of the corporal, the captain having already been freed. When they arrived, a Japanese officer told them they would not allow the Americans to attack the Cossacks, and that if they did, the Japanese would join the Cossacks against the Americans. The American officer in charge, Major Shamatoulski, told the commander he was going to rescue the corporal and the Japanese could resist at their own risk. The Japanese evidently thought better of it, for no fighting ensued. The major took three Cossack hostages, only to find that the corporal was no longer in Iman. When the soldier was later exchanged for the hostages, it was discovered that he had been "beaten unmercifully." Graves believed that the Japanese had contrived the whole incident to bring the Americans and Cossacks to blows, in the hope that open war between the two groups would cause an American withdrawal, leaving Japan in charge of eastern Siberia.[562]

General Graves began receiving independent confirmation of Japanese duplicity and news of a plot to attack American soldiers. General Dmitrii Leonidovich Horvat, a Kolchak supporter who had opposed Graves's non-interference policy, came to American Expeditionary Forces headquarters and warned Graves that Kalmikov was planning to attack American soldiers. He advised Graves to concentrate American detachments at once. He reported that the Japanese had sanctioned and financed the operation. Horvat's warning was later confirmed by Colonel Butenko, fortress commander at Vladivostok, who had access to all telegraphic messages coming through the city. He told Graves that Semenov had cabled Kalmikov to go ahead and attack the Americans, and to let him know if he needed any help. The Japanese had also informed Kalmikov that they could not give him active assistance but only moral support. Shortly after this, Kolchak's foreign minister told Major Slaughter in Omsk that the Americans did not have enough men in the Far East to meet the emergency that would arise if they had any trouble with Semenov and Kalmikov, because the Japanese had arranged to support Semenov in every way—with troops if necessary.[563]

As a result of these warnings, all American posts were put on alert on 12 September and given orders that "if any organized effort against Americans is made by these Cossacks, use your entire force to destroy or capture every Cossack in uniform within the limits of your sector." Lieutenant Sylvain Kindall wrote that shortly after the warning from Vladivostok another message followed with instructions "to abandon all stations along our sector as quickly and secretly as possible, and to concentrate our troops at Spasskoe. Apparently," he remarked, "the situation was graver than we first supposed."[564]

Graves seems to have taken Horvat's advice. The concentration of American troops was evidently sufficient to avert the immediate danger. Within a few weeks the troops were redeployed. Graves described the situation to Albert Galen, one of his former officers, even though he told Galen that "the situation is so critical over here that it is a very dangerous thing to communicate my views in a letter to anyone." The letter was a summation of everything that had happened during his stay in Siberia, and where it was all leading. He described the death-throes of a government and the dying influence of American efforts. He called Kolchak's lieutenants "the worst scoundrels in the world"; Kolchak was powerless over Kalmikov, Seminov, and Ivanov-Rinov, he wrote, and Kolchak knew it. "Notwithstanding this fact," he continued, "Kolchak gives them additional rank and additional responsibility, with the hope that he will be able to buy them. There is, of course, no chance to buy such men as they are. It enables them, however, to do just exactly as they please and claim that they are supporting the government and shedding their blood for the 'mother-land.'"[565]

Graves said he found the Railway Service Corps, except for Stevens, "absolutely disgusted." He told Galen "they know they have absolutely no authority over the railroad." Graves believed that Stevens was so anxious to make the railroad a success that he dismissed any disagreeable reports of conditions as mere pessimism. Concerning potential conflict with the Cossacks, Graves thought it was largely dependent upon the Japanese. Their objective, to Graves, was clear, "the establishment of a government in Eastern Siberia under the dictatorship of Seminof. They have also demanded from Kolchak that Kalmickoff be given the same rights that Seminof has in granting concessions. They have poor old Kolchak where they can demand anything and he consents to their demands." Japan's attitude towards the Americans was equally clear to Graves. "They want Americans out of Siberia before Seminof establishes his dictatorship. As I see it," he explained, "the United States has been a party to getting Japan in here and they must get Japan out if we withdraw, otherwise we have been a party to giving Japan Eastern Siberia and have done an incalculable harm to the Russians."[566]

As things turned out, Graves's post-mortem was somewhat premature: The AEF's stay was not quite over. A new crisis erupted when he refused to deliver 100,000 rifles that Kolchak had ordered because he feared they would fall into the hands of the Cossacks and be used against the AEF. Apart from being an irresponsible act, Graves claimed that it would be "helping to arm the worst criminals in Siberia."[567] Morris supported Graves in his decision. The Omsk government, however, claimed that it needed the rifles desperately, and that it was unable to control the Cossacks. After urgent appeals from the State Department and British representatives, and with the consent of the War Department, Graves agreed to deliver the rifles—directly to the Omsk government outside the Cossack zone.[568]

The first trainload of rifles and ammunition went through to Irkutsk without mishap. Trouble began when the second train reached Chita on 24 October. Semenov stopped the train and demanded 15,000 rifles. Lieutenant Ryan, who was in charge of the fifty men guarding the train, refused to turn them over without orders from Vladivostok. Semenov threatened to take the rifles, if they were not surrendered to him in thirty hours. He followed up this threat by surrounding the train with two armored cars and a battalion of Cossacks. Ryan telegraphed General Graves for instructions and was told not to give Semenov a single rifle. Graves was reasonably confident that the Japanese would not permit the Cossacks to attack the train in the Japanese sector. His estimate of the situation was accurate; after forty hours Semenov let Ryan leave with the rifles.[569]

As the Omsk government declined and chaos spread throughout Siberia, many of the reasons for American involvement disappeared. August Heid, the representative of the War Trade Board in Vladivostok, reported that he believed his work was finished. The economic, military, and political situation was too unsettled to attempt any further economic relief in Siberia.[570]

While Heid was washing his hands of aid for Siberia, Consul General Harris was still pressing for at least de facto recognition of Kolchak. Harris wanted Wilson to write to Kolchak expressing his confidence in his motives and methods. Harris reported that the Siberian Army was making progress and that Omsk was secure.[571] His report directly contradicted Major Slaughter's, which had reported a high desertion rate and low morale. Polk was disturbed by this conflict, and he ordered Harris to confer with Slaughter so the two could come to some agreement.[572] Harris's reports also disagreed with those of Morris, who had become increasingly pessimistic about the situation, since Kolchak had agreed to recognize Semenov and Kalmikov officially. Morris painted a grim picture. "As it is impossible for our agencies to cooperate with these Atamans," he explained, "we now find ourselves in disagreement not only with the Japanese policy but also with the official representatives of the Kolchak government in Eastern Siberia. We thus have the doubly anomalous situation that the Czechs by their presence are responsible for the continued existence of the Government against which they are now intriguing." Furthermore, he added, "we are endeavoring to find a means of Cooperation with a Government many of whose representatives are openly hostile."[573]

The position of the Americans at Vladivostok worsened when Kolchak appointed General Sergei N. Rozanov to succeed General Horvat as his representative in the Far East. Rozanov was already well-known for his anti-American views. He brought 4,000 Cossacks into the city. Kalmikov and his men were allowed to roam the city at will. Shortly after their arrival, Russian officers murdered an American and a Czech soldier. The Allied military representatives, with the exception of the Japanese, demanded Rozanov's recall, and threatened to force him out of the city if he did not leave by noon on 29 September.[574] The Omsk government refused to comply, claiming that the Allies had no extraterritorial rights in Vladivostok. It did promise, however, to investigate the crimes. In an extraordinary report, the Omsk government blamed the incident on General Graves, "whose conduct recently has become entirely incomprehensible to Omsk." The report warned that "his remaining at Vladivostok will lead to perpetual misunderstanding and the growing of public discontent with Americans."[575]

Afterwards the Cossack and Japanese threats increased; both army and naval reports indicated that Kalmikov, Semenov, and Rozanov were plotting to attack the American detachments.[576] In Washington, Baker was now firmly convinced that the United States should either send a large force to Siberia or withdraw completely.[577]

Despite the rising tide of contrary sentiment, Harris continued to urge that Kolchak be formally recognized and given increased aid. Even Polk was in favor of recognizing the Omsk government. All decisions on Siberia were in abeyance, however, because of Wilson's illness.[578] Lansing, too, was alarmed, and he called a cabinet meeting. Wilson was still incapable of handling the situation following his stroke. Lansing felt that some action was necessary, and he suggested that the vice president, Thomas R. Marshall, should take charge of the government. Dr. Grayson appeared before the cabinet, saying that Wilson was better, but that "no business should come before him now." His condition was improving but "we are not out of the woods." He said Wilson wanted to know why the cabinet meeting was held and "did not like it." In fact, he ultimately dismissed Lansing because of it.[579]

Baker was distressed by a cable from Graves indicating that the Cossacks would soon attack the AEF and that the Japanese would aid them. He and Lansing met informally with Daniels to discuss the situation. Baker asked Daniels if the American navy could "whip" the Japanese navy in the event war broke out. Daniels said "Yes, but we must have bases and supplies and they are wanting and we would require time." Wilson, wrote Daniels, did not wish to close down the railroad and leave starving people to their fate, which is what he feared would happen if American troops withdrew. Baker asked Grayson to raise the issue with

Wilson, for none of the cabinet could see the president. "Government cannot stop because [the] President is sick," Lansing remarked.[580]

Wilson's response, according to Grayson, was to order Lansing to insist upon an immediate answer to his protest to the Japanese Foreign Ministry. Baker, fearing the American forces would be "cut off and killed far from help," asked Daniels to keep a ship with a powerful wireless in Vladivostok and stand ready to send other ships to evacuate the AEF.[581]

Meanwhile, Harris continued to urge that Kolchak be formally recognized and given aid. Even Polk was in favor of recognizing the Omsk government. On the other hand, now Dr. Teusler, the Red Cross head in Siberia and a former Kolchak supporter, indicated that he believed the fall of the Omsk government was imminent.[582]

By early November the stage was set for the final confrontation. The Bolsheviks were advancing on Omsk, and all the foreign missions were evacuating the city. Harris continued to send confident reports as he packed to leave.[583] Colonel Eichelberger predicted to his wife that "the Kolchak government is about finished. I look for Bolshevism to follow right on the trail of the Czechs as they withdraw. As for the Siberian Army with its British uniforms—They will join the other side in all probability."[584]

The diplomatic evacuation of Omsk signaled the start of a mass exodus from Central Siberia. The Czech decision on 16 November to withdraw from Siberia added to the rising chaos. Citing the atrocities of the White forces, and the Czechs' distaste for their own role in Siberia, Girsa protested that "in protecting the railway and maintaining order in the countryside, our Army is forced to act contrary to its convictions when it supports and maintains an arbitrary absolute power…. This passiveness is the direct result of our neutrality and nonintervention in Russian internal affairs, and, thanks to our being loyal to this idea, we have become, in spite of ourselves, accomplices to a crime." He thus announced that "we see no other way out of this situation than to evacuate immediately the sector which was given us to guard."[585] While Girsa's criticisms were completely valid, the Czechs Legion had scarcely been neutral and had chosen a very convenient time for a final bout of moral revulsion—just as the Kolchak government was about to fall.

On the heels of the Czech announcement, General Gajda came to the forefront once more. After returning to Vladivostok, Gajda had joined forces with the Social Revolutionaries. They began to plan for the overthrow of Rozanov while in a railway car only 300 yards from his headquarters.[586] On 17 November, when Gajda found Kolchak abandoning Omsk, he began his revolt. Gajda and 100 men captured the Vladivostok telegraph station and wired news of the uprising to their colleagues in the west. They then moved to capture Rozanov at his headquarters. The attempted coup was a failure.[587] The population of Vladivostok did not rush to join them as they had hoped, although many of Rozanov's forces did. Nevertheless, the rest of Rozanov's troops pinned the insurgents down at an intersection in the center of Vladivostok.

Gajda had also launched a simultaneous assault on the railway yard. There he and 300 men held out against the Cossack counterattack until the British forces provided Rozanov with cadets from Russian Island and artillery to use against them. General Graves's son, Sidney, went down to the station, rescued General Romanovsky and his family from their railway car, and brought them back, complete with their cats, to the AEF Headquarters under heavy fire.[588]

The Czech Legion remained neutral throughout the fighting. But the Japanese supported Rozanov, who attacked Gajda again.[589] Now Gajda's men began to surrender. The Americans saw Rozanov's troops take their prisoners into a shed and execute them. The Cossacks then went into a warehouse that was being used as a hospital and shot all the wounded. Gajda, seriously wounded, was finally discovered. Rozanov's soldiers beat him until he was unconscious. Gajda's life was spared only by the direct appeals of Čeček and Syrový, the commander of the Czech Legion. Rozanov finally agreed to let Gajda go if he left Siberia within twenty-four hours and never returned.[590] The democratic cause in Eastern Siberia was finished.

Gajda's departure would have put an end to the incident, except that during the fighting Colonel Krakovetsky and four other of Gajda's followers forced their way into American headquarters and asked for asylum. General Graves was in a very awkward position. If he turned them away Rozanov would kill them. American headquarters, however, was not legally US territory. Graves decided to cable Washington for instructions. On 19 November, he received an answer: "Secretaries of State and War agree, not possible to constitute your headquarters American territory."[591] Graves cabled back, explaining that Rozanov was shooting prisoners and would surely shoot the five men if they were turned over to him. The problem was fortuitously solved by Colonel Fred Bugbee of the 31st Infantry, the man to whom General Graves had entrusted the prisoners. While Graves was awaiting further instructions, Bugbee called to inform him that the prisoners had "escaped" (which they had done with Bugbee's help). This effectively solved Graves's problem. On 10 December, Graves finally received a reply to his second cable which said "State Department advises that you cause refugees to leave your headquarters as soon as consistent with general principles of humanity and before question of surrender arises."[592] The whole incident generated a renewed burst of anti-American propaganda. Rozanov claimed that the United States had financed the revolt.

While these events were underway in Vladivostok, Kolchak had abandoned Omsk to the advancing Red Army.[593] On 24 November, Colonel Stevens cabled Lansing to inform him of the scope of the Red victory at Omsk. The Red Army had captured 35,000 White troops, ten generals, 1,000 officers, 2,000 machine guns, 1,000,000 rifles, 3,000,000 shells, plus uniforms and equipment for 30,000 men, and sixteen armored trains. "Kolchak's army," Stevens reported, "is entirely demoralized and scattered. Czechs have all left Novo Nikoliaevsk and foreigners with them. It is probable that Reds will capture 157 trains on the way east. I see no chance for the Government."[594] Two days later, Kolchak expressed contrition "for faults of the past and giving assurances of good conduct in the future. The reign of requisition and military terror is to be abolished." He added that he was no longer opposed to granting legislative powers to a new assembly if that would save the situation.[595] It was far too little, and far too late.

Kolchak's retreat rapidly turned into a rout. Reports of degenerating conditions poured into Vladivostok and Washington. Typhus was rampant among the retreating hordes. Shortages of food and coal along the line made things even worse. The Czechs were seizing all available locomotives to secure their retreat and leaving Kolchak and his forces to manage as best they could.[596] The dreadful cold of the Siberian winter added to the catastrophe. Lansing now knew that the situation was hopeless. "We will gain nothing and help nobody by keeping forces there," he wrote in his diary. "As it is, I think it will be difficult to withdraw without loss of life."[597]

The retreat of the anti-Bolshevik forces was a struggle for survival in which very few conducted themselves with distinction. The circumstances inspired little human decency. The Czech Legion fared better than most, in part because it had entered the fray with several distinct advantages. It was occupying most of the Central Siberian Railway stations, and it had its own engineers and mechanics to repair and maintain the locomotives.[598] Consul General Harris reported that "the Czechs are apparently seeking their own evacuation without thought to other foreigners who may still be to their rear." The Czechs had seized one track for themselves and left everyone else to use the other track on which traffic scarcely moved at all. Kolchak accused the Czechs of "cruelty in leaving women and children to suffer and doing other deeds of violence which completely hamper movements of his army."[599]

Kolchak and his entourage were stalled at Krasnoyarsk. Relations between the Czechs and the Whites were strained to the breaking point. Kolchak was outraged at the way the Czechs were treating him. He appealed to General Janin for help, but Janin ignored him, and remarked to Syrový that Kolchak was travelling with five more trains than the tsar had ever found necessary. The implication was that he should abandon a few of them. Desperate and angered by the remark, Kolchak's chief of staff, Vladimir Kappel, challenged Syrový to a duel. Syrový refused. The incident was typical of the bizarre behavior born of extreme circumstances.[600]

In a foolish, desperate, and self-destructive act, Kolchak telegraphed Semenov and ordered him to blow up the Baikal tunnels to stop the Czech evacuation. In exchange Kolchak promised to make Semenov commander of all White forces east of Irkutsk. Kolchak even secured the support of General Oi for Semenov's appointment.[601] But the Czechs were in control of the telegraph wires and immediately picked up the message. Kolchak's fate was sealed.

On Christmas Eve 1919, Semenov issued an ultimatum to the legion to cease from interfering with the railway; otherwise he would stop their retreat by force.[602] But Stevens reported on 27 December that he was reliably informed by his inspectors that the "Kolchak government is completely overthrown." The Czechs were openly defying Semenov. He also said that they were providing protection for the Americans in their area of jurisdiction. He warned Lansing to disregard any criticism of the Czechs that he heard; "they are fully justified in their acts."[603] By 28 November, even Kolchak's most loyal champion, Consul General Harris, had at last lost all hope. "Kolchak's mentality is breaking up under the tremendous strain of the past two months," he declared. "The tone of the telegrams which he has forwarded to Czechs and foreign representatives here would almost indicate this." He added that it seemed that there were sufficient Czech, American, and Japanese forces in the Baikal Sector to protect the tunnels from Semenov.[604]

Kolchak's position was precarious. The White government at Irkutsk had collapsed, to be replaced by the Social Revolutionaries. Many of the smaller cities and towns along the railroad were now under the control of anti-Kolchak, if not pro-Bolshevik, factions. They would not allow Kolchak to pass through them alive. Janin ordered that Kolchak be kept at Nizhni-Udinsk until he could decide what to do with him. A Czech "storm" battalion was ordered to guard Kolchak and the gold trains even as Kolchak's underlings were beginning to desert him.

The situation altered, but not favorably for Kolchak. The Bolshevik Revolutionaries seized power in Irkutsk. The Czech detachment guarding Kolchak was unaware of the change in government at Irkutsk. It decided that it was time to leave Nizhni-Udinsk. As they passed through village after village full of anti-Kolchak demonstrators, the Czechs grew increasingly concerned. They contrived to leave these villages only by persuading the demonstrators that they were taking Kolchak to Irkutsk to turn him over to the Revolutionary Committee.

The final crisis came on 13 January 1920, when the echelon reached Polovina station. The Czechs guarding Kolchak needed a new engine. The skeptical railwaymen refused to provide one unless they were allowed to place their own guards on Kolchak's car to insure that the Czechs actually turned Kolchak over to the Irkutsk authorities.

After lengthy discussion, the Czechs gave way. Red guards were posted. At 6:00 P.M. on 14 January, the admiral, on General Janin's instructions, was turned over to the Red Guard at Glaskov along with the imperial gold reserves in exchange for clear passage for the Czech Legion.[605] Janin had little choice; if he had refused to surrender Kolchak, the legion would have been placed in enormous danger. If the coal from west of Irkutsk had been interdicted, the tracks sabotaged, or a single tunnel blown up, the Czechs would have been forced to make their way to Vladivostok on foot.[606] Apart from that, Kolchak had frequently abused the Czechs in the past and they had little desire to jeopardize their safety for his.

In the midst of this debacle, the United States was compelled to reach a final decision on what American policy in Siberia would be. Kolchak's collapse brought a rapid disintegration of the State Department's enthusiasm for him. On 2 December 1919, Breckinridge Long told Boris Bakhmetev, who had been appointed as ambassador to the US by the Provisional Government and stayed on after the Bolshevik Revolution, "we could not get any sentiment in this country for fighting the Bolsheviki...." He pointed out that "each of the anti-Bolsheviks fought the Bolsheviks only a little harder than they were fighting each other."[607]

Lansing was also losing what little enthusiasm he had for military intervention. He wrote Wilson, now reiterating what the president had said all along, that Bolshevism is "pre-eminently an economic and moral phenomenon against which economic and moral remedies alone will prevail."[608] On the 7 December, in response to requests for American aid for the collapsing Kolchak, Lansing cabled Morris that "this government does not propose to depart in any way from its principles on non-interference in Russian internal affairs."[609]

In Siberia, Graves and Harris were still operating at cross purposes. A controversy arose over the arrival of an American officer in Vladivostok with orders to report to Harris, an extremely unusual arrangement at the best of times. Graves believed that the State Department and Harris, working through General Marlborough Churchill, had had the orders issued because Graves's reports and those of the Army differed materially from those of the consul general. It was Graves's conclusion that the officer was sent in order to dispatch reports that contradicted the official army reports. The officer in question also had in his possession a document provided by the Military Intelligence Division that stated that "American troops are in Siberia primarily to support Kolchak against Bolsheviks by keeping his line of communications open along the Trans-Siberian railroad." This contradicted Graves's repeated statements on non-interference in Russian internal affairs. The whole affair incensed Graves, and he cabled General March asking that the officer report to him and burn the offending passage in his presence. March agreed, and the document was destroyed.[610]

Meanwhile Lansing was drafting a memorandum to the president. He advised the withdrawal of the AEF as the only reasonable course. He argued that the United States had done everything possible to encourage the Siberians in their efforts at self-government. Secondly, arrangements had been made for the repatriation of the Czechs. Thirdly, the Bolshevik advance had put an end to all railway work west of Lake Baikal. But most importantly, if American troops remained in Siberia, there was a strong possibility that they might get into a war with the Bolsheviks. Lansing's opinion was that the United States should not consult the British and French since the United States had made the intervention arrangements only with Japan.[611] The State Department, this memorandum revealed, at last realized—as did the War Department—that nothing positive could come of a continued American presence in Siberia. Baker read the memorandum and agreed with Lansing's recommendation.

Graves was thinking along the same lines in Vladivostok. He cabled the War Department that "the safety of American troops demands concentration which results in abandoning parts of our sector. We are fast arriving at the place where we join Kalmikoff, Semeonoff, and Rozanoff in fighting the Russians who claim they are trying to establish a republican government in the East."[612]

On New Year's Eve 1919, Graves received a reply from the War Department. It stated that within a few days he would receive "orders for the withdrawal of your entire command." He was warned to keep the information secret until he received those orders.[613] Graves received the withdrawal order on 5 January 1920. It was published in Washington on 7 January and in Vladivostok on 8 January. The American evacuation began as soon as the last Czech left Vladivostok.[614]

Wilson released a public statement on 16 January. He observed that American efforts to support Russian self-government and self-defense had met with little success. "The United States," he observed, "is disposed to view that further military effort to assist the Russians in the struggle for self-government may lead to complications which would have exactly the opposite effect prolonging the period of readjustment and involving Japan and the United States in ineffective and needless sacrifices."[615]

Wilson's unilateral decision outraged the British and the French. As the Senate had failed to ratify the Versailles Treaty, however, and Wilson no longer required their cooperation or goodwill. It was difficult, moreover, to take their accusations of desertion seriously, because the Allies were themselves rapidly withdrawing their own missions from Siberia.

On 23 April 1920, the remaining members of the American Expeditionary Force in Siberia departed. The last to leave Vladivostok were Major General William S. Graves and his staff. His orders remained unchanged from the day in August 1918 that he had received them from Newton Baker in a Kansas City hotel. His convictions were intact. The evacuation was complete.

Conclusion

Just before General Graves and the last of the AEF left Siberia in April 1920, the Japanese government announced its intention to remain in Siberia contrary to American requests for withdrawal. Once the Europeans and Americans evacuated the region the Bolsheviks and Japanese came into direct and brutal conflict. After two more years, in November 1922, Japanese forces finally evacuated Vladivostok. By the end of 1923 all of Siberia was under Soviet control.

Woodrow Wilson never recovered his physical or intellectual vigor after his stroke of October 1919. He continued as president until early 1921, but he remained an invalid until his death in 1924.

In his last years Wilson broke with most of his former associates. He never saw Edward House again after he left Paris; he never saw Robert Lansing after dismissing him as secretary of state. Josephus Daniels and Newton Baker, however, enjoyed Wilson's undiminished regard for the remainder of his life.

After leaving Siberia, General Graves served as commander of the 1st Division and later as commander of the Panama Canal Zone. In 1922 Graves and other members of the AEF testified in a Senate committee hearing on the activities of Ataman Semenov. During these days of the infamous Red Scare the FBI kept Graves under surveillance on suspicion of being a Bolshevik sympathizer.

In 1931 Graves published his memoirs of the Siberian intervention, but this failed to rehabilitate him in the public mind. He continued to be popularly perceived as the man who had refused to destroy Bolshevism when he had the chance. By the 1930s the Soviet government's notoriety began to increase, while memories of White excesses faded. Graves remained politically suspect until his death in 1940.

During his lifetime Graves kept up a close friendship with Robert Eichelberger. After leaving Vladivostok, Eichelberger served in the Far East and on the General Staff. During World War II, having attained the rank of lieutenant general, he served in a variety of commands under Douglas MacArthur in the South Pacific. Instrumental in retaking the Philippines, Eichelberger later commanded the first occupation forces in Japan. From 1946 until his retirement in 1948 he commanded all US and Allied ground forces in Japan. In the course of his duties he occasionally met some of the Japanese officers whom he had encountered in Siberia a quarter-century before.[616]

Grigorii Semenov left Siberia after the Japanese departure and finally settled in Manchuria. During World War II he continued his work for the Japanese and commanded a Japanese division. When the Soviets invaded Manchuria in August 1945 they captured Semenov and shipped him to Moscow. He was imprisoned in Lubianka, tried and convicted as an enemy of the Soviet people, and finally hanged in August 1946.

Rudolph Gajda returned to Czechoslovakia after fleeing Vladivostok. He served for a time as chief of staff of the Czech Army, but he never lost his taste for coups. In 1926 he organized a conspiracy against the Czech Republic, and upon its failure he was court-martialed and dismissed from the army. Gajda went on to found the Czech Fascist party, leading an uncertain life under German occupation.

After the Czechs turned Admiral Kolchak over to the Red Guards in January 1920, an Extraordinary Investigation Committee spent three weeks taking testimony from him. When the Committee finished, Kolchak was executed by a firing squad and his body shoved into the Angara through a hole chopped in the ice.

The history of the AEF in Siberia reveals that Wilson's policy there was essentially one of neutrality, as outlined in his aide memoire. According to the aide memoire, and the War Department's strict construction of it, the AEF in Siberia had several missions. The first was to rescue the Czech Legion. Another objective was to have American troops help restore commerce, communication, and transportation on the Trans-Siberian

Railway, and to assist in distributing humanitarian relief. Finally Graves's superiors decided, with Wilson's approval, that Graves's orders allowed him to attempt to prevent excesses by all political factions against the Siberian civilian population.

Once Graves arrived he discovered that the rescue of the Czechs was not possible, because not only were they in no need of help, but they were embroiled in the Russian Civil War and were unwilling to leave Siberia. At the same time the Japanese were active in a way totally at odds with Wilson's original understanding. Washington did not learn of these changed circumstances for several months, during which time the AEF undertook another mission by default; Graves turned his attention to keeping an eye on the Japanese and serving as a brake upon their imperialist ambitions in Siberia. During this time Graves also endeavored to carry out his mission of humanitarian relief. He was unsuccessful because of Japanese and White Army obstruction. Only the Whites benefited from this aid because of their control of the railway. Finally, Graves attempted to prevent excesses of all factions in the region. In practice the AEF directed almost all of its efforts against White, Cossack, and Japanese forces, Bolsheviks being a relatively minor problem in the area before early 1920.

Throughout his stay in Siberia, Graves was under considerable pressure from the Allies as well as the State Department to adopt an active anti-Bolshevik policy. But Graves ignored these appeals and adhered strictly to the chain of command, taking his orders from Wilson via the War Department. For his part Wilson reviewed Graves's actions on several occasions and in every instance he sustained his general's decisions. Even when Baker himself voiced doubts about Graves, Wilson continued to support him. Thus Graves's conduct reflected what Wilson wanted, and allowed, from the AEF.

During this time the State Department was frequently out of touch with Wilson's wishes. Much of this was Wilson's own fault. From 1918 on he cloistered himself from Lansing and neglected to consult or inform the secretary and his department of developments on many foreign policy issues. The views and opinions of State Department officials on the proper role of the AEF, therefore, were not always representative of Wilson's Siberian policy.

What did Wilson hope to accomplish by keeping Graves in Siberia during a time of such extreme changes? By instructing him to carry out a neutral policy, Wilson gained time to consider what action he should take in Russia. Between 1918 and 1920 he considered recognizing first the Bolshevik, and then the Kolchak regimes. In the end he drew back from the latter course because of his fears that Kolchak, despite his assurances of democracy, was on the way to becoming a reactionary dictator.

To judge from his general views on democratic government and international relations, Wilson probably hoped to use the AEF to stabilize the situation in Siberia. His intention appeared to be to keep the warring factions apart, and to keep foreign governments from exploiting the situation in Russia, until some moderate group could emerge. Wilson wanted the Russian people to have self-determination. No doubt he assumed that self-determination would result in Russia choosing a liberal democratic government. Wilson feared both the Bolsheviks and the Whites, not on ideological grounds, but because neither regime contemplated a popularly-elected government. He feared them not for their beliefs, but for their actions.

To realize his aim of Russian self-determination in Siberia (as he understood the term), Wilson used the AEF in a novel fashion—to prevent war, by more limited military action if necessary, and to encourage and maintain peace, rather than to wage war outright—to allow a popular government time to evolve and take control. In a sense this amounted to a constructive use of force—a use of force to create an even field for the contending parties, to allow the Russian people to determine the outcome for themselves in a democratic manner. Wilson wished to facilitate the political process and bring about self-government in a foreign country rather than to impose American will (other than in the broadest possible sense) upon that country. Wilson did want something from Russia: he wanted it to develop self-determination. To this end he would use force against those who had other, more selfish, ideas.

Unfortunately, however, what moderates there were in Russia proved unable to take charge of the situation. The government that Wilson longed to see in the end never took shape. Discouraged by White excesses on one hand, and Allied intrigues on the other, Siberian peasants either acquiesced to Bolshevik control or, in desperation, supported it, only to find later that the Soviets could be as ruthless as the counter-revolutionaries, and much more efficient. In the end, when Wilson was overcome by illness and the strength of forces arrayed against the AEF grew, the mission came to an abortive end.

Throughout his presidency Wilson used the military in a new and untraditional manner; he used it not to wage war, but to restore peace. During his time as president he created a more benign role for the military while using it as a major agent of his foreign policy. He employed it frequently, unilaterally, and with great effect in the Western Hemisphere.

In Russia, however, Wilson tried to act in concert (at least to some degree) with the Allied Powers in a highly unstable political environment. The Allies, and particularly Japan, had very different goals in Russia from Wilson. Wilson conspicuously lacked imperialist motives in that he sought no pecuniary gain for the United States. This was not true of Japan or any other country involved in the Siberian intervention.

The activities of the AEF in Siberia reflected Wilson's policies there very accurately. They reflected Wilson's intention to follow a policy of neutrality towards various Russian factions. In a larger sense, however, they reflected Wilson's belief in a new style of military action, aimed at achieving a new sort of diplomatic order. But just as Wilson's dream of a world based on the Fourteen Points was crippled at Versailles and died a lingering death in Washington, so, too, did his new concept of military peace-keeping flounder and fail on the steppes of Siberia. In Versailles, the Fourteen Points fell victim to the selfish interests of European governments. In Siberia, the AEF likewise found itself literally outgunned by the forces of imperialism, revolution, and counter-revolution, and under the

control of commander in chief thousands of miles away who was fast losing his capacity to command.

But just as the United Nations arose from the ashes of Wilson's doomed
League of Nations, so, too, did the Wilsonian concept of military peace-
keeping see a renaissance in the years after World War II. Military
peace-keeping today, then, hearkens back to the Great War, and Wilson's
new use of the American Expeditionary Force that was neither fully war,
nor fully peace.

NOTES

---

[1] David Lloyd George, *The War Memoirs of David Lloyd George* (London: Ivor, Nicholson and Watson 1936) 2577–78.

[2] Polk to Wilson, 28 January 1918, *The Papers of Woodrow Wilson*, ed. Arthur S. Link, et al. (Princeton: Princeton University Press, 1984) 46:154–55.

[3] House to Wilson, 31 January 1918, ibid., 181–83.

[4] In November 1917 the Allied and Associated Powers created an organization designed to coordinate strategy. This was a result of the appalling casualties they had sustained in the preceding year. The council included the head of each government and a political representative of the governments of Britain, France, and Italy. Each nation also had a permanent military representative to provide expert analysis. The council met monthly at Versailles. Wilson agreed to send a military representative, General Tasker H. Bliss, but declined to send a political representative.

[5] Lansing to Wilson, 9 February 1918, *Wilson Papers*, 46:301–304.

[6] Lansing to Page, 13 February 1918, ibid., 339–41.

[7] Lansing to Wilson, 26 February 1918, ibid., 451–52.

[8] Bliss to March, 20 February 1918, Tasker Howard Bliss Papers, Library of Congress, Manuscript Division, Washington, DC, file 162-1.

[9] Wiseman to Drummond, 4 March 1918, *Wilson Papers*, 46:531; Draft Aide Memoire, 1 March 1918, *Wilson Papers*, 46:498–99. See also Diary of Colonel House, 4 March 1918; 532.

[10] Balfour to Reading, 26 February 1918, *Wilson Papers*, 46:470–71.

[11] House to Balfour, 4 March 1918, *Wilson Papers*, 46:530–31; Wiseman to Drummond, 4 March 1918, *Wilson Papers*, 46:531; Wiseman to Foreign Office, 9 March 1918. *Wilson Papers*, 46:590–91.

[12] Polk to Morris, 5 March 1918, ibid., 545.

[13] Reading to Balfour, 19 March 1918, *Wilson Papers*, 47:78–82.

[14] Page to Wilson, 16 March 1918, ibid., 59–61; 81.

[15] Knight to Department of the Navy, rec'd 18 March 1918, ibid., 70–71.

[16] Drummond to Wiseman, 26 March 1918, ibid., 156–57.

[17] Wilson to Swope, 2 April 1918, ibid., 224.

[18] Richard Luckett, *The White Generals* (New York: The Viking Press, 1971) 163; Betty Miller Unterberger, *The United States, Revolutionary Russia, and the Rise of Czechoslovakia* (Chapel Hill: University of North Carolina Press, 1989) 173–74.

[19] V. Maksakov and I. A. Turunov, eds., *Khronika grazdanskoi voiny v Sibiri, 1917–1918*, quoted in John Bunyan, ed., *Intervention, Civil War, and Communism in Russia: April–December 1918 Documents and Materials* (New York: Octagon Books, 1977) 91.

[20] Memorandum by Robert Lansing, 3 June 1918, *Wilson Papers*, 48:236.

[21] Richard Goldhurst, *The Midnight War: The American Intervention in Russia 1918–1920* (New York: McGraw-Hill Book Co., 1978) 23–24.

[22] United States Department of State, *Papers Relating to the Foreign Relations of the United States, 1918, Russia*, 3 vols. (Washington DC: US Government Printing Office, 1931–1932) 2:484–85.

[23] March to Bliss, 28 May 1918, *Wilson Papers*, 48:182.

[24] Ray Stannard Baker, ed., *Armistice*, vol. 8 of *Woodrow Wilson, Life and Letters* (Garden City NY: Doubleday, Doran and Company, Inc., 1939) 147.

[25] Reinsch to State Department, 13 June 1918, *Wilson Papers*, 48:335–36.

[26] Peyton C. March, *The Nation at War* (New York: Doubleday, Doran, and Company, 1932) 116.

[27] Ibid., 116–20.

[28] Baker to Wilson, 19 June 1918, Newton D. Baker Papers, Library of Congress, Manuscript Division.

[29] Victor S. Matamey, *The United States and East Central Europe 1914–1918: A Study in Wilsonian Diplomacy and Propaganda* (Princeton: Princeton University Press, 1957) 285–86.

[30] Frederick Palmer, ed., *Bliss, Peacemaker: The Life and Letters of General Tasker Howard Bliss* (New York: Dodd and Mead, 1934) 293.

[31] Foch to Wilson, 27 June 1918, *Wilson Papers*, 48:446.

[32] House to Wilson, 21 June 1918, ibid., 390–91.

[33] He sent troops to Mexico twice, and once each to Haiti and the Dominican Republic. In the course of World War I he dispatched troops to the Western Front, North Russia, and finally to Siberia.

[34] Carl von Clausewitz, *On War*, ed. Michael Howard and Peter Paret (Princeton: Princeton University Press, 1976) 87.

[35] He continues, foreshadowing some of his difficulties with the Senate over the Versailles Treaty: "The President cannot conclude a treaty with a foreign power without the consent of the Senate, but he may guide every step of diplomacy, and to guide diplomacy is to determine what treaties must be made, if the faith and prestige of the government are to be maintained. He need disclose no step of negotiation until it is complete and when in any critical matter it is completed the government is virtually committed. Whatever its disinclination, the Senate may feel itself committed also."

Woodrow Wilson, *Constitutional Government in the United States* (New York: Columbia University Press, 1921) 77–78.

[36] Frederick S. Calhoun, *Power and Principle: Armed Intervention in Wilsonian Foreign Policy* (Kent OH: Kent State University Press, 1986) 2.

[37] Lord Reading to A. J. Balfour, 3 June 1918, and Joint Note No. 31, 3 June 1918, "Allied Intervention at the White Sea Ports," *Wilson Papers*, 48:286–88. See below for a more detailed discussion of the Aide Memoire, as well as American policy in North Russia.

[38] Woodrow Wilson, Aide Memoire, 17 July 1918, *Wilson Papers*, 48:642.

[39] An Address to the Joint Session of Congress, 8 January 1918, *Wilson Papers*, 45:536.

[40] Ibid., 537.

[41] Wilson to Eliot, 21 January 1918, *Wilson Papers*, 46:53.

[42] Wilson to Gompers, 21 January 1918, *Wilson Papers*, 46:53; Wiseman to Reading, 12 February 1918, *Wilson Papers*, 46:333–34; Lansing to David R. Francis, 14 February 1918, in US Department of State, *Foreign Relations of the United States, 1918, Russia*, 1:381.

[43] Wilson to Tumulty, 23 February 1918, *Wilson Papers*, 46:422.

[44] "A Proclamation," 8 April 1918, *Wilson Papers*, 47:284–85.

[45] Reading to Balfour, 23 May 1918, *Wilson Papers*, 48:133.

[46] Lansing to Wilson, 13 June 1918, ibid., 305–306.

[47] Wiseman to Drummond, 14 July 1918, *Wilson Papers*, 48:315–16; Reading to Balfour, 25 June 1918, *Wilson Papers*, 48:429–30.

[48] Balfour to Reading, 2 July 1918, ibid., 496.

[49] Ibid., 498–99.

[50] Ibid., 500.

[51] Ibid., 501. Bliss was not part of this "unanimous opinion." For his views see Bliss to War Department, 2 July 1918, *Wilson Papers*, 48:503–506.

[52] Ibid., 500.

[53] Ibid., 501.

[54] Ibid., 501.

[55] Ibid., 501.

[56] J. F. N. Bradley, *Civil War in Russia, 1917–1920* (New York: St. Martin's Press, 1975) 89.

[57] Lansing to Wilson, 4 July 1918, file 861.oo/2292 1/2, General Records of the Department of State, National Archives, Washington, DC.

[58] March, *The Nation at War*, 124.

[59] March, *The Nation at War*, 126.

[60] Memorandum from Col. E. D. Anderson, General Staff, Chief of Operations Branch to the Chief of Staff, subject: Expedition to Vladivostok, 6 July 1918, Historical Files of

the American Expeditionary Forces in Siberia, 1918–1920, National Archives, Washington, DC, file 21-19.3.

[61] March, *The Nation at War*, 126.

[62] Baker to Hayes, 29 December 1929, quoted in Daniel R. Beaver, *Newton D. Baker and the American War Effort* (Lincoln: University of Nebraska Press, 1966) 184.

[63] Memorandum of a Conference at the White House in Reference to the Siberian Situation by Robert Lansing, 6 July 1918, *Wilson Papers*, 48:542–43. See also Josephus Daniels Diary, 6 July 1918, *Wilson Papers*, 48:544.

[64] Memorandum of a Conference at the White House in Reference to the Siberian Situation by Robert Lansing, 6 July 1918, ibid., 542–43.

[65] Josephus Daniels to Austin M. Knight, 6 July 1918, ibid., 543.

[66] Wilson to Edward M. House, 8 July 1918, ibid., 550.

[67] Memorandum from Admiral Knight to the Secretary of the Navy, 9 July 1918, Historical Files of the AEF, file 21-19.3.

[68] Memorandum of Conference with Japanese Ambassador Concerning a Siberian Program, 8 July 1918, *Wilson Papers*, 48:559–61.

[69] Wilson to Polk, 17 July 1918, ibid., 639–40.

[70] Woodrow Wilson, Aide Memoire, 17 July 1918, ibid., 639–41.

[71] Ibid.

[72] Ibid.

[73] Ibid.

[74] Ibid., 642.

[75] Ibid., 642.

[76] Ibid., 642–43.

[77] Ibid., 643.

[78] For details of these missions see Calhoun's *Power and Principle*.

[79] Reading to Balfour, 3 July 1918, *Wilson Papers*, 48:511–14.

[80] Balfour to Reading, 22 July 1918, *Wilson Papers*, 49:57–60.

[81] Polk to Wilson, 24 July 1918, ibid., 75–76.

[82] Polk to Wilson, 26 July 1918, ibid., 107–109.

[83] Press Release, 3 August 1918, ibid., 49:170–72.

[84] Diary of Colonel House, 25 July 1918, ibid., 96.

[85] C. K. Cummings and Walter W. Pettit, eds., *Russian-American Relations, March 1917–March 1920, Documents and Papers* (New York: Harcourt, Brace, & Howe, 1920) 239.

[86] Ishii to Polk, 2 August 1918, in US Department of State, *Foreign Relations of the United States, 1918, Russia*, 2:324–25.

[87] W. B. Fowler, *British American Relations, 1917–1918: The Role of Sir William Wiseman* (Princeton: Princeton University Press, 1969) 190–92.

[88] Wiseman to Murray, 4 July 1918, *Wilson Papers*, 48:523 (emphasis mine).

[89] Thomas Garrigue Masaryk, *The Making of a State; Memories and Observations 1914–1918* (London: George Allen and Unwin Ltd., 1927) 259.

[90] Betty Miller Unterberger, *The United States, Revolutionary Russia, and the Rise of Czechoslovakia* (Chapel Hill: University of North Carolina Press, 1989) 199–200. This volume contains an excellent account of how various American State Department officials, and particularly George H. Emerson (commander of the Russian Railroad Service Corps) attempted to mediate between the Bolsheviks and the Czechs to secure a cease-fire and the peaceful removal the Czech Legion. They failed largely because of the intransigence of Rudolph Gajda and other young Czech hardliners who refused to believe in the sincerity of any Bolshevik offer; they remained convinced that the Bolsheviks were German puppets. See pp. 170–200. For a detailed account of Emerson's activities and transcripts of his conversations see "Report of American Railway Engineers Who Were in Siberia with the Czecho-Slovacs from May 5, to September 9th 1918." Historical Files of the American Expeditionary Forces in Siberia, 1918–1920, National Archives, Washington, DC, file 21-42.2, pp. 6–52.

[91] Luckett, *The White Generals*, 163; Unterberger, *The United States, Revolutionary Russia, and the Rise of Czechoslovakia*, 91.

[92] Luckett, *The White Generals*, 167–68.

[93] Ibid., 169.

[94] Goldhurst, *The Midnight War: The American Intervention in Russia, 1918–1920*, 67–68.

[95] George F. Kennan, *Russia and the West: Under Lenin and Stalin* (Boston: Little, Brown and Co., 1960) 283.

[96] George F. Kennan, *The Decision to Intervene* (Princeton: Princeton University Press, 1958) 71.

[97] Ibid., 73–74.

[98] John Bunyan, ed., *Intervention, Civil War, and Communism in Russia: April–December, 1918 Documents and Materials* (New York: Octagon Books, 1977) 93.

[99] US Department of State, Confidential Report on Matters Relating to Russia, No. 16, 16 August 1918, quoted in Bunyan, *Intervention, Civil War, and Communism in Russia*, 96–98; "Report of American Railway Engineers who were in Siberia...," Historical Files of the AEF, file 21-42.2, p. 18.

[100] Unterberger, *The United States, Revolutionary Russia, and the Rise of Czechoslovakia*, 181–83.

[101] Lansing to Wilson, 24 March 1918, *Wilson Papers*, 47:231–32; Caldwell to Lansing, 25 June 1918, *Wilson Papers*, 48:428–29; Knight to Daniels, 5 July 1918, *Wilson Papers*,

48:527–28. Lansing did mention to Wilson, however, that the Czechs were being opposed by the "Bolsheviks" and "Red Guards" and did not mention Austrians and Germans specifically. Lansing to Wilson, 23 June 1918, *Wilson Papers*, 48:398.

[102] Caldwell to Lansing, 20 August 1918, in Gaddis Smith, "Canada and the Siberian Intervention 1918–1919," *American Historical Review* (July 1959): 868.

[103] United States Department of State, *Papers Relating to the Foreign Relations of the United States, 1918, Russia*, 3 vols. (Washington DC: US Government Printing Office, 1931–1932) 2:352.

[104] Kennan, *The Decision to Intervene*, 425.

[105] Peyton C. March, *The Nation at War* (New York: Doubleday, Doran, and Company, 1932) 74.

[106] Charles Bracelen Flood, *Lee: The Last Years* (Boston: Houghton, Mifflin Co., 1981) 237.

[107] T. Harry Williams, *The History of American Wars* (New York: Alfred A. Knopf, 1985) 400.

[108] Ibid.

[109] Witherspoon to Bliss, 15 June 1914, quoted in Frederick S. Calhoun, *Power and Principle: Armed Intervention and Wilsonian Foreign Policy* (Kent OH: Kent State University Press, 1986) 50–51.

[110] "Address at Biltmore Hotel" in Ray S. Baker and William E. Dodd, eds., *The Public Papers of Woodrow Wilson: The New Democracy*, 2 vols. (New York: Harper & Brothers, 1926) 1:331.

[111] March, *The Nation at War*, 68.

[112] John J. Pershing, *My Experience in the World War* (New York: Frederick A. Stokes Co., 1931) 1:17.

[113] Pershing, *Experience*, 37.

[114] March, *The Nation at War*, 193–96.

[115] Calhoun, *Power and Principle*, 20.

[116] Ibid., 32.

[117] Ibid., 28–29.

[118] Ibid., 27.

[119] Arthur S. Link, *Wilson the Diplomatist: A Look at his Major Foreign Policies* (New York: New Viewpoints, 1974) xiii.

[120] Lansing and Wilson's working relationship was at its high watermark during the summer of 1918, when they worked to draft the plans for the American Expeditionary Force in Siberia.

[121] Lansing to Francis, 25 March 1918, Francis Papers, quoted in David S. Fogelsong, "America's Secret War Against Bolshevism: United States Intervention in the Russian

Civil War, 1917–1920" (Ph.D. diss., University of California, Berkeley, 1991) 66. For a more complete discussion of anti-Bolshevik activity by the State Department, see also David S. Fogelsong, *America's Secret War Against Bolshevism: US Intervention in the Russian Civil War, 1917–1920* (Chapel Hill: University of North Carolina Press, 1995).

[122] Francis Papers, quoted in Fogelsong, *America's Secret War Against Bolshevism*. Fogelsong argues that while Francis, Consul General Maddin Summer, and his successor Dewitt C. Poole acted on their own responsibility, Wilson was conducting covert actions against the Bolsheviks while remaining ignorant of the details.

[123] March, *The Nation at War*, 127.

[124] Betty Miller Unterberger, "William Sidney Graves," in Roger J. Spiller, ed., *Dictionary of American Military Biography* (Westport CT: Greenwood Press, 1984) 401.

[125] William S. Graves, *America's Siberian Adventure, 1918–1920* (New York: Peter Smith, 1941) ix.

[126] Graves, *Adventure*, 1–2.

[127] Betty Miller Unterberger, "William Sidney Graves," 400–401.

[128] Lansing to Baker, 18 July 1918, quoted in John Silverlight, *The Victor's Dilemma* (New York: Weybright and Talley, 1970) 71.

[129] Graves, *Adventure*, 3.

[130] Ibid., 4.

[131] Ibid.

[132] Memorandum to General Graves at Camp Fremont, California, from McCain, Manila, 6 August 1918, Historical Files of the American Expeditionary Forces in Siberia, 1918–1920, National Archives, Washington, DC, file 21-19.3.

[133] Millard S. Curtis Papers, "History of the 27th Infantry Regiment," 10, US Army Military History Institute, Carlisle Barracks, Pennsylvania.

[134] General Order Number 5, Historical Files of the AEF, file 21-19.3.

[135] The War Diary of the Replacement Troops of the AEF Siberia, 14 August 1918, Historical Files of the AEF, file 21-19.3.

[136] Sylvain Kindall, *American Soldiers in Siberia* (New York: Richard R. Smith, 1945) 17.

[137] Graves, *Adventure*, 55.

[138] Styer to AGWAR, No. 5, 19 August 1918, Historical Files of the AEF, file 21-23.11.

[139] General Headquarters at Vladivostok from Ussuri Front, 25 August 1918, Historical Files of the AEF, file 21-32.3.

[140] Curtis Papers, "History of the 27th Infantry Regiment," 11.

[141] Ibid.

[142] Ibid.

[143] Graves to AGWAR, Washington, no. 14, 3 September 1918, Historical Files of the AEF, file 21-21.3.

[144] William S. Graves, *America's Siberian Adventure, 1918–1920* (New York: Peter Smith, 1941) 67.

[145] Ibid., 57 (emphasis mine).

[146] Ibid., 63.

[147] Ibid., 59.

[148] Ibid., 58.

[149] United States Army War College, *Order of Battle of the United States' Land Forces in the World War* (Washington: US Government Printing Office, 1937). This was true, although no one ever informed Graves. Graves believed a diplomat unfamiliar with military terms had given this impression.

[150] Graves, *Adventure*, 57.

[151] Goldhurst, *The Midnight War: The American Intervention in Russia, 1918–1920*, 79.

[152] Graves, *Adventure*, 60.

[153] Goldhurst, *The Midnight War*, 79.

[154] Eichelberger to Director of Military Intelligence, 13 March 1919, file 861.00/4967, General Records of the Department of State, National Archives, Washington, DC; Graves to Adjutant General, 1 December 1918, Office of the Adjutant General, file 370.22, Russian Expedition, Siberian War Records, National Archives, Washington, DC; Goldhurst, *The Midnight War*, 82–83.

[155] Ibid.

[156] Goldhurst, *The Midnight War*, 126.

[157] J. W. Morley, *The Japanese Thrust into Siberia* (New York: Columbia University Press, 1957) 88–89.

[158] Luckett, *The White Generals*, 163; Unterberger, *The United States, Revolutionary Russia, and the Rise of Czechoslovakia*, 212.

[159] George F. Kennan, *The Decision to Intervene* (Princeton: Princeton University Press, 1958) 62–67.

[160] Sylvain Kindall, *American Soldiers in Siberia* (New York: Richard R. Smith, 1945) 154.

[161] Graves, *Adventure*, 90–91.

[162] Kennan, *Russia and the West: Under Lenin and Stalin*, 116.

[163] Sir Brian G. Horrocks, *A Full Life* (London: Collins, 1960) 38.

[164] Peter Fleming, *The Fate of Admiral Kolchak* (New York: Harcourt, Brace and World, Inc., 1963) 94.

[165] Reading to Lloyd George, 12 July 1918, *Wilson Papers*, 48:603.

[166] Janin was a dapper and intelligent man, if somewhat vain and self-important. As a result of these failings his arrival in Siberia was considerably delayed. On the journey he felt it was necessary to stop in Washington and Tokyo to see everyone of importance, including Woodrow Wilson and the emperor of Japan. Ibid., 98.

[167] Quoted in ibid., 97.

[168] Morley, *The Japanese Thrust into Siberia*, 227.

[169] Goldhurst, *The Midnight War*, 81.

[170] For an overview of the revolution and civil war in Russia, see Orlando Figes, *A People's Tragedy: The Russian Revolution 1891–1924* (London: Jonathan Cape, 1996).

[171] Fleming, *The Fate of Admiral Kolchak*, 97.

[172] March, *The Nation at War*, 96–98.

[173] French Ambassador to Quinet, 23 June 1918, quoted in "Report of American Railway Engineers Who Were in Siberia with the Czecho-Slovaks from May 5th–September 9th 1918," Historical Files of the American Expeditionary Forces in Siberia, 1918–1920, National Archives, Washington, DC, file 21-42.2, p. 56.

[174] United States Department of State, *Papers Relating to the Foreign Relations of the United States, 1918, Russia*, 3 vols. (Washington DC: US Government Printing Office, 1931–1932) 2:366.

[175] Carl William Ackerman, *"Trailing the Bolsheviki"* (New York: Charles Scribner's Sons, 1919) 167–68.

[176] US Department of State, *Foreign Relations of the United States, 1918, Russia* 2:387–90.

[177] Graves, *Adventure*, 85.

[178] Quoted in Goldhurst, *The Midnight War*, 82.

[179] Graves, *Adventure*, 72–73.

[180] Harris to State Department, 30 August 1918, *The Papers of Woodrow Wilson*, ed. Arthur S. Link, et al. (Princeton: Princeton University Press, 1984) 49:448–49. Harris's information here is puzzling. He stresses that the Czechs are only fighting Austrians and Germans, but it is clear in Emerson's Report of American Engineers with the Czecho-Slovaks that Harris was aware that the Czechs were fighting the Bolsheviks earlier in the summer.

[181] Wilson to Lansing, 5 September 1918, *Wilson Papers*, 49:448.

[182] Lansing to American Embassy, London, 11 September 1918, ibid., 516–17.

[183] Memorandum for General Graves of an Interview between Morris and Vologodsky, 21 September 1918, Vladivostok, Historical Files of the AEF, file 21-21.3.

[184] Graves, *Adventure*, 66–67.

[185] Lansing to Wilson, 9 September 1918, *Wilson Papers*, 49:491–93.

[186] Graves to Adjutant General #20, received 12 September 1918, Robert L. Eichelberger Papers, box 53, Special Collections Department, William R. Perkins Library, Duke University.

[187] Baker to Wilson, 17 October 1918, Newton D. Baker Papers, Library of Congress, Manuscript Division, box 8, in Edward M. Coffman, *The Hilt of the Sword; The Career of Peyton C. March* (Madison: University of Wisconsin Press, 1966) 102. There is no record

of Wilson's response, but we may assume that he was not as alarmed as Baker. Whatever Wilson's feelings, Graves kept his command.

[188] March to Wilson and Bliss to March, 12 September 1918, *Wilson Papers*, 49:530–32.

[189] Ibid.

[190] Ibid.

[191] Knox to Milner, 16 September 1918, Clemenceau to Janin, 16 September 1918, quoted in John Bradley, *Allied Intervention in Russia* (New York: Basic Books, 1968) 109.

[192] Wilson to Lansing, 17 September 1918, *Wilson Papers*, 51:25–26.

[193] Ibid., 25.

[194] Lansing to Wilson, 21 September 1918, *Wilson Papers*, 51:87.

[195] Wilson to Lansing, 23 September 1918, ibid., 91.

[196] Graves, *Adventure*, 68.

[197] Ibid., 68.

[198] Paris to Clemenceau, quoted in Bradley, *Allied Intervention in Russia*, 108.

[199] Lansing to Wilson, 21 September 1918, *Wilson Papers*, 51:86–87.

[200] Masaryk to Lansing, 23 September 1918, ibid., 96–97.

[201] Lansing to Wilson, 18 September 1918, ibid., 61–62.

[202] Lansing to Wilson, 24 September 1918, ibid., 97–98.

[203] Graves, *Adventure*, 85.

[204] Morris to State Department, 23 September 1918, *Wilson Papers*, 51:99. Morris supported this move. He felt that Graves could protect the railroad, organize civilian relief, and check Gajda's exuberance better from Omsk.

[205] Graves to March, 24 September 1918, William S. Graves Papers, box 1, GW1, Hoover Institution on War, Revolution, and Peace, Stanford University, Stanford, California.

[206] Lansing to Morris, 26 September 1918, in US Department of State, *Foreign Relations of the United States, 1918, Russia*, 2:392–94.

[207] Graves, *Adventure*, 67.

[208] Ibid., 79–80.

[209] Ackerman, *"Trailing the Bolsheviki,"* 42.

[210] Graves, *Adventure*, 80–81.

[211] Final Report of Operations, Historical Files of the AEF, file 21-33.6.

[212] "Summary of the Proposal of General Graves," 21 September 1918, Historical Files of the AEF, file 21-21.3.

[213] Clarence Manning, *The Siberian Fiasco* (New York: Library Publishers, Inc., 1952) 98.

[214] 12 October 1918, Historical Files of the AEF, file 21-4.7.

[215] Joseph S. Loughran, 1 April 1975, The World War I Survey, AEF, Siberia, US Army Military History Institute, Carlisle Barracks, Pennsylvania.

216 Kindall, *American Soldiers in Siberia*, 25–27.

217 Ibid., 25–27.

218 Russell C. Swihart, Joseph Longuevan Papers, US Army Military History Institute, Carlisle Barracks, Pennsylvania.

219 Millard S. Curtis Papers, "History of the 27th Infantry Regiment," 17, US Army Military History Institute, Carlisle Barracks, Pennsylvania.

220 Loughran, The World War I Survey, US Army Military History Institute.

221 Graves, *Adventure*, 119–20.

222 Ibid., 120–21.

223 March, *The Nation at War*, 226–27.

224 Goldhurst, *The Midnight War*, 120.

225 Graves, *Adventure*, 121.

226 Ackerman, *"Trailing the Bolsheviki,"* 186.

227 Ibid., 186–88.

228 Syrový to Graves, 1 October 1918, Historical Files of the AEF, file 21-23.11.

229 Girsa, Czechoslovak National Council to Graves, 29 September 1918, Historical Files of the AEF, file 21-21.3; Goldhurst, *The Midnight War*, 116.

230 *Civil War in Russia, 1917–1920*, 93.

231 Lansing Diaries, 26 October 1918, quoted in Linda Killen, *The Russian Bureau* (Lexington KY: The University Press of Kentucky 1983) 79.

232 Ibid., 6.

233 Graves, *Adventure*, 143.

234 Graves to the Adjutant General, 31 October 1918, file 370.22, Russian Expedition War Records Collection, National Archives.

235 Miles to Lansing, 28 October 1918, *Wilson Papers*, 51:478.

236 Miles to Lansing, 8 November 1918, file 861.00/3214 1/2, General Records of the Department of State, National Archives.

237 Baker to Wilson, 6 November 1918, *Wilson Papers*, 51:608.

238 Betty Miller Unterberger, *America's Siberian Expedition, 1918–1920: A Study in National Policy* (Durham NC: Duke University Press, 1956) 3–4.

239 Otani to Graves, 21 November 1918, Historical Files of the AEF, file 21-4.7.

240 Graves, *Adventure*, 108; and Roger W. Straus to Graves, 19 November 1918, Historical Files of the AEF, file 21-21.1.

241 E. Davis to AEF Headquarters, Historical Files of the AEF, file 21-23.11.

242 Kindall, *American Soldiers in Siberia*, 190–91.

243 Ibid.

244 Graves, *Adventure*, 148.

245 Alexievski to Graves, 11 October 1918, Historical Files of the AEF, file 21-21.3.

[246] Graves, *Adventure*, 87.

[247] Benjamin Dickson Papers, Special Collections, US Military Academy Library, quoted in Goldhurst, *The Midnight War*, 127.

[248] Graves to the Adjutant General, 1 October 1918, Historical Files of the AEF, file 21-21.3.

[249] Ibid.

[250] Ibid.

[251] The Russian Railway Service Corps was staffed by American experts. Their job was to administer the stretches of the Trans-Siberian Railroad, not under Bolshevik control, and the entire Chinese Eastern Railroad as well.

[252] J. E. Greiner, "The American Railway Commission in Russia," *Railway Review* 5/3 (August 1918): 171.

[253] Graves to March, 24 September 1918, Historical Files of the AEF, file 21-21.3.

[254] Graves, *America's Siberian Adventure, 1918–1920*, 144.

[255] Ibid.

[256] Ibid., 96.

[257] Ibid.

[258] John Bradley, *Allied Intervention in Russia* (New York: Basic Books, 1968) 114.

[259] Goldhurst, *The Midnight War: The American Intervention in Russia, 1918–1920*, 142–43; Luckett, *The White Generals*, 163; Miller Unterberger, *The United States, Revolutionary Russia, and the Rise of Czechoslovakia*, 222.

[260] Patrick R. Taylor, "Aleksandr Vasil'evich Kolchak," in Joseph L. Wieczynski, ed., *Modern Encyclopedia of Russian and Soviet History*, 60 vols. (Gulf Breeze FL: Academic International Press, 1980) 17:110–13.

[261] Morris to Lansing, 4 August 1919, in United States Department of State, *Papers Relating to the Foreign Relations of the United States, 1919, Russia* (Washington DC: US Government Printing Office, 1931–1932) 403.

[262] Colonel John Ward, *With the "Die-Hards" in Siberia* (New York: George H. Doran Co., 1920) 227.

[263] Quoted in Peter Fleming, *The Fate of Admiral Kolchak* (New York: Harcourt, Brace and World, Inc., 1963) 95, and John Silverlight, *The Victor's Dilemma* (New York: Weybright and Talley, 1970) 235.

[264] United States Department of State, *Papers Relating to the Foreign Relations of the United States, 1918, Russia*, 3 vols. (Washington DC: US Government Printing Office, 1937) 2:433–35.

[265] Ibid., 440–41.

[266] Ishii to Wilson, 20 November 1918, *The Papers of Woodrow Wilson*, ed. Arthur S. Link, et al. (Princeton: Princeton University, Press, 1984) 53:144–47.

[267] Graves to Adjutant General, in Baker to Wilson, 22 November 1918, *Wilson Papers*, 53:168–69.

[268] Baker to Wilson, 23 November 1918, ibid., 184–85.

[269] Baker to Wilson, 27 November 1918, ibid., 227–29.

[270] Ibid.

[271] See Chicherin to Wilson, 29 October 1918, *Wilson Papers*, 51:508–510.

[272] Chicherin to Wilson. 2 November 1918, ibid., 555–61.

[273] Ibid.

[274] Lansing to Wilson, 21 November 1918, *Wilson Papers*, 53.151–52.

[275] Wilson to Macfarland, 27 November 1918, ibid., 221.

[276] Elena Varneck and H. H. Fischer, eds., *The Testimony of Admiral Kolchak and Other Siberian Materials* (Stanford CA: Stanford University Press, 1935) 186–87.

[277] Quoted in Graves, *Adventure*, 107.

[278] Ibid., 97.

[279] Ibid.

[280] Ibid., 98.

[281] Ibid. 191–92; and George Stewart, *The White Armies of Russia* (New York: MacMillan and Co., 1933) 279.

[282] Graves, *Adventure*, 147.

[283] Graves to Morris, 11 November 1918, William S. Graves Papers, box 1, GW1, Hoover Institution on War, Revolution, and Peace, Stanford University, Stanford, California.

[284] John Albert White, *The Siberian Intervention* (Princeton: Princeton University Press, 1950) 232.

[285] Quoted in Silverlight, *The Victor's Dilemma*, 237.

[286] Baker's forward to Graves, *Adventure*, x–xi.

[287] Ibid., xiv.

[288] Diary of William Christian Bullitt, 9 December 1918, *Wilson Papers*, 53:352. See also Bell to Winslow, 31 December 1918, *Wilson Papers*, 53:574–76.

[289] Polk to Lansing, 21 December 1918, *Wilson Papers*, 53:463–66.

[290] Polk to Lansing, 30 December 1918, ibid., 555–58.

[291] Wilson believed that a just peace treaty would eliminate the necessity of dealing with many separate problems. Smuts's Memorandum on the League of Nations, 26 December 1918, ibid., 515. This memorandum made a great impression upon Wilson. In point 2 Smuts recommended that concerning the peoples and territories formerly belonging to Russia, Austria-Hungary, and Turkey, the League of Nations should have the right of ultimate disposal of these problems in accordance with certain fundamental principles. Point 3 outlined what these fundamental principles were. First, there would be no annexation of

any of these territories by the victors, including Japan, and second any future government of these territories and peoples should be allowed to exercise self-determination. Point 4 stated that any authority, or administration necessary in these territories apart from their own should be the exclusive function of the League of Nations and be exercised by or on behalf of it.

[292] Imperial War Cabinet #47 Draft Minutes of a Meeting Held at 10 Downing Street SW on Monday, 30 December 1918, at 3:30 P.M. *Wilson Papers*, 53:558–60.

[293] Ibid., 568.

[294] Ibid., 568.

[295] Baker to Wilson, 1 January 1919, *Wilson Papers*, 53:582–83. See also *Congressional Record*, 65th Cong., 3rd sess., 30, pt. 1:342–46, 864.

[296] Polk to Lansing, 6 January 1919, *Wilson Papers*, 53:627.

[297] Ibid., 628–32.

[298] Ibid., 632–33.

[299] Lansing to Wilson, 9 January 1919, *Wilson Papers*, 53:706; Wilson to Lansing, 10 January 1919, *Wilson Papers*, 53:709.

[300] Litvinov to Wilson, 24 December 1918, *Wilson Papers*, 53:492–94.

[301] Wilson to Lansing, 10 January 1919, *Wilson Papers*, 53:709.

[302] Wilson to Tumulty, 10 January 1919, *Wilson Papers*, 53:709.

[303] Hankey's Notes, Meeting of the Supreme War Council, 12 January 1919, 2.30 P.M., *Wilson Papers*, 54:8.

[304] Hankey's Notes, Meeting of the Supreme War Council, 12 January 1919, 4:00 P.M., ibid., 54:21–23.

[305] Hankey's Notes of Two Meetings of the Council of Ten, 21 January 1919, ibid., 54:179–89; Hankey's Notes of a Meeting of the Council of Ten, 22 January 1919, *Wilson Papers*, 54:205–206; Diary of Dr. Grayson, 22 January 1919, ibid. 199. See Appendix B.

[306] Chicherin to Allied and Associated Governments, in US Department of State, *Foreign Relations of the United States, 1919, Russia*, 39–42.

[307] Minister of Foreign Affairs at Omsk to Russian Embassy at Washington, 19 February 1919, in US Department of State, *Foreign Relations of the United States, 1919, Russia*, 71.

[308] John Silverlight, *The Victor's Dilemma* (New York: Weybright and Talley, 1970) 153–54; Lansing to Wilson, 17 February 1919, *Wilson Papers*, 55:202–203; House to Wilson, 17 February 1919, *Wilson Papers*, 55:303–304.

[309] Wilson to American Commissioners, 19 February 1919, *Wilson Papers*, 55:208.

[310] US Department of State, *Foreign Relations of the United States, 1919, Russia*, 461.

[311] Baker to Department of State, 14 January 1919, file 861.00/3651, General Records of the Department of State, National Archives, Washington, DC, quoted in Betty Miller

Unterberger, *America's Siberian Expedition, 1918–1920: A Study in National Policy* (Durham NC: Duke University Press, 1956) 114.

[312] Lansing to Polk, 31 January 1919, *Wilson Papers*, 54:411–13.

[313] Ibid., 248–49.

[314] Graves, *Adventure*, 176, 181.

[315] Ibid., 122.

[316] Ibid., 84.

[317] Ibid., 68.

[318] Ibid., 124–25.

[319] William Henry Chamberlin, *The Russian Revolution, 1917–1921*, 2 vols. (New York: MacMillan Co., 1935) 2:163.

[320] Sylvain Kindall, *American Soldiers in Siberia* (New York: Richard R. Smith, 1945) 21.

[321] Gustav Becvar, *The Lost Legion* (London: Stanley Paul and Co., 1939) 205.

[322] Ibid. 195.

[323] Graves, *Adventure*, 113.

[324] Dr. Svoboda, Russian Branch of the Czecho-Slovak National Council, 6 December 1918, Historical Files of the American Expeditionary Forces in Siberia, 1918–1920, National Archives, Washington, DC, file 21-33.5.

[325] Quoted in Henry Baerlein, *The March of the Seventy Thousand* (London: Leonard Parsons, 1926) 198.

[326] Lt. Col. David P. Barrows, Intelligence Summary, No. 36, to AEF Headquarters, 30 November 1918, Historical Files of the AEF, file 21-33.5.

[327] Goldhurst, *The Midnight War*, 147.

[328] Baerlein, *The March of the Seventy Thousand*, 222–23.

[329] Quoted in Silverlight, *The Victor's Dilemma*, 235.

[330] Baerlein, *The March of the Seventy Thousand*, 269.

[331] Sharp to Department of State, 12 February 1919, file 861.00/3837, General Records of the Department of State, National Archives, quoted in Unterberger, *America's Siberia Expedition*, 127–28; and Harris to Department of State, 25 January 1919, and Phillips to Lansing, 29 March 1919, in US Department of State, *Foreign Relations of the United States, 1919, Russia*, 274–75, 279–80.

[332] Millard S. Curtis Papers, "History of the 27th Infantry Regiment," 19, US Army Military History Institute, Carlisle Barracks, Pennsylvania.

[333] Graves, *Adventure*, 130.

[334] Curtis Papers, "History of the 27th Infantry Regiment," 19.

[335] Graves, *Adventure*, 130.

[336] Curtis Papers, "History of the 27th Infantry Regiment," 19.

[337] Graves, *Adventure*, 130–31.

[338] Ibid., 132–33.

[339] Ibid., 137.

[340] Styer to AEF Headquarters, 11 February 1919; Graves to Styer, 12 February 1919; Historical Files of the AEF, file 21-21.3; and Curtis Papers, "History of the 27th Infantry Regiment," 20.

[341] Graves, *Adventure*, 134.

[342] Quoted in ibid., 135.

[343] Intelligence Summary No. 34, 26 November 1918, Historical Files of the AEF, file 21-33.5.

[344] Straus to Intelligence Officer, AEF Siberia, 29 November 1918, Historical Files of the AEF, file 21-33.5.

[345] David P. Barrows, Intelligence Summary No. 41, 6 December 1918, Historical Files of the AEF, file 21-33.5.

[346] Kolchak to Major General Volkoff, 6 December 1918, Historical Files of the AEF, file 21-33.5.

[347] Kolchak to Bakmetev, 8 December 1918, file 861.00/3462, General Records of the Department of State, National Archives, quoted in Unterberger, *America's Siberian Expedition*, 120.

[348] R. L. Eichelberger, Intelligence Officer, 15 December 1918, Historical Files of the AEF, file 21-33.5.

[349] Barrows to Eichelberger, 19 December 1918, Intelligence Summary No. 50, Historical Files of the AEF, file 21-33.5.

[350] Schuyler to Intelligence Section, 20 December 1918, No. 50, Historical Files of the AEF, file 21-33.5.

[351] Reinsch to Polk, 27 March 1919, in US Department of State, *Foreign Relations of the United States, 1919, Russia*, 484–85.

[352] Ward, *With the "Die-Hards" in Siberia*, 49.

[353] Graves, *Adventure*, 186.

[354] Ibid., 187.

[355] White, *The Siberian Intervention*, 272–73.

[356] Graves, *Adventure*, 183–84.

[357] Ibid., 187–88.

[358] Ibid., 150.

[359] Kindall, *American Soldiers in Siberia*, 84.

[360] Polk to Commission to Negotiate the Peace, 10 January 1919, in US Department of State, *Foreign Relations of the United States, 1919, Russia*, 195–96.

[361] Reinsch to Polk, 30 January 1919, ibid., 198.

[362] In J. F. N. Bradley, *Civil War in Russia, 1917–1920* (New York: St. Martin's Press, 1975) 100–101.

[363] Graves, *Adventure*, 145.

[364] Quoted in White, *The Siberian Intervention*, 115.

[365] Morris to Lansing, 4 August 1919, in US Department of State, *Foreign Relations of the United States, 1919, Russia*, 403–404.

[366] Polk to Commission to Negotiate Peace, 29 March 1919, in ibid., 200.

[367] In Graves, *Adventure*, 189.

[368] Ibid. 190.

[369] Ibid. 191.

[370] Ibid. 196.

[371] Quoted in Silverlight, *The Victor's Dilemma*, 237.

[372] Graves, *Adventure*, 112; Polk to Lansing and McCormick, 13 March 1919, *Wilson Papers*, 55:493–94.

[373] Ibid., 159.

[374] Polk to Lansing, 13 March 1919, *Wilson Papers*, 55:494–95.

[375] Ibid., 165.

[376] Ibid., xxi.

[377] Ibid., 165–66.

[378] Lansing to Wilson, *Wilson Papers*, 56:186.

[379] British Foreign Office to Lansing, in US Department of State, *Foreign Relations of the United States, 1919, Russia*, 499–500.

[380] Graves, *Adventure*, 18–19.

[381] Ibid., 169–71.

[382] Morris to Polk, 8 March 1919, file 861.77/736, General Records of the Department of State, National Archives.

[383] Lansing to Wilson, 22 March 1919, *Wilson Papers*, 56:184–85.

[384] Ibid., 56:184.

[385] Phillips to Lansing, 28 March 1919, file 861.00/417a, General Records of the Department of State, National Archives.

[386] 31 March 1919, file 861.00/4967, General Records of the Department of State, National Archives.

[387] Graves, *Adventure*, 118–19.

[388] Ibid., 93.

[389] Baker to Wilson, 3 March 1919, *Wilson Papers*, 55:399.

[390] Graves, *Adventure*, 160.

[391] Bullitt to Wilson, Lansing, and House, 16 March 1919, *Wilson Papers*, 55:540–45.

[392] Grayson Diary, 25 March 1919, *Wilson Papers*, 56:247; R. S. Baker Diary, 27 March 1919, *Wilson Papers*, 56:338.

[393] Mantoux's Notes of Two Meetings of the Council of Four, *Wilson Papers*, 56:254.

[394] Ibid., 252–57.

[395] Mantoux's Notes of Two Meetings of the Council of Four, *Wilson Papers*, 56:320.

[396] Ibid., 328–29.

[397] Graves, *Adventure*, 93.

[398] House Diary, 27 March 1919, *Wilson Papers*, 56:336–37.

[399] Hoover to Wilson, 28 March 1919, *Wilson Papers*, 56:377.

[400] Tumulty to Wilson, 2 April 1919, *Wilson Papers*, 56:551–52.

[401] Nansen to Wilson, 3 April 1919, *Wilson Papers*, 56:575–76.

[402] House Diary, 5 April 1919, *Wilson Papers*, 57:34–35.

[403] Nansen to Lenin, 17 April 1919, *Wilson Papers*, 57:438–39.

[404] House Diary, 19 April 1919, *Wilson Papers*, 57:503–505.

[405] *Wilson Papers*, 58:vii–viii, 625–28.

[406] Baker to Wilson, 4 April 1919, *Wilson Papers*, 56:576–77.

[407] Baker to Wilson, 4 April 1919, *Wilson Papers*, 56:576–77; Phillips to American Commissioners, 4 April 1919, *Wilson Papers*, 56:606–607.

[408] Lansing to Wilson, 12 April 1919, *Wilson Papers*, 57:313–15.

[409] American Commission to Negotiate the Peace to State Department, 11 April 1919, *Wilson Papers*, 57:315.

[410] Lansing and McCormick to Polk, 16 April 1919, *Wilson Papers*, 57:420–22.

[411] Bliss to Wilson, 18 April 1919, *Wilson Papers*, 57:460–61; Wilson to Benson, 2 May 1919, *Wilson Papers*, 58:354.

[412] Polk to American Commission, 6 May 1919, *The Papers of Woodrow Wilson*, ed. Arthur S. Link, et al. (Princeton: Princeton University Press, 1984) 58:494–96.

[413] Hankey and Mantoux's Notes of the Meeting of the Council of Four, *Wilson Papers*, 58:506–507.

[414] Several observers remarked that Wilson's behavior had changed as a result of his illness. Herbert Hoover pointed out that beforehand Wilson had been willing to listen to advice and had a quick and incisive grasp of essentials. Afterwards Wilson "groped for ideas" and others remarked that his memory was affected. Edwin A. Weinstein, *Woodrow Wilson: A Medical and Psychological Biography* (Princeton: Princeton University Press, 1981) 344.

[415] Hankey's Notes, Meeting of the Council of Four, 9 May 1919 *Wilson Papers*, 58:573–75.

[416] Ibid.

[417] Ibid.

[418] Mantoux's Notes, Meeting of the Council of Four, 9 May 1919, *Wilson Papers*, 58:575–78.

[419] Mantoux's Notes, Meeting of the Council of Four, 9 May 1919, *Wilson Papers*, 58:575–78.

[420] Hankey's Notes of a Meeting of the Council of Four, 10 May 1919, *Wilson Papers*, 59:14–21.

[421] Hankey's Notes of a Meeting of the Council of Four, 10 May 1919, *Wilson Papers*, 59:14–21.

[422] Mantoux's Notes, Meeting of the Council of Four, 10 May 1919, *Wilson Papers*, 59:29–31.

[423] Ibid., 29–31.

[424] Ibid.

[425] Wilson to Polk, 14 May 1919, *Wilson Papers*, 59:148.

[426] Wilson to McCormick, 16 May 1919, *Wilson Papers*, 59:188.

[427] Hoover to Wilson, 16 May 1919, *Wilson Papers*, 59:192–97.

[428] Hankey's Notes, Meeting of the Council of Four, 20 May 1919, *Wilson Papers*, 59:300–301n8.

[429] Mantoux's Notes, Meeting of the Council of Four, 20 May 1919, *Wilson Papers*, 59:301

[430] Hankey's Notes, Meeting of the Council of Four, 20 May 1919, *Wilson Papers*, 59:301.

[431] Mantoux's Notes, Meeting of the Council of Four, 20 May 1919, *Wilson Papers*, 59:311–12.

[432] Mantoux's Notes, Meeting of the Council of Four, *Wilson Papers*, 59:310–12.

[433] Hankey's Notes, Meeting of the Council of Four, 17 May 1919, *Wilson Papers*, 59:225; McCormick to Wilson, 17 May 1919, *Wilson Papers*, 59:235–36.

[434] McCormick to Wilson, 17 May 1919, *Wilson Papers*, 59:233.

[435] Polk to Lansing and McCormick, 9 May 1919, *Wilson Papers*, 59:234–35.

[436] Ibid.

[437] Wilson to Baker, 19 May 1919, *Wilson Papers*, 59:281.

[438] Polk to Auchincloss, 22 May 1919, *Wilson Papers*, 59:409–410.

[439] Ibid.

[440] Polk to Auchincloss, 22 May 1919, *Wilson Papers*, 59:409–10.

[441] Wilson to Tumulty, 23 May 1919, *Wilson Papers*, 59:449.

[442] Hankey's Notes, Meeting of the Council of Four, 23 May 1919, *Wilson Papers*, 59:421.

[443] Hankey's Notes, Meeting of the Council of Four, 23 May 1919, *Wilson Papers*, 59:435–38. Wilson was wary of committing himself to Kolchak, despite the wishes of the British and the French. His physician, Dr. Grayson reported that Wilson was unwilling to accept "a pig in a poke," and would not support Kolchak without explicit assurances that

his triumph would lead to democracy and not dictatorship. Grayson Diary, 24 May 1919, *Wilson Papers*, 59:453.

[444] Hankey's Notes, Meeting of the Council of Four, 24 May 1919, 11:00 A.M., *Wilson Papers*, 59:457–58.

[445] Hankey's Notes, Meeting of the Council of Four, 24 May 1919, *Wilson Papers*, 59:461–65.

[446] Lansing to Wilson, 28 May 1919, *Wilson Papers*, 59:572.

[447] Lansing to Wilson, 30 May 1919, *Wilson Papers*, 59:619.

[448] Stewart, *The White Armies of Russia: A Chronicle of Counter Revolution and Allied Intervention*, 281–83.

[449] Mantoux's Notes, Meeting of the Council of Four, 3 June 1919, *Wilson Papers*, 60:95.

[450] Kolchak to Clemenceau, 4 June 1919, *Wilson Papers*, 60:141–44.

[451] Mantoux's Notes, Meeting of the Council of Four, 17 June 1919, *Wilson Papers*, 60:261–62.

[452] Mautoux's Notes, Meeting of the Council of Four, 12 June 1919, *Wilson Papers*, 60:477.

[453] Phillips to Lansing and McCormick, 16 June 1919, *Wilson Papers*, 60:608.

[454] Ibid., 609.

[455] Mantoux's Notes, Meeting of the Council of Four, 17 June 1919, *Wilson Papers*, 60:636.

[456] Ibid., 637.

[457] Ibid., 636–38. Wilson had blockaded Mexico without a declaration of war a few years earlier. He was willing to use his authority as commander-in-chief in creative ways to further his conception of foreign policy. But he could fall back on convention when it served his purposes, as was the case here.

[458] McCormick Diary, 23 June 1919, *Wilson Papers*, 61:110–11.

[459] McCormick to Wilson, 24 June 1919, *Wilson Papers*, 61:130–31.

[460] Hankey and Mantoux's Notes of a Meeting of the Council of Four, 25 June 1919, *Wilson Papers*, 61:154–55; see also ibid., 164–66.

[461] Hankey's Notes, Meeting of the Council of Four, 23 June 1919, *Wilson Papers*, 61:201–202.

[462] Hankey's Notes, Meeting of Council of Four, 26 June 1919, *Wilson Papers*, 61:196–97.

[463] Hankey's Notes, Meeting of the Council of Four, 27 June 1919, *Wilson Papers*, 61:271.

[464] Notes of a Press Conference by Walter Edward Weyl, 27 June 1919, *Wilson Papers*, 61:244.

[465] *Congressional Record*, 66th Cong. 1st sess., 1864.

[466] Polk to Lansing and McCormick, 27 June 1919, *Wilson Papers*, 61:288.

[467] *Wilson Papers*, 61:viii.

[468] Report of a Press Conference in the East Room of the White House, 10 July 1919, *Wilson Papers*, 61:424.

[469] Polk to Wilson, 12 July 1919, *Wilson Papers*, 61:465–66.

[470] Baker to Wilson, 15 July 1919, *Wilson Papers*, 61:485.

[471] Polk to Wilson, 16 July 1919, *Wilson Papers*, 61:494.

[472] *Wilson Papers*, 62:vii.

[473] Phillips to Wilson, 21 July 1919, *Wilson Papers*, 61:571–73.

[474] Wilson to President of the Senate, 22 July 1919, *Wilson Papers*, 61:580–82.

[475] Ibid., 581.

[476] Ibid.

[477] Ibid., 579–82.

[478] Caldwell to Lansing, 25 July 1919, *Wilson Papers*, 61:636–38.

[479] Desk Diary of Robert Lansing, 25 July 1919, *Wilson Papers*, 61:629.

[480] Baker to Wilson, 31 July 1919, *Wilson Papers*, 62:82–83.

[481] Ibid., 84.

[482] Ibid.

[483] Ibid., 85–86.

[484] Ibid.

[485] Graves to Adjutant General, 21 June 1919, *Wilson Papers*, 62:89–90.

[486] Lansing Desk Diary, 7 August 1919, *Wilson Papers*, 62:202; Lansing to Wilson, *Wilson Papers*, 62:203.

[487] Statement by Dewitt C. Poole, Jr., 7 August 1919, *Wilson Papers*, 62:203–205.

[488] Poole to Lansing, 21 August 1919, *Wilson Papers*, 62:441–48.

[489] Wilson to Baker, 21 August 1919, *Wilson Papers*, 62:433–34.

[490] Lansing to Wilson, 30 August 1919, *Wilson Papers*, 62:588–89.

[491] Ibid., 590–91.

[492] Lansing to Japanese Minister of Foreign Affairs, 28 August 1919, *Wilson Papers*, 62:589–93.

[493] Wilson's Address in Kansas City, 6 September 1919, *Wilson Papers*, 63:70. See also, Wilson's Address in the Des Moines Coliseum, 6 September 1919, *Wilson Papers*, 63:76–77 in which he warns against the spread of Bolshivism to the United States.

[494] Lansing to Wilson, 17 September 1919, *Wilson Papers*, 63:337–38.

[495] Joseph Patrick Tumulty, *Woodrow Wilson As I Knew Him* (Garden City NY: The Literary Digest, 1921) 441–43.

[496] *Wilson Papers*, 63:339n4.

[497] Phillips to Wilson, 19 September 1919, *Wilson Papers*, 63:394.

[498] Phillips to Wilson, 19 September 1919, *Wilson Papers*, 63:394–95.

[499] Bert E. Parks, "Woodrow Wilson's Stroke of 2 October 1919," *Wilson Papers*, 63:639–40.

[500] Ibid., 640.

[501] Ibid., 641–42.

[502] Ibid., 646.

[503] Memoir by Irwin Hood Hoover, undated, *Wilson Papers*, 63:634–35.

[504] Ibid., 632–38.

[505] Millard S. Curtis Papers, "History of the 27th Infantry Regiment," 20, US Army Military History Institute, Carlisle Barracks, Pennsylvania.

[506] Sylvain Kindall, *American Soldiers in Siberia* (New York: Richard R. Smith, 1945) 94–95.

[507] Ibid., 105.

[508] Goldhurst, *The Midnight War: The American Intervention in Russia 1918–1920*, 189.

[509] Quoted in John Albert White, *The Siberian Intervention* (Princeton: Princeton University Press, 1950) 119.

[510] William S. Graves, *America's Siberian Adventure, 1918–1920* (New York: Peter Smith, 1941) 93–95.

[511] Robinson to Graves, 17 September 1918, Historical Files of the American Expeditionary Forces in Siberia, 1918–1920, National Archives, Washington, DC, file 21-20.7.

[512] Graves, *Adventure*, 95.

[513] Notes from a dictation on Siberia made by General Robert L. Eichelberger in February 1946, 1-2, Robert L Eichelberger Papers, box 56, Special Collections Department, William R. Perkins Library, Duke University.

[514] "Report by R.L. Eichelberger of his visit to Suchan Mines Siberia," 26 April 1919, Eichelberger Papers, box 1-A.

[515] "Report of 2nd Lt. G.S. Rumans. 31st Infantry on Activity near Pyratin and Novitskaya, 25 April 1919, Eichelberger Papers, box 1-A.

[516] R. L. Eichelberger, "Report on visit to the Suchan Mines." 26 April 1919, Eichelberger Papers, box 1-A.

[517] Eichelberger to Mrs. R. L. Eichelberger, 19 April 1919, Eichelberger Papers, box 1-A.

[518] Eichelberger to Eichelberger, 25 April 1919, Eichelberger Papers, box 1-A.

[519] Eichelberger to Eichelberger, 26 April 1919, Eichelberger Papers, box 1-A. Also Graves to Ivanoff-Rinov, box 1, folder 1.

[520] Ibid.

[521] Eichelberger to Eichelberger, 15 April 1919, Eichelberger Papers, box 1-A.

[522] "Additional memorandum on Siberia (Semenoff)," dictated 7 February 1948, Eichelberger Papers, box 56.

[523] Some of these photographs are in the Eichelberger Papers.

[524] Notes from a dictation on Siberia made by General Robert L. Eichelberger, in February 1946, 3–4, Eichelberger Papers, box 69.

[525] Graves to Morris, 15 April 1919, Graves Papers, box 1, GW4

[526] Graves to Morris, 15 April 1919, ibid.

[527] Graves to Morris, 30 April 1919, ibid.

[528] From *Golos Rabochego*, Number 3, 25 May 1919, quoted in William Henry Chamberlin, *The Russian Revolution, 1917–1921*, 2 vols. (New York: MacMillan Co., 1935) 1:484.

[529] Curtis Papers, "History of the 27th Infantry Regiment," 20.

[530] Graves to Morris, 7 May 1919, Grave Papers, box 1, GW5.

[531] Graves to Adjutant General, 17 May 1919, Graves Papers, box 1, File 1.

[532] "Report of Operations in the Suchan Valley, Siberia: June 22 to July 5," and "Headquarters Mine Guard: Report in Compliance with Memorandum Number 36," Historical Files of the AEF, file 21-33.6.

[533] Fribley to Williams, 25 June 1919, Historical Files of the AEF, file 21-33.5.

[534] Eichelberger to Eichelberger, 27 June 1919, Eichelberger Papers, box 1-B.

[535] Graves to Morris, 24 June 1919, Graves Papers, box 1, GW5.

[536] "Regimental History of the Thirty-first US Infantry, July 1916–July 1920," 29, US Army Military History Institute, Carlisle Barracks, Pennsylvania.

[537] Alan Ferguson to Joseph Longuevan; "Much Ado About Nothing;" and "The Prelude and Aftermath of the Romanovka Massacre As Told to Virginia Cooper Westfall by Russell C. Swihart," Joseph Longuevan Papers, US Army Military History Institute, Carlisle Barracks, Pennsylvania.

[538] Goldhurst, *The Midnight War*, 199–200.

[539] "Prelude and Aftermath of the Romanovka Massacre;" and "September 14, 1919," Longuevan Papers, US Army Military History Institute.

[540] "Headquarters Mine Guard: Report in Compliance with Memorandum Number 36," Historical Files of the AEF, file 21-33.6.

[541] John Wilmer Blue to Flora Blue, 22 August 1919, Blue Papers, in the possession of Mrs. W. G. Lowe, Raeford, North Carolina.

[542] Bliss to Baker, 5 October 1919, Tasker Howard Bliss Papers, Library of Congress, Manuscript Division, Washington, DC, quoted in Betty Miller Unterberger, *America's Siberian Expedition, 1918–1920: A Study in National Policy* (Durham NC: Duke University Press, 1956) 164.

[543] Graves, *Adventure*, 209.

[544] Ibid., 216.

[545] United States Department of State, *Papers Relating to the Foreign Relations of the United States, 1919, Russia* (Washington, DC: US Government Printing Office, 1937) 205.

[546] Henry Baerlein, *The March of the Seventy Thousand* (London: Leonard Parsons, 1926) 231.

[547] US Department of State, *Foreign Relations of the United States, 1919, Russia*, 390–91.

[548] Morris to Secretary of State, 22 June 1919, in ibid., 394.

[549] Morris to Acting Secretary of State, 22 July 1919, in ibid., 395–96.

[550] Graves, *Adventure*, 216–19.

[551] Ibid., 235.

[552] Sargent to AGWAR, #417, 9 August 1919, Eichelberger Papers, box 55.

[553] Sargent to AGWAR, 16 August 1919, #425, Eichelberger Papers, box 55.

[554] Morris to Acting Secretary of State, 8 August 1919, FR 1919, Russia, 407–408.

[555] Ibid.

[556] Ibid.

[557] Lansing to Morris, 12 August 1919, ibid., 412–13.

[558] Ibid., 415.

[559] Lansing toMorris, 25 August 1919, ibid., 421–22.

[560] Graves, *Adventure*, 242–44.

[561] Baker to Lansing, 29 August 1919, Newton D. Baker Papers, Library of Congress, Manuscript Division, quoted in Unterberger, *America's Siberian Expedition*, 167–68.

[562] Graves, *Adventure*, 248–50.

[563] Ibid., 250–55.

[564] Kindall, *American Soldiers in Siberia*, 224–25.

[565] Graves to Galen, 15 September 1919, Graves Papers, box 1, folder 1.

[566] Ibid.

[567] US Department of State, *Foreign Relations of the United States, 1919, Russia*, 540–41.

[568] Ibid., 519, 522.

[569] Graves, *Adventure*, 260–62.

[570] US Department of State, *Foreign Relations of the United States, 1919, Russia*, 426–27.

[571] Ibid., 427–30.

[572] Ibid., 215.

[573] Morris to Phillips, 23 September 1919, file 861.00/5264, General Records of the Department of State, National Archives, Washington, DC, quoted in Unterberger, *America's Siberian Expedition*, 163.

[574] US Department of State, *Foreign Relations of the United States, 1919, Russia*, 522–23.

[575] Ibid., 530–31.

[576] Graves to the Adjutant General, 8 October 1919, file 861.00/5472; and Macgowan to Lansing, 8 October 1919, file 861.00/5360, General Records of the Department of State, National Archives, quoted in Unterberger, *America's Siberian Expedition*, 172.

[577] Baker to Grayson, 9 October 1919, Baker Papers, quoted in ibid.

[578] US Department of State, *Foreign Relations of the United States, 1919, Russia*, 444–45.

[579] E. David Cronon, ed., *Josephus Daniels Cabinet Diaries, 1913–1921* (Lincoln: University of Nebraska Press, 1963) 6 October 1919, 445.

[580] Ibid., 8 October 1919, 446–47.

[581] Ibid., 10 October 1919, 447–48.

[582] US Department of State, *Foreign Relations of the United States, 1919, Russia*, 444–45, and Eichelberger to Chief of Staff, Memos on Conversation with Dr. Teusler, 23 October 1919, Eichelberger Papers, box 54.

[583] US Department of State, *Foreign Relations of the United States, 1919, Russia*, 222.

[584] Eichelberger to Eichelberger, 1 November 1919, Eichelberger Papers, box 1-B.

[585] Quoted in Graves, *Adventure*, 277–78.

[586] Clarence Manning, *The Siberian Fiasco* (New York: Library Publishers, Inc., 1952) 161.

[587] Goldhurst, *The Midnight War*, 238–48.

[588] Eichelberger to Eichelberger, 17 November 1919, Eichelberger Papers, box 1-B.

[589] Intelligence Summary Number 357, 18 November 1919, Historical Files of the AEF Siberia, file 21-33.5.

[590] Eichelberger to Eichelberger, 18 November 1919, Eichelberger Papers, box 1-B.

[591] Graves, *Adventure*, 283–86.

[592] Ibid.

[593] US Department of State, *Foreign Relations of the United States, 1919, Russia*, 225–26.

[594] Ibid., 226.

[595] Graves to AGWAR. 26 November 1919, Eichelberger Papers, box 55.

[596] Ibid., 229.

[597] Lansing Diary, 30 November 1919, Lansing Papers, box 2 in Edward M. Coffman, *The Hilt of the Sword; The Career of Peyton C. March* (Madison: University of Wisconsin Press, 1966) 217.

[598] David Footman, *Civil War in Russia* (London: Faber and Faber, 1961) 225.

[599] US Department of State, *Foreign Relations of the United States, 1919, Russia*, 230–31.

[600] Ibid., 231–32.

[601] Ibid., 232.

[602] Ibid., 232–33.

[603] Ibid., 234–35.

[604] Ibid., 235.

⁶⁰⁵ Peter Fleming, *The Fate of Admiral Kolchak* (New York: Harcourt, Brace and World, Inc., 1963) 195–97.

⁶⁰⁶ Baerlein, *The March of the Seventy Thousand*, 252.

⁶⁰⁷ Memorandum of a Conversation between Long and the Russian Ambassador, 2 December 1919, Long Papers, Library of Congress, Washington, DC, quoted in Unterberger, *America's Siberia Expedition*, 177.

⁶⁰⁸ Lansing to Wilson, 4 December 1919, *The Papers of Woodrow Wilson*, ed. Arthur S. Link, et al. (Princeton: Princeton University Press, 1984) quoted in Killen, 7.

⁶⁰⁹ Graves, *Adventure*, 295.

⁶¹⁰ Ibid., 296–97.

⁶¹¹ Lansing to Wilson, 23 December 1919, file 861.00/6107, General Records of the Department of State, National Archives, quoted in Unterberger, *America's Siberia Expedition*, 176–77.

⁶¹² Graves, *Adventure*, 302.

⁶¹³ Ibid., 302–303.

⁶¹⁴ Poole to Lansing, 9 January 1920, file 861.00/0126, General Records of the Department of State, National Archives, quoted in Unterberger, *America's Siberia Expedition*, 178.

⁶¹⁵ Quoted in Stanley S. Jados, *Documents on Russian-American Relations* (Washington, DC: Catholic University of America, 1965) 45.

⁶¹⁶ Paul Chwialkowski, "A 'Near Great' General: The Life and Career of Robert L. Eichelberger" (Ph.D. diss. Duke University, Durham NC, 1991).

Aide Memoire[1]

The whole heart of the people of the United States is in the winning of this war. The controlling purpose of the Government of the United States is to do everything that is necessary and effective to win it. It wishes to cooperate in every practicable way with the Allied governments, and to cooperate ungrudgingly; for it has no ends of its own to serve and believes that the war can be won only by common counsel and intimate concert of action. It has sought to study every proposed policy or action in which its cooperation has been asked in this spirit, and states the following conclusions in the confidence that if it finds itself obliged to decline participation in any undertaking or course of action, it will be understood that it does so only because it deems itself precluded from participating by imperative considerations either of policy of fact.

In full agreement with the Allied governments and upon the unanimous advice of the Supreme War Council, the Government of the United States adopted, upon its entrance into the war, a plan for taking part in the fighting on the western front into which all its resources of men and material were to be put, and put as rapidly as possible, and it has carried out that plan with energy and success, pressing its execution more and more rapidly forward and literally putting into it the entire energy and executive force of the nation. This was its response, its very willing and hearty response, to what was the unhesitating judgment alike of its own military advisers and of the advisers of the Allied governments. It is now considering, at the suggestion of the Supreme War Council, the possibility of making very considerable additions even to this immense programme which, if they should prove feasible at all, will tax the industrial processes of the United States and the shipping facilities of the whole group of associated nations to the utmost. It has thus concentrated all its plans and all its resources upon this single absolutely necessary object.

In such circumstances it feels it to be its duty to say that it cannot, so long as the military situation on the western front remains critical, consent to break or slacken the force of its present effort by diverting any part of its military force to other points or objectives. The United States is at a great distance from the field of action on the western front; it is at a much greater distance from any other field of action. The instrumentalities by which it is to handle its armies and its stores have at great cost and with great difficulty been created in France. They do not exist elsewhere. It is practicable for her to do a great deal in France; it is not practicable for her to do anything of importance or on a large scale upon any other field. The American Government, therefore, very respectfully requests its Associates to accept its deliberate judgment that it should not dissipate its forces by attempting important operations elsewhere.

It regards the Italian front as closely coordinated with the western front, however, and is willing to divert a portion of its military forces from France to Italy if it is the judgment and wish of the Supreme Command that it should do so. It wishes to defer to the decision of the Commander-in-Chief in this matter, as it would wish to defer in all others, particularly because it considers these two fronts so closely related as to be practically but separate parts of a single line and because it would be necessary that any American troops sent to Italy should be subtracted from the number used in France and be actually transported across French territory from the ports now used by armies of the United States.

It is the clear and fixed judgment of the Government of the United States, arrived at after repeated and very searching reconsiderations of the whole situation in Russia, that military intervention there would add to the present sad confusion in Russia rather than cure it, injure her rather than help her, and that it would be of no advantage in the prosecution of our main design, to win the war against Germany. It cannot, therefore, take part in such intervention or sanction it in principle. Military intervention would, in its judgment, even supposing it to be efficacious in its immediate avowed object of delivering an attack upon Germany from the east, be merely a method of making use of Russia, not a method of serving her. Her people could not profit by it, if they profitted by it at all, in time to save them from their present distresses, and their substance would be used to maintain foreign armies, not to reconstitute their own. Military action is admissible in Russia, as the Government of the United States sees the circumstances, only to help the Czecho-Slovaks consolidate their forces and get into successful cooperation with their Slavic kinsmen and to steady any efforts at self-government or self-defence in which the Russians themselves may be willing to accept assistance. Whether from Vladivostok or from Murmansk and Archangel, the only legitimate object for which American or Allied troops can be employed, it submits, is to guard military stores which may subsequently be needed by Russian forces and to render such aid as may be acceptable to the Russians in the organization of their own self-defense. For helping the Czecho-Slovaks there is immediate necessity and sufficient justification. Recent developments have made it evident that that is in the interest of what the Russian people themselves desire, and the Government of the United States is glad to contribute the small force at its disposal for that purpose. It yields, also, to the judgment of the Supreme Command in the matter of establishing a small force at Murmansk, to guard the military stores at Kola and to make it safe for Russian forces to come together in organized bodies in the north. But it owes it to frank counsel to say that it can go not further than these modest and experimental plans. It is not in a position, and has no expectation of being in a position, to take part in organized intervention in adequate force from either Vladivostok or Murmansk and Archangel. It feels that it ought to add, also, that it will feel at liberty to use the few troops it can spare only for the purposes here stated and shall feel obliged to withdraw these forces, in order to add them to the forces at the western front, if the plans in whose execution it is now intended that they should cooperate, should develop into others inconsistent with the policy to which the Government of the United States feels constrained to restrict itself.

At the same time the Government of the United States wishes to say with the utmost cordiality and good will that none of the conclusions here stated is meant to wear the least colour of criticism of what the other governments associated against Germany may think it wise to undertake. It wishes in no way to embarrass their choices of policy. All that is intended here is a perfectly frank and definite statement of the policy which the United States feels obliged to adopt for herself and in the use of her own military forces. The Government of the United States does not wish it to be understood that in so restricting its own activities it is seeking, even by implication, to set limits to the action or to define the policies of its Associates.

It hopes to carry out the plans for safeguarding the rear of the Czecho-Slovaks operating from Vladivostok in a way that will place it and keep it in close cooperation with a small military force like its own from Japan, and if necessary from the other Allies, and that will assure it of the cordial accord of all the Allied powers; and it proposes to ask all associated in this course of action to unite in assuring the people of Russia in the most public and solemn manner that none of the governments uniting in action either in Siberia or in northern Russia contemplates any interference of any kind with the political sovereignty of Russia, any intervention in her internal affairs, or any impairment of her territorial integrity either now or hereafter, but that each of the associated powers has the single object of affording such aid as shall be acceptable, and only such aid as shall be acceptable, to the Russian people in their endeavor to regain control of their own affairs, their own territory, and their own destiny.

It is the hope and purpose of the Government of the United States to take advantage of the earliest opportunity to send to Siberia a commission of merchants, agricultural experts, labour advisers, Red Cross Representatives, and agents of the Young Men's Christian Association accustomed to organizing the best methods of spreading useful information and rendering educational help of a modest sort, in order in some systematic manner to relieve the immediate economic necessities of the people there in every way for which opportunity may open. The execution of this plan will follow and will not be permitted to embarrass the military assistance rendered in the rear of the westward-moving forces of the Czecho-Slovaks.

Woodrow Wilson
Washington, July 17, 1918

[1] *Wilson Papers*, 48:640–43.

———

Hankey's Notes of a Meeting
of the Council of Ten, Quai D'Orsay
January 22, 1919, 3:15 P.M.
Prinkipo Declaration[2]

The single object the representatives of the Associated Powers have had in mind in their discussions of the course they should pursue with regard to Russia has been to help the Russian people, not to hinder them, or to interfere in any manner with their right to settle their own affairs in their own way. They regard the Russian people as their friends not their enemies, and are willing to help them in any way they are willing to be helped. It is clear to them that the troubles and distresses of the Russian people will steadily increase, hunger and privation of every kind become more and more acute, more and more widespread, and more and more impossible to relieve, unless order is restored, and normal conditions of labour, trade, and transportation once more created, and they are seeking some way in which to assist the Russian people to establish order.

They recognize the absolute right of the Russian people to direct their own affairs without dictation or direction of any kind from outside. They do not wish to exploit or make use of Russia in any way. They recognise the revolution without reservation and will in no way and in no circumstances, aid or give countenance to any attempt at a counter-revolution. It is not their wish or purpose to favor or assist any one of those organized groups now contending for the leadership and guidance of Russia as against the others. Their sole and sincere purpose is to do what they can to bring Russia peace and an opportunity to find her way out of her present troubles.

The Associated Powers are now engaged in the solemn and responsible work of establishing the peace of Europe and of the world, and they are keenly alive to the fact that Europe and the world cannot be at peace if Russia is not. They recognize and accept it as their duty, therefore, to serve Russia in this matter as generously, as unselfishly, as thoughtfully, as ungrudgingly as they would serve every other friend and ally. And they are ready to render this service in the way that is most acceptable to the Russian people.

In this spirit and with this purpose, they have taken the following action: they invite every organized group that is now exercising or attempting to exercise, political authority or military control anywhere in Siberia, or within the boundaries of European Russia as they stood before the war just concluded (except in Finland) to send representatives, not exceeding three representatives for each group, to the Princes Islands, Sea of Marmara, where they will be met by representatives of the Associated Powers, provided, in the meantime, there is a truce of arms amongst the parties invited, and that all armed forces anywhere sent or directed against any people or territory outside the boundaries of European Russia or as they stood before the war, or against Finland, or against any people or territory whose autonomous action is in contemplation in the fourteen articles upon which the present negotiations are based, shall be meanwhile withdrawn, and aggressive military action cease. These representatives are invited to confer with the representatives of the Associated Powers in the freest and frankest way, with a view to ascertaining the wishes of all sections of the Russian people, and bringing about, if possible, some understanding and agreement by which Russia may work out her own purposes and happy cooperative relations be established between her people and the other peoples of the world.

A prompt reply to this invitation is requested. Every facility for the journey of the representatives, including transport across the Black Sea, will be given by the Allies, and the parties concerned are expected to give the same facilities. The representative[s] will be expected at the place appointed by 15th February 1919.

---

[2] *Wilson Papers*, 54:205–206.

Hankey's Notes of a Meeting of the Council of Four[3]

President Wilson's House,
Paris, May 27, 1919, 4:00 p.m.
Despatch to Admiral Koltchak
Paris, 26th May, 1919

The Allied and Associated Powers feel that the time has come when it is necessary for them once more to make clear the policy they propose to pursue in regard to Russia.

It has always been a cardinal axiom of the Allied and Associated Powers to avoid interference in the internal affairs of Russia. Their original intervention was made for the sole purpose of assisting those elements in Russia which wanted to continue the struggle against German autocracy and to free their country from German rule, and in order to rescue the Czech-Slovaks [sic] from the danger of annihilation at the hands of the Bolshevik forces. Since the signature of the armistice on November 11th, 1918, they have kept forces in various parts of Russia. Munitions and supplies have been sent to assist those associated with them at a very considerable cost. No sooner, however, did the Peace Conference assemble than they endeavored to bring peace and order to Russia by inviting representatives of all the warring Governments within Russia to meet them in the hope that they might be able to arrange a permanent solution of Russian problems. This proposal and a later offer to relieve the distress among the suffering millions of Russia broke down through the refusal of the Soviet Government to accept the fundamental condition of suspending hostilities while negotiations or the work of relief was proceeding. Some of the Allied and Associated Governments are now being pressed to withdraw their troops and to incur no further expense in Russia on the ground that continued intervention shows no prospect of producing an early settlement. They are prepared, however, to continue their assistance on the lines laid down below, provided they are satisfied that it will really help the Russian people to liberty, self-government, and peace.

The Allies and Associated Governments now wish to declare formally that the object of their policy is to restore peace within Russia by enabling the Russian people to resume control of their own affairs through the instrumentality of a freely elected Constituent Assembly and to restore peace along its frontiers by arranging for the settlement of disputes in regard to the boundaries of the Russian state and its relations with its neighbours through the peaceful arbitration of the League of Nations.

They are convinced by their experiences of the last twelve months that it is not possible to attain these ends by dealing with the Soviet Government in Moscow. They are therefore disposed to assist the Government of Admiral Koltchak and his Associates with munitions, supplies and food, to establish themselves as the governments of all Russia, provided they receive from them definite guarantees that their policy has the same objects in view of the Allied and Associated Powers. With this object they would ask Admiral Koltchak and his Associates whether they will agree to the following as the conditions upon which they accept continued assistance from the Allied and Associated Powers.

In the first place, that, as soon as they reach Moscow they will summon a Constituent Assembly elected by a free, secret and democratic franchise as the Supreme Legislature for Russia to which the Government of Russia must be responsible, or if at that time order is not sufficiently restored they will summon the Constituent Assembly elected in 1917 to sit until such time as new elections are possible.

Secondly, that throughout the areas which they at present control they will permit free elections in the normal course for all local and legally constituted assemblies such as municipalities, Zemtsvos, etc.

Thirdly, that they will countenance no attempt to revive the special privileges of any class or order in Russia. The Allied and Associated Powers have noted with satisfaction the solemn declaration made by Admiral Koltchak and his associates that they have no intention of restoring the former land system. They feel that the principles to be followed in the solution of this and other internal questions must be left to the free decision of the Russian Constituent Assembly; but they wish to be assured that those whom they are prepared to assist stand for the civil and religious liberty of all Russian citizens and will make no attempt to reintroduce the regime which the revolution has destroyed.

Fourthly, that the independence of Finland and Poland be recognised, and that in the event of the frontiers and other relations between Russia and these countries not being settled by agreement, they will be referred to the arbitration of the League of Nations.

Fifthly, that if a solution of the relations between Esthonia, Latvia, Lithuania, and the Caucasian and Transcaspian territories and Russia is not speedily reached by agreement the settlement will be made in consultation and co-operation with the League of Nations, and that until such settlement is made the Government of Russia agrees to recognise these territories as autonomous and to confirm the relations which may exist between the de facto Governments and the Allied and Associated Governments.

Sixthly, the right of the Peace Conference to determine the future of the Roumanian part of Bessarabia, be recognized.

Seventhly, that as soon as a Government for Russia has been constituted on a democratic basis, Russia should join the League of Nations and co-operate with the other members in the limitation of armaments and of military organization throughout the world.

Finally, that they abide by the declaration made by Admiral Koltchak on November 27th, 1918, in regard to Russia's national debts.

The Allied and Associated Powers will be glad to learn as soon as possible whether the Government of Admiral Koltchak and his associates are prepared to accept these conditions, and also whether in the event of acceptance they will undertake to form a single government and army command as soon as the military situation makes it possible.

> (Sd.) G. Clemenceau
> D. Lloyd George
> V. E. Orlando
> Woodrow Wilson
> Saionji

[3] *Wilson Papers*, 59:543–46

SOURCES

I. Primary Sources

A. Unpublished Sources

Armée de Terre, Service Historique Archives de la Mission Militaire en Sibérie, 1918–1920, 17N593–17N643. Chateau Vincennes, Paris. This is the collection of the Archives of the French Military Mission in Siberia. It contains a wealth of information on the activities and views of the French military in Siberia. Particularly useful is volume 17N632, the intelligence reports. These reports are highly critical of America's sympathy with the so-called "advanced" or Bolshevik parties.

Newton D. Baker Papers. Library of Congress Manuscript Division, Washington, DC. An important and extensive collection of the papers of Wilson's secretary of war. Most of what has been useful for this study has been reproduced in *The Papers of Woodrow Wilson*, below.

Tasker Howard Bliss Papers. Library of Congress Manuscript Division, Washington, DC. Bliss was the American representative to the Supreme War Council. As is the case with the Baker Papers, all of Bliss's direct correspondence with Wilson found in this collection is reproduced in *The Papers of Woodrow Wilson*.

Captain John W. Blue Papers. Collection of Mrs. W. G. Blue, Raeford, North Carolina. A small private collection consisting of a few letters and photographs. One letter illustrates growing impatience in the AEF with the Bolsheviks.

Fred William Bugbee Papers. US Army Military History Institute, Carlisle Barracks, Pennsylvania. Bugbee was the colonel of the 31st Infantry in Siberia. This is a small collection of his correspondence.

Millard S. Curtis Papers. US Army Military History Institute, Carlisle Barracks, Pennsylvania. The principal item here is a memoir of Curtis's adventures with the AEF while guarding the Trans-Siberian Railroad.

Robert L. Eichelberger Papers. Manuscript Department, William R. Perkins Library, Duke University, Durham, North Carolina. The Eichelberger Papers are a very valuable, although a not-often-used, source on the AEF in Siberia. Eichelberger's daily letters give a vivid account of the activities of the American headquarters and the problems that General Graves faced.

Alva C. Gillem Papers. US Army Military History Institute, Carlisle Barracks,

Pennsylvania. The main feature of this collection is a thirty-page typescript of an oral history interview with General Gillem about his experiences in Siberia.

William S. Graves Papers. Hoover Institution, Stanford University, Stanford, California. Three boxes of correspondence, reports, monographs, and photographs relating to Graves's service as commanding officer of the AEF in Siberia. Some of the official documents are duplicated in the Historical Files of the AEF Siberia. The Graves Papers are a valuable, and much-neglected, source.

Nick Hociota Papers. US Army Military History Institute, Carlisle Barracks, Pennsylvania. The main element of this collection is Hociota's typed recollections of his service in the AEF Siberia.

Sylvester E. Kuhn. "Around Siberia and Back, August 1919–April 1920," US Army Military History Institute, Carlisle Barracks, Pennsylvania. A post-service recollection of conflict between the AEF Siberia and Semenov.

Robert Lansing Papers. Library of Congress Manuscript Division, Washington, DC. An extensive collection of Wilson's secretary of state. Lansing's papers are a valuable source on the attitude of the State Department during the Russian Civil War. Most of his direct correspondence with Wilson is published in *The Papers of Woodrow Wilson*.

Edward Larkin Papers. US Army Military History Institute, Carlisle Barracks, Pennsylvania. A brief memoir of Larkin's service with the AEF.

Joseph Longuevan Papers. US Army Military History Institute, Carlisle Barracks, Pennsylvania. Longuevan was the long-time head of the Siberian Veteran's Organization. He amassed an extensive collection of letters and reminiscences of the AEF members.

Joseph G. Loughran Papers. US Army Military History Institute, Carlisle Barracks, Pennsylvania. Loughran was a chaplain attached to the AEF; his papers deal mainly with the repatriation of German and Austrian prisoners-of-war.

Rodney S. Sprigg Papers. US Army Military History Institute, Carlisle Barracks, Pennsylvania. Another small collection of letters from Siberia.

World War I Survey, AEF Siberia. US Army Military History Institute, Carlisle Barracks, Pennsylvania. Part of a collection of questionnaires sent to veterans of the AEF.

B. Published Sources

Ackerman, Carl William. *"Trailing the Bolsheviki:" Twelve Thousand Miles with the Allies in Siberia.* New York: Charles Scribner's Sons, 1919.

Baker, Ray Stannard. *American Chronicle: The Autobiography of Ray Stannard Baker.* New York: Charles Scribner's Sons, 1945.

————, ed. *The Public Papers of Woodrow Wilson: War and Peace*. 2 Volumes. New York: Harper and Brothers, 1927.

————, ed. *Woodrow Wilson, Life and Letters*. Volume 7, *War Leader. April 6, 1917–February 28, 1918*. Volume 8, *Armistice, March 1–November 11, 1918*. New York: Doubleday, Doran and Co., Inc., 1939.

Baruch, Bernard M. *Baruch: The Public Years*. New York: Holt, Rinehart and Winston, 1960.

Bunyan, James and H. H. Fisher, eds. *The Bolshevik Revolution, 1917–1919, Documents and Materials*. Stanford: Stanford University Press, 1934.

Bunyan, James, ed. *Intervention, Civil War, and Communism in Russia, April-December 1918: Documents and Materials*. New York: Octagon Books, 1976.

Cronon, E. David, ed. *Josephus Daniels Cabinet Diaries 1913–1921*. Lincoln: University of Nebraska Press, 1963.

Cumming, C. K. and Walter W. Pettit, eds. *Russian-American Relations: March 1917–March 1920, Documents and Papers*. New York: Harcourt, Brace and Howe, 1920.

Farmborough, Florence. *With the Armies of the Tsar: A Nurse at the Russian Front, 1914–1918*. New York: Stein and Day, 1974.

Francis, David R. *Russia from the American Embassy: April 1916–November 1918*. New York: Charles Scribner's Sons, 1921.

Gidney, James B., ed. *Witness to Revolution: Letters from Russia, 1916–1919, by Edward T. Heald*. Kent, OH: Kent State University Press, 1972.

Graves, William S. *America's Siberian Adventure, 1918–1920*. New York: Peter Smith, 1941.

Horrocks, Sir Brian G. *A Full Life*. London: Collins, 1960.

Jados, Stanley S., ed. *Documents on Russian-American Relations*. Washington, DC: Catholic University of America, 1965.

Kindall, Sylvain G. *American Soldiers in Siberia*. New York: Richard R. Smith, 1945.

Lansing, Robert. *War Memoirs*. 2 volumes. Indianapolis: Bobbs-Merrill, Inc., 1935.

Link, Arthur S., ed. *The Deliberations of the Council of Four (March 24 – June 28, 1919): Notes of the Official Interpreter, Paul Mantoux*. 2 volumes. Princeton: Princeton University Press, 1992.

————, ed. *The Papers of Woodrow Wilson*. 69 volumes. Princeton University Press, 1966–1994.

Lloyd George, David. *War Memoirs of David Lloyd George*. 6 volumes. London: Ivor Nicholson and Watson, 1936.

March, Peyton C. *The Nation at War*. Garden City, New York: Doubleday, Doran and Co., Inc., 1932.

Masaryk, Thomas G. *The Making of a State: Memories and Observations, 1914–1918*. New

York: G. Allen and Unwin, Ltd., 1927.

Palmer, Frederick, ed. *Bliss: Peacemaker, The Life and Letters of Tasker H. Bliss.* New York: Dodd and Mead Co., 1934.

———, ed. *Newton D. Baker: America at War.* 2 volumes. New York: Dodd, Mead and Co., 1931.

Pershing, John J. *My Experiences in the World War.* New York: Frederick A. Stokes Company, 1931.

"Regimental History of the Thirty-first US Infantry, July 1916–July 1920." US Army Military History Institute, Carlisle Barracks, Pennsylvania.

Seymour, Charles, ed. *The Intimate Papers of Colonel House.* 4 volumes. Boston: Houghton, Mifflin Co., 1926–1928.

Silverlight, John. *The Victor's Dilemma: Allied Intervention in the Russian Civil War.* New York: Weybright and Talley, 1970.

Trotsky, Leon. *My Life: An Attempt at Autobiography.* New York: Charles Scribner's Sons, 1930.

Tumulty, Joseph P. *Woodrow Wilson as I Knew Him.* Garden City, New York: The Literary Digest, 1921.

Varneck, Elena and H. H. Fisher, eds. *The Testimony of Admiral Kolchak and Other Materials.* Stanford: Stanford University Press, 1935.

Ward, Colonel John. *With the "Die-Hards" in Siberia.* New York: George H. Doran Co., 1920.

II. Government Documents

Historical Files of the American Expeditionary Forces in Siberia, 1918–1920. 21-4.7–21-67.4, National Archives Microfilm Publication M917.

Siberia and Eastern Russia. US War Office, 4 volumes. Washington, DC: US Government Printing Office, 1918.

United States Army War College. *Order of Battle of the United States Land Forces in the World War, American Expeditionary Forces in the World War.* Washington, DC: US Government Printing Office, 1937.

United States Congress. *Congressional Record, Proceedings and Debates, 1918–1920.* Washington, DC: US Government Printing Office, 1918–1920.

United States Department of State. *Papers Relating to the Foreign Relations of the United States, 1918, Russia.* 3 volumes. Washington, DC: US Government Printing Office, 1931–1932.

United States Department of State. *Papers Relating to the Foreign Relations of the United States, 1919, Russia.* Washington, DC: US Government Printing Office, 1937.

United States Department of State. *Papers Relating to the Foreign Relations of the United States, 1920.* 3 volumes. Washington, DC: US Government Printing Office, 1936.

III. Secondary Sources

Baerlein, Henry. *The March of the Seventy Thousand.* London: Leonard Parsons, 1926.

Barrows, David P., "Japan as Our Ally in Siberia," *Asia* 19 (September 1919): 927–31.

Beaver, Daniel R. *Newton D. Baker and the American War Effort, 1917–1919.* Lincoln: University of Nebraska Press, 1966.

Becvar, Gustav. *The Lost Legion: A Czechoslovakian Epic.* London: Stanley Paul and Co., Ltd., 1939.

Blum, John Morton. *Woodrow Wilson and the Politics of Morality.* Boston: Little, Brown and Company, 1956.

Bradley, J. F. N. *Civil War in Russia, 1917–1920.* New York: St. Martin's Press, 1975.

Bradley, John. *Allied Intervention in Russia.* New York: Basic Books, Inc., Publishers, 1968.

Calhoun, Frederick S. *Power and Principle: Armed Intervention in Wilsonian Foreign Policy.* Kent OH: Kent State University Press, 1986.

Chamberlin, William Henry. *The Russian Revolution, 1917–1921.* 2 volumes. New York: The MacMillan Co., 1935.

Churchill, Winston S. *The Aftermath: The World Crisis, 1918–1928.* New York: Charles Scribner's Sons, 1929.

Chwialkowski, Paul. "A 'Near Great' General: The Life and Career of Robert L. Eichelberger." Ph.D. dissertation, Duke University, 1991.

Coates, W. P., and Coates, Zelda K. *Armed Intervention in Russia, 1918–1922.* London: Victor Gollancz, Ltd., 1935.

Coffman, Edward M. *The Hilt of the Sword: The Career of Peyton C. March.* Madison: University of Wisconsin Press, 1986.

Corwin, Edward S. *The President: Office and Powers, 1787–1957.* New York: New York University Press, 1957.

Cramer, Clarence H. *Newton D. Baker: A Biography.* Cleveland: World Publishers, 1961.

Curry, Roy Watson. *Woodrow Wilson and Far Eastern Policy, 1913–1921.* New York: Octagon Books, 1968.

Daniels, Josephus. *The Life of Woodrow Wilson, 1856–1924.* Philadelphia: Will H. Johnston, 1924.

———. *The Wilson Era: Years of Peace, 1910–1917.* Chapel Hill: University of North Carolina Press, 1944.

———. *The Wilson Era: Years of War and After, 1917–1923.* Chapel Hill: University of

North Carolina Press, 1946.

Davison, Henry Pomeroy. *The American Red Cross in the Great War*. New York: The MacMillan Company, 1920.

Ferrell, Robert H. *Woodrow Wilson and World War I, 1917–1921*. New York: Harper and Row Publishers, 1985.

Figes, Orlando, *A People's Tragedy: The Russian Revolution 1891–1924*. London: Jonathan Cape, 1996.

Fleming, Peter. *The Fate of Admiral Kolchak*. New York: Harcourt, Brace and World, Inc., 1963.

Foglesong, David S. *America's Secret War Against Bolshevism: US Intervention in the Russian Civil War, 1917–1920*. Chapel Hill: University of North Carolina Press, 1995.

Footman, David. *Civil War in Russia*. London: Faber and Faber, 1961.

Fowler, W. B. *British-American Relations, 1917–1918: the Role of Sir William Wiseman*. Princeton: Princeton University Press, 1969.

Goldhurst, Richard. *The Midnight War: The American Intervention in Russia, 1918–1920*. New York: McGraw-Hill Book Co., 1978.

Gorbachev, Mikhail. *Perestroika: New Thinking For Our Country and the World*. New York: Harper and Row, 1987.

Graves, Sidney C. "Japanese Aggression in Siberia," *Current History* 14 (May 1921): 239–45.

Greiner, J. E. "The American Railway Commission in Russia," Railway Review 5 (3 August 1988): 171.

Griswold, A. Whitney. *The Far Eastern Policy of the United States*. New York: Harcourt, Brace and Company, 1938.

Kennan, George F. "Russia and the Versailles Conference." *The American Scholar* 30 (Winter 1960): 13–42.

———. *Russia and the West: Under Lenin and Stalin*. Boston: Little, Brown and Co., 1960.

———. *Soviet-American Relations, 1917–1920*. Volume 1, *Russia Leaves the War*, and volume 2, *The Decision to Intervene*. Princeton: Princeton University Press, 1956 and 1958.

Kettle, Michael. *The Allies and the Russian Collapse, March 1917–March 1918*. London: Andrew Deutsch Ltd., 1981.

Killen, Linda. *The Russian Bureau: A Case Study in Wilsonian Diplomacy*. Lexington: University Press of Kentucky, 1983.

Klante, Margarete. *Von der Wolga zum Amur: Die tschechische Legion und der russische Burgerkrieg*. Berlin: Ost Europa Verlag, 1931.

Knox, Alfred. "General Janin's Siberian Diary." *The Slavonic Review* 3/9 (March 1925): 724.

————. *With the Russian Army 1914–1917, Being Chiefly Extracts from the Diary of as Military Attache.* 2 volumes. London: Hutchinson and Company, 1921.

Levin, N. Gordon, Jr. *Woodrow Wilson and World Politics: America's Response to War and Revolution.* New York: Oxford University Press, 1968.

Link, Arthur S. *The Higher Realism of Woodrow Wilson and Other Essays.* Nashville: Vanderbilt University Press, 1971.

————, ed. *The Impact of World War I.* New York: Harper and Row, 1969.

————. *Wilson the Diplomatist: A Look at His Major Foreign Policies.* New York: New Viewpoints, 1974.

————. *Woodrow Wilson: Revolution, War and Peace.* Arlington Heights, IL: A. H. M. Publishing Company, 1979.

————, ed. *Woodrow Wilson and a Revolutionary World, 1913–1921.* Chapel Hill: University of North Carolina Press, 1982.

Luckett, Richard. *The White Generals: An Account of the White Movement and the Russian Civil War.* New York: The Viking Press, 1971.

Maddox, Robert James. *The Unknown War with Russia: Wilson's Siberian Intervention.* San Rafael, California: Presidio Press, 1977.

Manning, Clarence. *The Siberian Fiasco.* New York: Library Publishers, Inc., 1952.

Matamey, Victor S. *The United States and East Central Europe, 1914–1918.* Princeton: Princeton University Press, 1957.

Mayer, Arno J. *Political Origins of the New Diplomacy, 1917–1918.* New York: Vintage Books, 1970.

————. *Politics and Diplomacy of Peacemaking: Containment and Counterrevolution at Versailles, 1918–1919.* New York: Vintage Books, 1967.

Medek, Rudolf. *The Czechoslovak Anabasis Across Russia and Siberia.* London: The Czech Society, 1929.

Morley, J. W. *The Japanese Thrust into Siberia.* New York: Columbia University Press, 1957.

Pergler, Charles. *America in the Struggle for Czechoslovak Independence.* Philadelphia: Dorrance and Company, Inc., 1926.

Rikhye, Indar Jit. *The Theory and Practice of Peacekeeping.* New York: St. Martin's Press, 1984.

Sakharow, Konstantin W. *Die tschechischen Legionen in Siberien.* Berlin-Charlottenburg: Heinrich Wilhelm Hendroick Verlag, 1930.

Schmickle, William E. "For the Proper Use of Victory: Diplomacy and the Imperatives of Vision in the Foreign Policy of Woodrow Wilson, 1916–1919." Ph.D. dissertation, Duke University, 1979.

Schmitt, Bernotte E. and Vedeler, Harold C. *The World in the Crucible, 1914–1919.* New York: Harper and Row, 1984.

Smith, Canfield. *Vladivostok Under Red and White Rule: Revolution and Counter-revolution in the Russian Far East, 1920–1922*. Seattle: University of Washington Press, 1975.

Smythe, Donald. *Pershing, General of the Armies*. Bloomington: Indiana University Press, 1986.

Snow, Russell E. *The Bolsheviks in Siberia, 1917–1918*. Granbury, NJ: Associated University Presses, Inc., 1977.

Stewart, George. *The White Armies of Russia: A Chronicle of Counter-Revolution and Allied Intervention*. New York: The MacMillan Co., 1933.

Strakhovsky, Leonid I. *American Opinion About Russia, 1917–1920*. Toronto: University of Toronto Press, 1961.

Sweetenham, John A. *Allied Intervention in Russia, 1918–1919*. London: Allen and Unwin, 1967.

Thompson, John M. *Russia, Bolshevism, and the Versailles Peace*. Princeton: Princeton University Press, 1967.

Tomkins, Pauline. *American-Russian Relations in the Far East*. New York: The MacMillan Co., 1949.

Ullman, Richard H. *Intervention and the War*. Volume 1 of *Anglo-Soviet Relations, 1917–1921*. Princeton: Princeton University Press, 1968.

Unterberger, Betty Miller. *American Intervention in the Russian Civil War*. Lexington, MA: D. C. Heath Company, 1969.

———. *America's Siberian Expedition, 1918–1920: A Study in National Policy*. Durham: Duke University Press, 1956.

———. *The United States, Revolutionary Russia, and the Rise of Czechoslovakia*. Chapel Hill: University of North Carolina Press, 1989.

Weinstein, Edwin A. *Woodrow Wilson: A Medical and Psychological Biography*. Princeton: Princeton University Press, 1981.

White, John Albert. *The Siberian Intervention*. Princeton: Princeton University Press, 1950.

Williams, William Appleman. *American-Russian Relations, 1781–1947*. New York: Rinehart and Company, Inc., 1952.

Wilson, Woodrow. *Constitutional Government in the United States*. New York: Columbia University Press, 1921.